TAPESTRY

by Steve Wiegand & Charlie Hayward

Corporate Profiles by Dennis Pottenger

Art Direction by Brian Groppe

Produced in Cooperation
with the Sacramento
Metropolitan
Chamber of Commerce

URBAN TAPESTRY SERIES
TOWERY Publishing, Inc.

Sacramento is a city of trees and trains, of gold and government, of dreams promised and dreams fulfilled. It's California's capital—and its contradiction. (preceeding pages)

Once they combined with river steamboats to make the area a major transportation hub. Now they serve mostly as backdrops for tourist photos at the California State Railroad Museum. But the trains still run through midtown Sacramento—to the delight of rail enthusiasts, young and old alike (above).

Library of Congress Cataloging-in-Publication Data

Wiegand, Steve, 1951-
    Sacramento tapestry / by Steve Wiegand; corporate profiles by Dennis Pottenger.
        p.   cm. — (Urban Tapestry Series)
    Includes index.
    ISBN 1-881096-10-6 : $39.50
    1. Sacramento (Calif.)—Pictorial works. 2. Sacramento (Calif.)—Description and travel.   I. Pottenger, Dennis. II. Title.   III. Series.
F869.S12W54   1994   94-24532
979.4'54—dc20   CIP

Copyright ©1994 by Towery Publishing, Inc.

All rights reserved. No part of this work may be reproduced or copied in any form or by any means, except for brief excerpts in conjunction with book reviews, without prior written permission of the publisher.

Towery Publishing, Inc., 1835 Union Avenue, Memphis, TN 38104

Publisher:	J. Robert Towery
Executive Publisher:	Jenny McDowell
Vice President of National Sales:	Steve Hung
Project Directors:	Susan Brown, Mel Merk
Executive Editor:	David Dawson
Senior Editors:	Michael James, Ken Woodmansee
Associate Editor:	Stinson Liles
Copy Editor:	Carlisle Hacker
Assistant Art Director:	Anne Castrodale
Assistant Profile Designers:	Jencie Escue, M. Paul Forsythe, Terri Jones, Lawanda McClellan
Technical Director:	William H. Towery

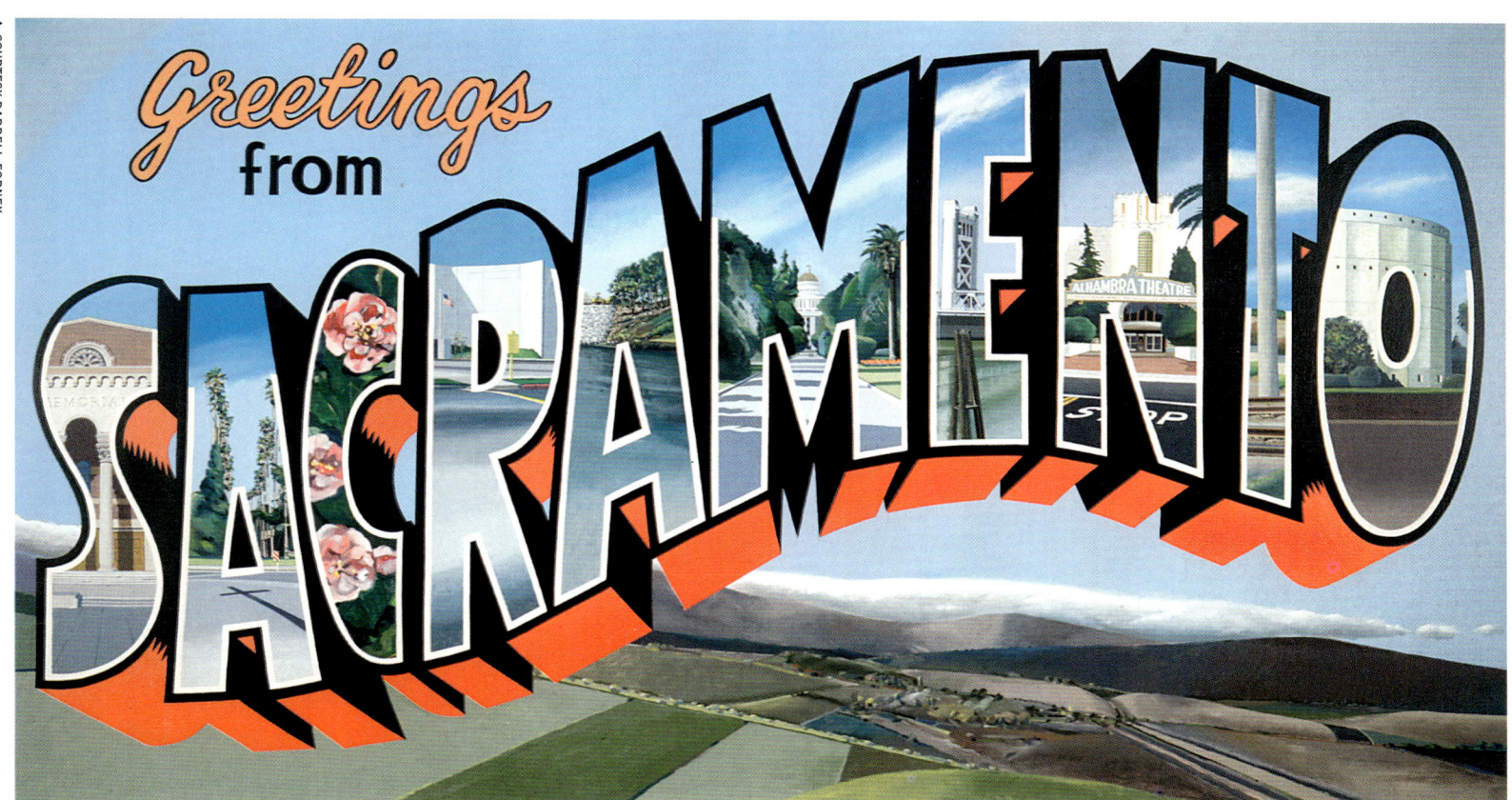

It's a big word that can speak volumes in just 10 letters (above). But local artist Darrell Forney's acrylic work uses scenes from Sacramento's past and present to spell out the essence of the city.

CONTENTS

SACRAMENTO TAPESTRY 11
by Steve Wiegand

"Sacramento has what has been an overriding California trait since the days of the Spanish conquistadors: the promise of a better tomorrow."

PROFILES IN EXCELLENCE 156
by Dennis Pottenger

A look at the corporations, businesses, professional groups, and community service organizations that have made this book possible.

ARTISTS & PHOTOGRAPHERS 236

INDEX TO PATRONS 239

So perennially abundant is the area's rice crop that potential markets extend far to the west, to Asia itself.
PAGES 6 & 7, PHOTO BY KURT FISHBACK

While the California State Capitol is no longer the skyline's dominant building, it is still the heart of the city—and the nerve center of the nation's largest state.
PAGES 8 & 9, PHOTO BY TOM MYERS

BY STEVE WIEGAND

SACRAMENTO IS CALIFORNIA'S contradiction. Says Phil Isenberg, a former city councilman and mayor who now makes his living representing Sacramento in the legislature, "Sacramento is probably less like the general stereotypes of California than any other big city in the state. There are times when it's hard to believe it's part of the same state as, say, Hollywood."

Sometimes it's even hard for Hollywood to believe it, which may help to explain why much of a recent movie supposedly set in Nebraska was filmed in Sacramento.

The writer and avowed New Yorker O. Henry confirmed this nearly a century ago, when he generalized that "Californians are a race of people; they are not merely inhabitants of a state." And while the state may generate an overall image distinct from the rest of the nation, it is true that the residents of California's capital are truly a breed apart from the rest of the state.

We don't hold this diversity to be anything but an asset. Sure, Sacramento is different from other California

ONCE THE DOMAIN OF DOWN-AND-OUTERS, THE K STREET MALL IS NOW HOME TO THE LIGHT-RAIL LINE AND COMMUNITY EVENTS, INCLUDING THE FESTIVAL DE LA FAMILIA (OPPOSITE) AND THE THURSDAY NIGHT MARKET, WHICH DRAWS CROWDS OF UP TO 10,000 (LEFT).

IN THE 1980S, THE PORT OF SACRAMENTO (ABOVE) SUFFERED FROM THE FACT THAT IT WAS NOT DEEP ENOUGH TO CONTAIN MANY OF THE PACIFIC RIM'S LARGER SHIPS. TODAY, HOWEVER, THE PORT IS CURRENTLY UNDERGOING A $76 MILLION CHANNEL DEEPENING THAT WILL ALLOW THE FACILITY TO RECEIVE 75 PERCENT OF ALL OCEANGOING VESSELS.

cities, but it's the array of moods, textures, and ways of life that keep the state, and its capital, such an interesting place to live. For instance, Sacramento lacks the laid-back hedonism of San Diego, the eccentric charm of San Francisco, or the frenetic exhibitionism of Los Angeles. Instead, Sacramento is characterized by a blend of more traditional American values. Like the Northeast, it can be zealously industrious. Like the South, it has its slow charms. And like the Midwest, it can be friendly and guileless.

Perhaps these traditional values are why Sacramento is, in fact, the fastest-growing urban area in California. Fed up with unrelenting crime, endless traffic jams, and soaring housing prices elsewhere, refugees from the rest of the state are flocking to the River City.

In 1992, for example, more than 5,000 families from

SYMBOLS OF THE CITY'S DOWNTOWN RENAISSANCE (OPPOSITE), THE WELLS FARGO CENTER (LEFT) AND CAPITOL BANK OF COMMERCE STAND AS SENTINELS ABOVE BUSY INTERSTATE 5.

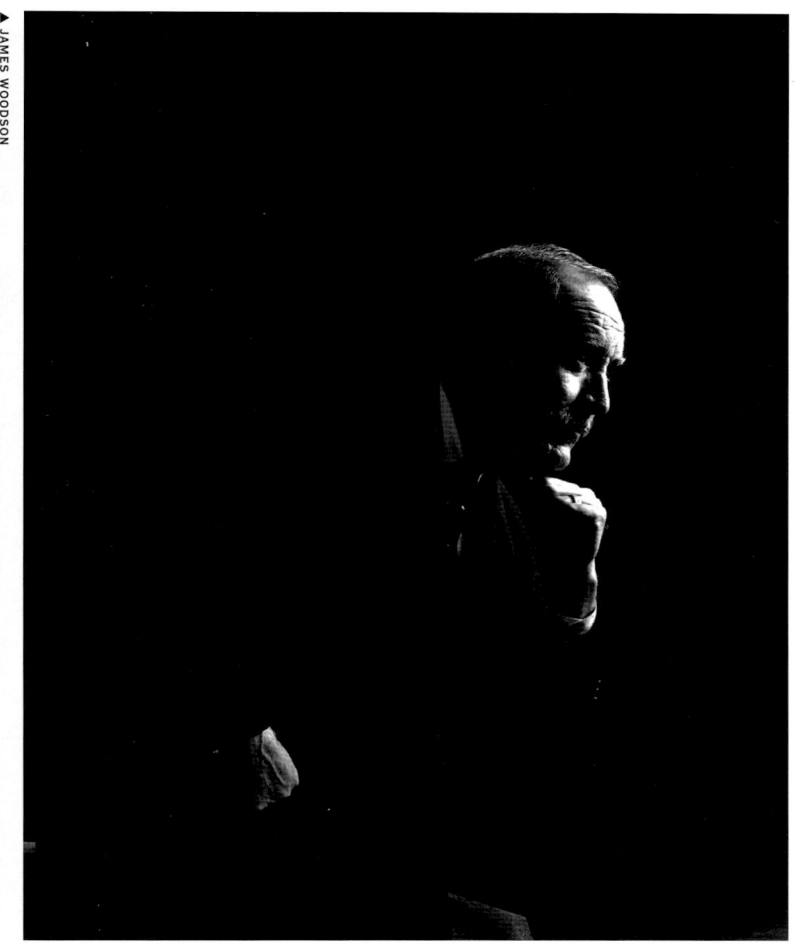

THE GALA OPENING OF THE DOWNTOWN PLAZA SHOPPING AND ENTERTAINMENT CENTER IN OCTOBER 1993 ATTRACTED A CROWD OF 20,000 AND GAVE MANY SACRAMENTANS A GOOD REASON TO COME TO THE CITY'S CENTER AFTER WORKING HOURS.

SURPRISINGLY, PERHAPS, IN A CITY CHOCK-FULL OF POLITICIANS, NOT ALL THE LEADERS ARE ELECTED. EXAMPLES: BUSINESS LEADER TOM HOBDAY (ABOVE LEFT) AND LOCAL FUTURIST ALAN EWEN (ABOVE RIGHT).

the Bay Area and another 2,300 from Los Angeles County relocated to Sacramento. What they found when they got here was an average daily commute that was the shortest of any California metropolitan area, a median house price that was the lowest of any metro area in the state, and a more relaxed pace.

How relaxed is the pace in Sacramento? A recent university study of stress-level indicators in 36 major urban American centers found Sacramentans walked slower, talked slower, and wore fewer wristwatches than any of their big-city counterparts.

"We like the pace," Natalie Needham said in explaining why she and her husband and two daughters moved to Sacramento in 1991 after living most of their lives in Los Angeles. "There are drawbacks to living anywhere, but you can come home here at the end of a long day and really unwind."

Once they get here, people tend to stay put. In most of California, mobility is a way of life. In Sacramento, however, more than half of the area's home owners have lived in the same house for at least five years.

True, it's a long commute to the beach if you're a surfer, and it's a good six- or seven-hour drive to Disneyland. You're unlikely to bump into many movie stars at the supermarket (although you might find yourself thumping melons with the governor). But we can live with that.

The reason: Sacramento always has held what has been an overriding California trait since the days of the Spanish conquistadores: the promise of a better tomorrow. A central city renaissance is radically transforming Sacramento's core from a rather run-down area that was deserted after dark to a vibrant center of commerce, shopping, and recreation. Innovative planning is under way to control urban sprawl. And most economists are predicting Sacramento's economic growth will outpace

CENTERED IN CALIFORNIA'S MIDSECTION, SACRAMENTO WAS THE IDEAL SITE FOR A RAILROAD CENTER. TODAY IT'S THE CENTER OF RAILROAD HISTORY, HOME TO THE LARGEST TRAIN MUSEUM IN THE COUNTRY. LOCATED IN OLD SACRAMENTO, THE CALIFORNIA STATE RAILROAD MUSEUM HAS 21 RESTORED TRAINS, 46 EXHIBITS, AND A HOST OF KNOWLEDGEABLE VOLUNTEERS WHO ARE HAPPY TO PRESERVE THE SPIRIT OF THE DAYS WHEN RAIL WAS KING.

THE 1930S BROUGHT VAUDEVILLE AND THE GREAT DEPRESSION TO J STREET—AND SACRAMENTO SURVIVED BOTH. AN INFUSION OF FEDERAL FUNDS FOR PUBLIC WORKS PROJECTS KEPT THE CITY GOING FINANCIALLY. IT WOULDN'T BE THE LAST TIME SACRAMENTO BENEFITED FROM ITS FRIENDSHIP WITH GOVERNMENT.

the rest of California in the coming decade.

"For years Sacramento was a city of big, styleless motels with overworked air conditioners," opined a recent story in the *New York Times*. "These days it's possible to find something considerably more elegant . . . Sacramento has become a city of the 1990s."

Which goes to show that even New Yorkers are right sometimes.

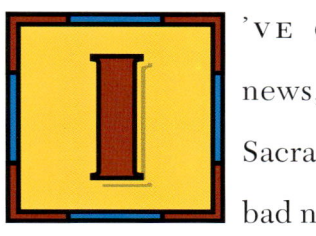"'VE GOT BAD NEWS AND GOOD news," Saint Peter tells the lifelong Sacramentan at the Pearly Gates. "The bad news is you have to go to Hell. The good news is that you won't mind a bit: it's a dry heat."

OK, it does get hot sometimes in Sacramento. Triple-digit hot. Then, in the winter, the city sometimes becomes shrouded in dense "tule fog," the kind of cold, wet fog that penetrates your heart with melancholy.

The key word here, however, is *sometimes*. The truth is that most of the time the weather in Sacramento is

IN THE WINTER, DENSE "TULE FOG" CAN GIVE THE SACRAMENTO VALLEY AN OTHERWORLDLY FEEL, MAKING A NIGHT TRAIN APPEAR AS A ROARING, ONE-EYED MONSTER, OR THE TOWER BRIDGE SEEM LIKE A BROODING GIANT (OPPOSITE).

mild and sunny: The average high temperature in January is 54 degrees; the average high in July is 93 degrees.

When it does get hot, locals like to point out that most of the time the humidity is quite low, which makes it almost comfortable. And when it gets foggy, you can always drive up to the foothills, above the tule, and have a nice lunch with all the money you save from not having to buy a snow shovel. The white stuff—and some of the best ski areas in the United States—stays comfortably up the road in the Sierra Nevada, 90 minutes away.

Did we say sunny? During daylight hours, the sun shines 78 percent of the time, according to the U.S. Census. That makes Sacramento sunnier than Miami and sunnier than Honolulu—in fact, it's the fourth-sunniest big city in the country. And all that sun exerts a magnetizing force, drawing all but the most determined couch potato outdoors.

And what Sacramentans see when they get outside their front doors is a city that in many respects could be picked up and plunked down in the middle of Iowa and not

BY THE END OF THIS DECADE, THERE WILL BE A TREE FOR EVERY TWO PEOPLE IN SACRAMENTO. IT'S THAT KIND OF ARBOREAL ABUNDANCE, AS EVIDENCED ALONG THE AMERICAN RIVER BIKE TRAIL, THAT MAKES THE CITY SO NATURALLY APPEALING.

THE TREES AREN'T SACRAMENTO'S ONLY GREENERY. GOLF COURSES—FROM PITCH-AND-PUTT TO PRO-CALIBER—OFFER PLAYERS OF ALL LEVELS AN EXCUSE TO ENJOY THE AREA'S GENERALLY FINE WEATHER.

CROCKER ART MUSEUM, SACRAMENTO, CA: GIFT OF FIRST INTERSTATE BANK OF CALIFORNIA

"Sacramento River,"
1981, oil on canvas,
(48" x 60"),
by Gregory Kondos,
American b. 1923,
Crocker Art Museum
collection

look out of place. It's a green, living place, smack in the middle of some of the best farm and vineyard country in the United States.

Unlike any of California's other big cities, Sacramento is a city of rivers. From the east, the American River spills and tumbles down from the Sierra Nevada, past the white-water rafters and the salmon and steelhead fishermen, through the heart of the metropolitan area. From the north comes the wide and—by California standards—mighty Sacramento, formidable enough to have served as a stand-in for the wide, muddy Mississippi River in dozens of Hollywood movies. (It even impressed Humphrey, a 40-foot-long humpback whale that appar-

▲ SACRAMENTO ARCHIVES & MUSEUM COLLECTION CENTER

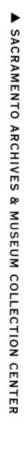

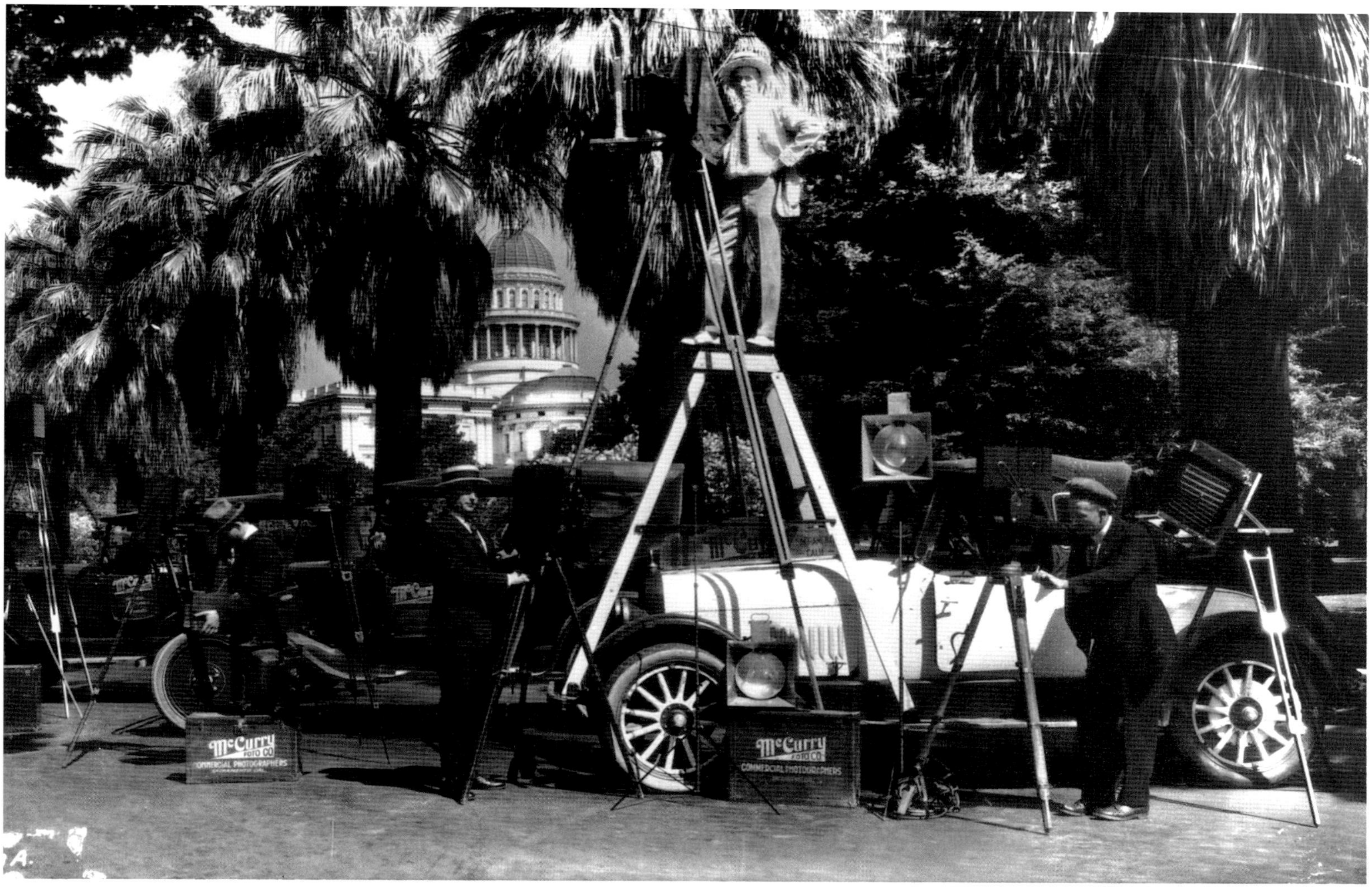

ently liked the river and its delta so much he spent nearly a month there in 1985 before eventually returning to the Pacific.) The two rivers join just north of downtown and flow along the city's western boundary into the labyrinthine delta region and ultimately into San Francisco Bay.

Moreover, Sacramento is a city of trees—more than 300,000 of them, more than any city its size anywhere in the country. There are oaks and elms, eucalyptus and fir trees, even a redwood or two. And more are on the way: Through public and private efforts, the city is planting an average of 130 trees a day, or more than 500,000 by the end of the 1990s.

Throw in a tabletop topography, and the results are an

BUILT IN THE 1860S AT A COST OF $2 MILLION AND REBUILT IN THE 1970S AT A COST OF ABOUT $70 MILLION, THE COPPER-DOMED CAPITOL IS SURROUNDED BY A SEA OF PLANT LIFE, INCLUDING AT LEAST ONE SPECIMEN OF EVERY KIND OF TREE IN THE STATE.

ideal location for bike rides along the parkway that parallels 23 miles of the American River, softball at one of the 108 diamonds, golf at one of the 18 public and private courses sprinkled throughout the region, or simply picnicking at the 10,000-plus acres of public parkland.

SACRAMENTO HAS PRODUCED A PLETHORA OF PROMINENT PUGILISTS OVER THE YEARS: MAX BAER, SR., PETE RANZANY, BOBBY CHACON, LORETO GARZA, AND RICHARD DURAN. THE BEST MIGHT JUST BE TONY "THE TIGER" LOPEZ, A THREE-TIME WORLD CHAMP.

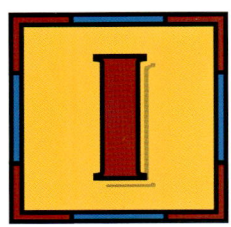

IN FACT, IF THERE'S ONE THING that Sacramento does share with the rest of California, it's a wonderfully eclectic assortment of things to do. Professional sports? Take in a Kings game at Arco Arena—that is, if you can get a ticket. The National Basketball Association club has sold out every home game since they arrived in 1985, despite a frankly woeful won-lost record.

And for the culture-oriented, there's everything from frogs to phantoms: from the Crawdad Festival in nearby Isleton and the world-famous frog-jumping contest in Calaveras County to Sacramento's much-lauded sym-

BIG-TIME SPORTS ACTION CAN BE FOUND AT ARCO ARENA, HOME OF THE NBA'S SACRAMENTO KINGS. THOUGH THEIR RECORD HAS NOT ALWAYS BEEN IMPRESSIVE, THE KINGS ATTRACT SELL-OUT CROWDS, GAME AFTER GAME.

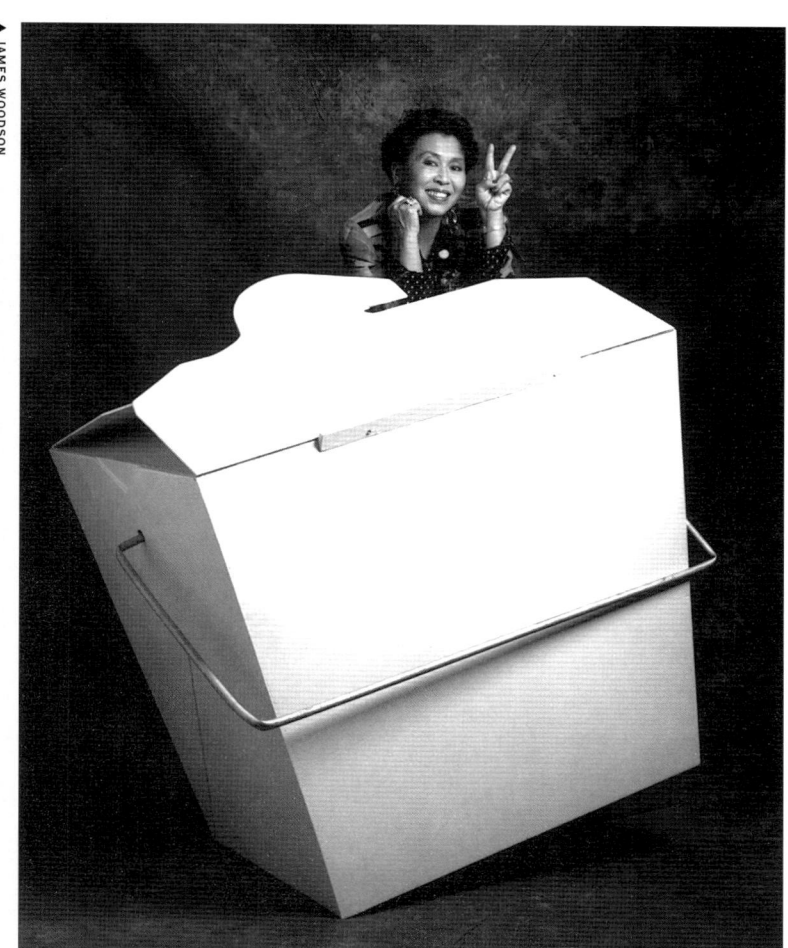 

EAST MEETS WEST AND BLENDS TASTILY TOGETHER IN RESTAURANTS SUCH AS CALIFORNIA FAT'S IN OLD SACRAMENTO. CHINESE CUISINE HAS BEEN AN INTEGRAL PART OF LOCAL FARE SINCE THE GOLD RUSH DAYS.

phony, opera, and ballet companies, and top touring shows such as the Broadway version of *Phantom of the Opera*. More than 30 local professional and amateur theatrical troupes stage productions in Sacramento, and the city is also a regular stop for big-name singers and groups that range from Guns 'n' Roses to Barry Manilow, from Billy Ray Cyrus to Paul Simon. Local festivals round out the calendar with such offerings as the Italian Cultural Festival, the Greek Food Festival, and the Japanese Food Bazaar.

RESTAURATEUR LINA FAT (ABOVE LEFT) AND PR/ADVERTISING MATRIARCH JEAN RUNYON (ABOVE RIGHT) ARE JUST KIDDING: SACRAMENTO'S DINING SCENE HAS EVOLVED LIGHT YEARS FROM TAKE-OUT CARTONS AND GREASY SPOONS.

Summer starts more or less officially with the Dixieland Jazz Jubilee weekend, which attracts bands and more than 100,000 Dixieland fans from all over the world. They can watch a jazz band from Poland belt out "Won't You Come Home, Bill Bailey?" in front of a hotel restored from the

"Sunday Morning in the Mines."
1872, Oil on Canvas.
(72" x 108"),
by Charles Christian Nahl,
American, 1818-1878,
Crocker Art Museum collection

In the gold fields near Sacramento, they played hard and worked even harder. Imagine what Saturday night was like.

Gold Rush era in Old Sacramento, then stroll a quarter mile to a splendidly restored Victorian mansion that houses the oldest art museum west of the Mississippi, with art exhibits spanning the centuries.

In the waning days of summer comes the California State Fair—a Sacramento mainstay since 1858—complete with horse racing, livestock and crafts exhibitions, taffy apples, and midway rides that can quickly quell one's appetite for any more taffy apples.

Despite its physical charms, however, most Sacramentans are modest in showing off their city, displaying a small-town affection for the familiar as well as the grand. Sure, they'll take Mom and Dad over to visit the splendidly ornate Capitol, which cost $2 million to build in the late 1860s and $65 million to rebuild and reopen in 1982, after engineers decided it wasn't earthquake-proof (Note: we do feel earthquakes in Sacramento every once in a while, but they're usually just the outermost aftershocks of the temblors from somewhere else in the state). But they'll also take them over to Vic's for an ice-cream cone and a view of one of the only places left in the civilized world with a working penny gum ball machine. ➤

THE HISTORICAL, IF NOT GEOGRAPHICAL, CENTER OF THE CITY IS SUTTER'S FORT, ONCE THE HOME OF SWISS ADVENTURER AND SACRAMENTO FOUNDER, JOHN SUTTER. EVERY YEAR, VOLUNTEERS DON 1840S GARB AND AND BRING THE ERA AND ITS CUSTOMS BACK TO LIFE.

TILL, A CITY IS BEST MEASURED not by its cultural offerings, its amusements, or its weather, but by its people. In Sacramento, that would include the well known: renowned artist Wayne Thiebaud, Major League baseball manager Dusty Baker, and actor Timothy Busfield. Rush Limbaugh launched his career here. So did model/singer Barbi Benton, baseball star Steve Sax, and actor Tom Hanks.

"If I ever left town, which I won't, I'd miss the people most," said Anne Rudin, who served two terms as Sacramento's mayor and presided over the first big-city council with a majority of women members. "The people here are friendly, down-to-earth, and unpretentious."

All of which confirms what former Mayor Isenberg had to say: Sacramento is a city unto itself, proud and unique, with an identity all its own. Despite the shadows cast by

THE CENTER OF THE SACRAMENTO ART SCENE SINCE THE LATE 1950S HAS BEEN WAYNE THIEBAUD. ARTIST, TEACHER, AND CHEERLEADER FOR THE ARTS, THIEBAUD HAS A PENCHANT FOR COLOR AND A FLAIR FOR THE EXUBERANT, TRAITS THAT REFLECT HIS TOWN.

"FARM POND"
1967-88
BY WAYNE THIEBAUD,
OIL ON CANVAS 50" X 50"
PRIVATE COLLECTION

IT'S SAID THE CALIFORNIA ASSEMBLY CHAMBERS IS BEST ADMIRED WHEN IT'S EMPTY—THE PERFECT TIME TO REFLECT ON ITS ORNATE SPLENDOR.

JOE SERNA, JR. (ABOVE) TEACHES POLITICAL SCIENCE AT CALIFORNIA STATE UNIVERSITY, SACRAMENTO, AND MOONLIGHTS AS THE CITY'S MAYOR.

some of its glitzier, headline-grabbing sister cities in the Golden State, Sacramentans don't suffer from any kind of inferiority complex. Just the opposite. As those who are migrating here from the rest of California already know, the River City might just be California's prototypical place to make a home.

"I DONT WANT TO SPOIL THE ENDING OF THIS BOOK, BUT I CAN'T KEEP SACRAMENTO A SECRET ANYMORE. THE CONCLUSION GOES LIKE THIS: 'DYNAMIC MAYOR LEADS HARDWORKING CITIZENRY TO NEW PROSPERITY IN A PLEASANT, HIGHLY LIVABLE COMMUNITY.' DON'T WAIT FOR THE MOVIE. COME AND SEE SACRAMENTO FOR YOURSELF."

—MAYOR JOE SERNA

A CITY IS NO MORE THAN THE SUM OF ITS PEOPLE, AND SACRAMENTO'S PEOPLE ARE A RICHLY DIVERSE MIX, AS REFLECTED BY A HOST OF ETHNIC FESTIVALS. "THE BALLET FOLKLORICO," ESTEEMED LOCAL ARTS CRITIC ALFRED KAY ONCE WROTE, "DEFIES CRITICAL ANALYSIS, LIKE WILDFLOWERS OR A CONGENIAL SUNRISE."

The Downtown Plaza is home to $1.2 million worth of public art, a 68,000-square-foot entertainment complex, more than 100 stores, and most of the hopes of local leaders for a revitalized city center.

Sacramento symmetry: Festival dancers in the Downtown Plaza rotunda; street codes for locating underground utility lines; detail from a downtown railing; and a manhole cover, the name of which the city council once tried to change because it was "sexist."

TAPESTRY 41

When legislators decided to restore the Capitol to the grandeur of 1906, they spared no expense, and artisans paid strict attention to detail. To replicate the rotunda's ornamental curlicues, workers used cake decorator bags filled with plaster.

"You're not expected to love everything," said consultant Susan Willoughby of public art. "The worst thing that could happen would be for people not to notice at all." Among Sacramento's noticeable displays: the Central Library Galleria (opposite); an installation at the Arden Fair Mall (left); and a skylight in downtown's 5th Street Market (right).

Sacramento is ready to take a chance when it comes to commercial building design. Owned by the California Dental Association, the 12th and K Building (opposite) is better known as the "Ban Roll-On Building" because of its distinctive dome. The Lincoln Plaza, home of the massive Public Employees Retirement System, relies on clean geometric shapes and pyramid layering to make its statement (this page).

Art in public places, public places as art. Clockwise from top left: Works by local artist Jeff Myers; two lobbies at the Center City complex; the terrazzo floor at the Carol Miller Justice Center; Victoria Rivers' "Neon Sunset" in the corporate lobby of Raley's grocery store chain; the new Roseville Corporation yard facade; and the entrance to the Apple Computer facility in Laguna.

Technology truly shapes Sacramento's future: a Pacific Bell worker (top) and IBM cable data storage (bottom). The Sacramento Municipal Utility District's solar cell field (opposite) basks while the closed Rancho Seco Nuclear Power Plant broods just behind it.

"OUR TECHNOLOGY GOAL IS TO GET THE MACHINES TO DO WHAT THE MACHINES DO WELL," SAYS GREG KUSIAK, CHIEF OPERATING OFFICER OF THE SACRAMENTO RADIOLOGY MEDICAL GROUP.

The light board is ready (opposite), but the lights have been off at Sacramento's Memorial Auditorium since 1986, when it was closed for repairs. Built in 1927, it's set to reopen in 1996. But the show must go on somewhere—here, it's a concert at the Cathedral of the Blessed Heart (left).

"I FIND THE QUALITY OF LIFE HERE SO DELIGHTFUL, SO CIVILIZED," SAYS OCTOGENARIAN ARTS ACTIVIST LUCY RITTER (OPPOSITE). "I'D HATE TO SEE US INCREASE IN SO MANY DIRECTIONS THAT WE INHERIT BIG-CITY PROBLEMS." BESIDES, IT WOULD CUT INTO CONVERSATION TIME BETWEEN FOLKS AT THE J STREET MASONIC TEMPLE (RIGHT).

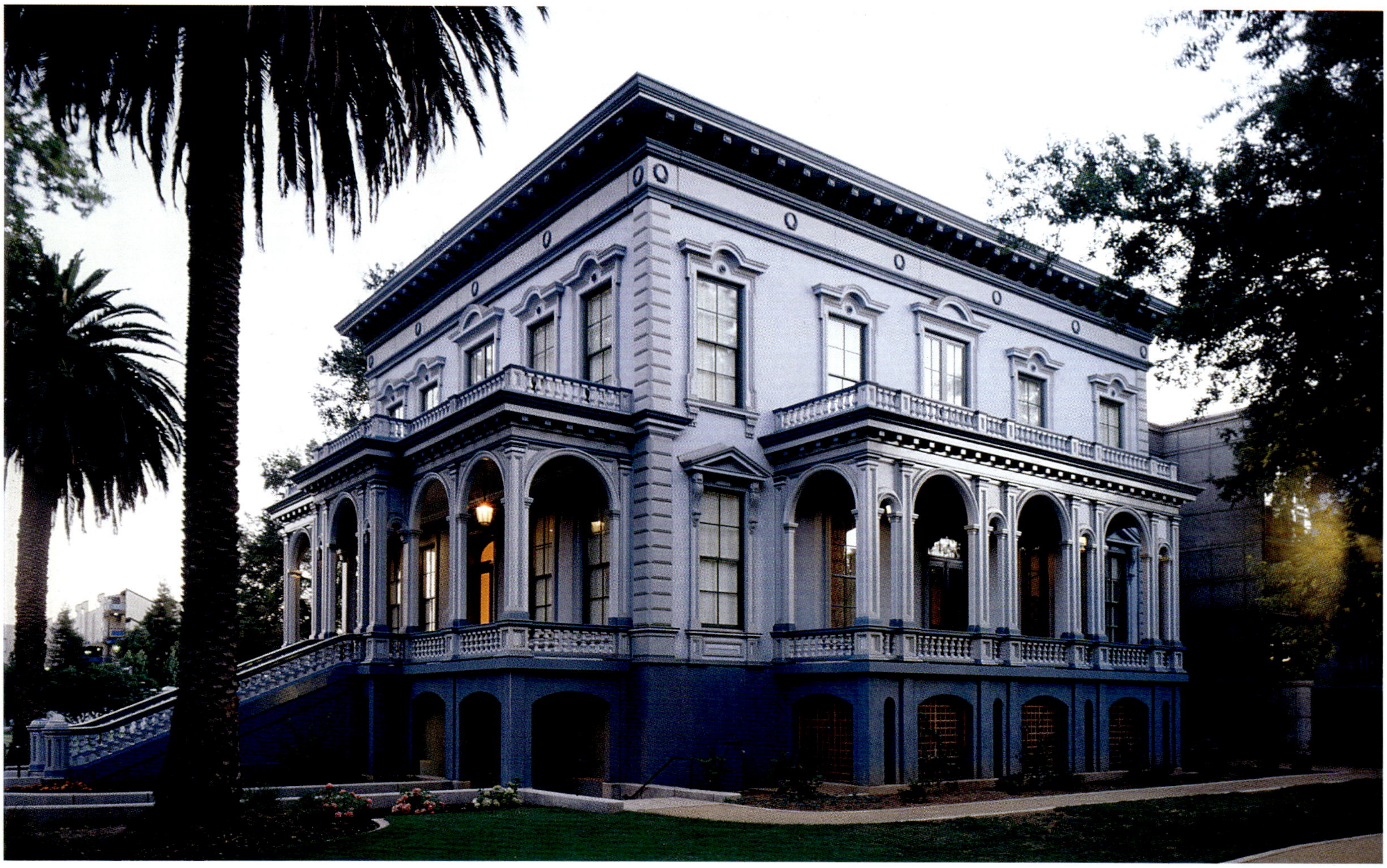

▲ CATHY KELLY

▲ CATHY KELLY

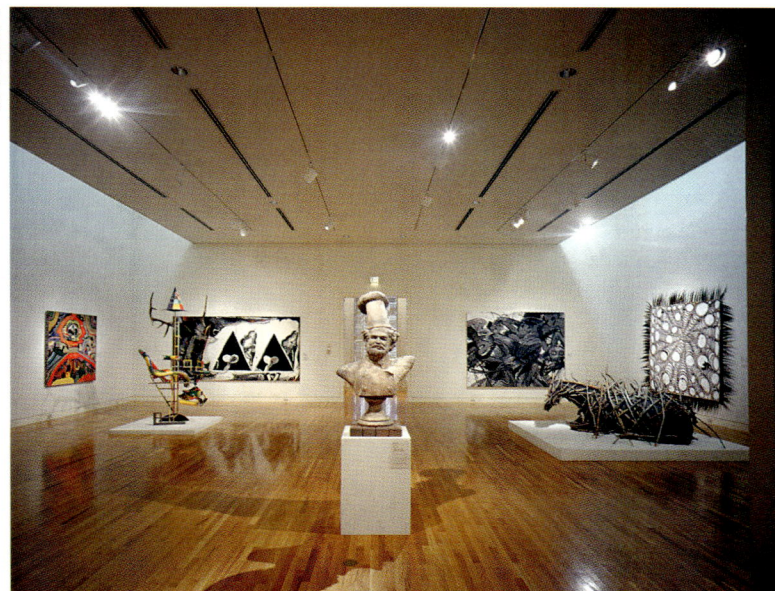

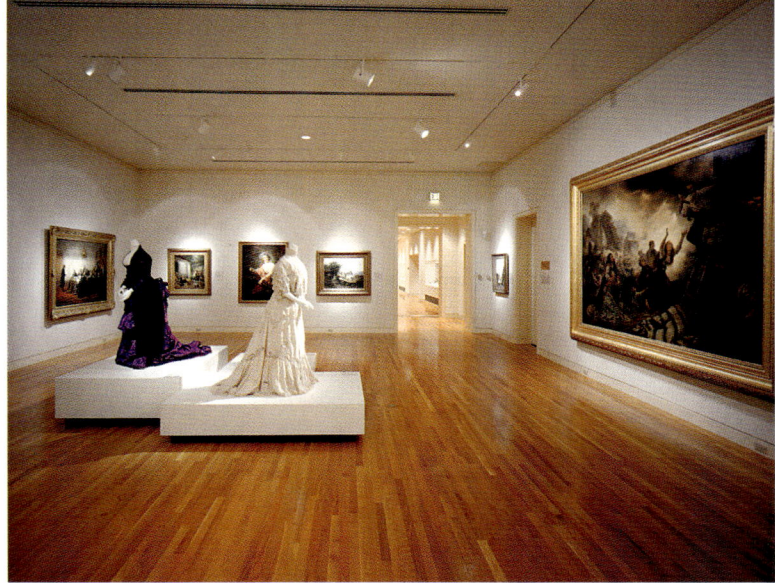

FORMER GOVERNOR PAT BROWN USED TO AMBLE FROM IT IN HIS BATHROBE TO SWIM IN THE HOTEL POOL ACROSS THE STREET. FORMER FIRST LADY NANCY REAGAN HATED THE RATS THERE. THESE DAYS, THE FORMER GOVERNOR'S MANSION (OPPOSITE), BUILT IN 1877, IS A MUSEUM AND POPULAR PLACE FOR WEDDINGS. BUILT ABOUT THE SAME TIME BY STATE SUPREME COURT JUSTICE E.B. CROCKER, THE CROCKER ART MUSEUM (THIS PAGE) IS THE OLDEST ART MUSEUM WEST OF THE MISSISSIPPI. AFTER HIS DEATH, THE JUDGE'S WIDOW GAVE THE MUSEUM AND ITS CONTENTS TO THE CITY.

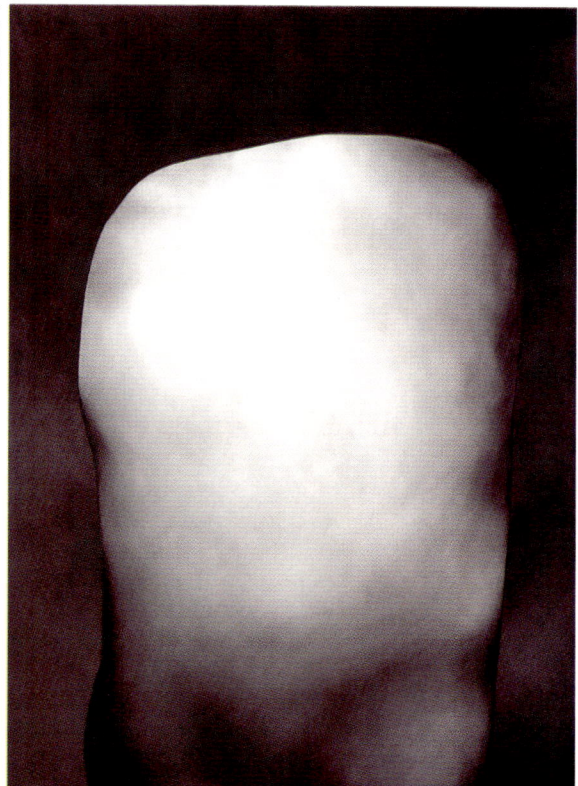

Sacramento's art scene is nothing if not eclectic, whether it's the oil work of Frank Damiano (opposite), the charcoal works of Julia Couzens (top), or the mixed-media, three-dimensional efforts of Rebecca Gozion (bottom).

The brainchild of Mayor Joe Serna, the Thursday Night Market takes over the K Street Mall once a week during summer months, drawing thousands to peruse arts and apples, crafts and cucumbers (opposite).

Practicing what they preach: Father Dan Madigan's Food Bank distributes food to more than 400,000 people each year (left), while Sister Bridget McCarthy (right) supervises four Catholic hospitals in the area and 5,000 employees—and has never received a paycheck for it.

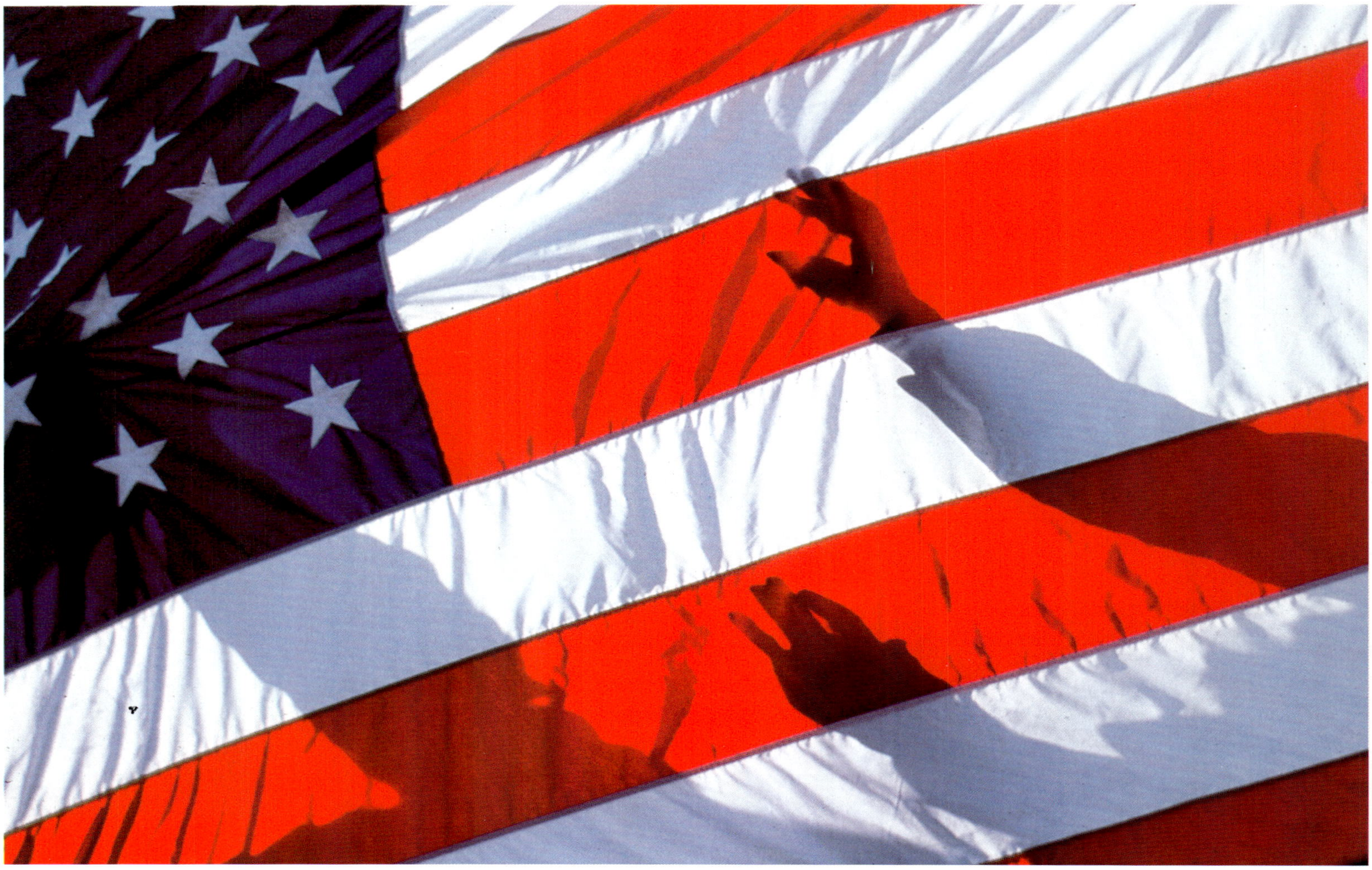

▼ TOM MYERS

▼ TOM MYERS

▼ JEFF MYERS

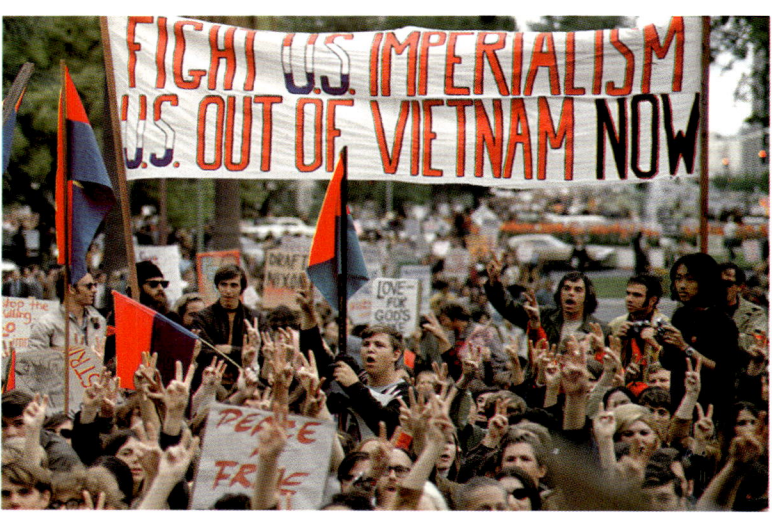

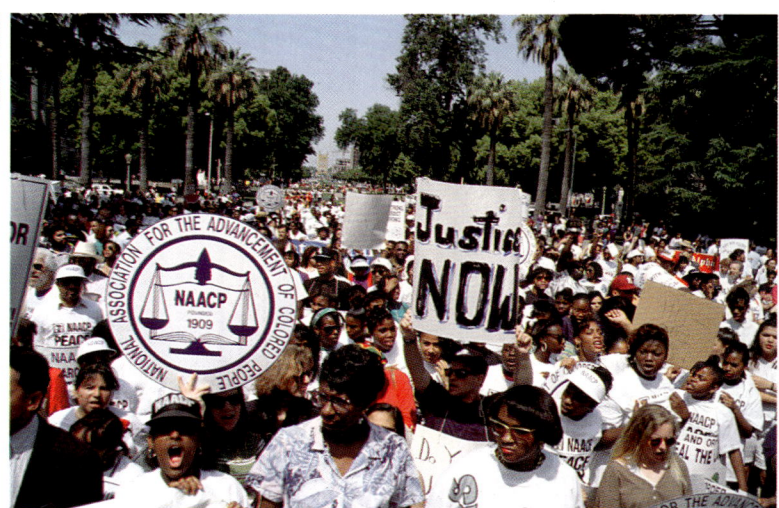

Capitol Park is said to have a representative of every kind of tree in the state, and it's been home to just about every kind of gathering too, from anti-war protests to gay-rights demonstrations.

TAPESTRY 65

Veteran TV newsman Stan Atkinson (top left) is probably the most recognizable media figure in city history, famous for his periodic jaunts to world hot spots. TV newsman Dick Cable (top right) may be a close second. Less visible but far more influential is *Sacramento Bee* Executive Editor Gregory Favre (bottom left), who has led the paper to two Pulitzer Prizes.

Pete Wilson first came to Sacramento in 1966 as an assemblyman from San Diego. He must have liked it—he gave up a seat in the U.S. Senate to come back as governor in 1990.

Want sizzling Chicago blues, Sacramento-style? Little Charlie and the Nightcats (opposite) are an internationally known band that has played everywhere, except maybe in a jail.

Built in the 1870s and made famous in song by Johnny Cash, Folsom Prison (left) has in recent years lost its "status" as California's toughest lockup. But the area isn't bereft of law-and-order symbols. Among them are U.S. Supreme Court Justice Anthony Kennedy (bottom left), a longtime Sacramento resident, and Police Chief Arturo Venegas, Jr. (bottom right).

Help in an emergency can take many forms: the University of California, Davis Medical Center's Life-Flight helicopter; dedicated firefighters; or a reassuring voice at the police communications center.

TAPESTRY 71

IF A CITY IS BEST DEFINED BY ITS PEOPLE, ITS SENSE OF HUMOR—INTENDED OR NOT—MIGHT BEST BE MEASURED BY THE SIGNS OF THE TIMES.

LISTING THE 5,822 CALIFORNIA CASUALTIES OF THE WAR, THE VIETNAM MEMORIAL IN CAPITOL PARK ATTRACTS THOSE WHO WERE THERE AND THOSE WHO REMEMBER. MANY OF THESE VISITORS ARRIVE VIA THE SACRAMENTO MUNICIPAL AIRPORT, THROUGH WHICH NEARLY A MILLION PASSENGERS PASS EACH YEAR (OPPOSITE).

John Sutter, a fugitive from a Swiss debtors' prison, came to the area that would become Sacramento in 1839. For a decade he ruled a mini-empire from an adobe fort with 18-foot-high walls. Then they found gold nearby and Sutter's empire was overrun by forty-niners. But the fort, now restored, is still there, and is one place where the past is cause for celebration.

What was the city's most important district in the 1850s had become its sorriest slum by the 1950s. But two decades of redevelopment—using original materials—turned Old Sacramento into a six-block slice of California history on the banks of the Sacramento River, complete with costumed characters and cobbled streets.

EVERY MEMORIAL DAY WEEKEND, OLD SACRAMENTO BECOMES THE DIXIELAND JAZZ CAPITAL OF THE WORLD, WHEN THE SACRAMENTO JAZZ JUBILEE BEGINS.

While the drinking policy isn't really as liberal as the misprinted sign indicates (top left), "Old Sac" still offers a varied collection of restaurants and watering holes.

▶ TOM MYERS

▶ TOM MYERS

▶ CATHY KELLY

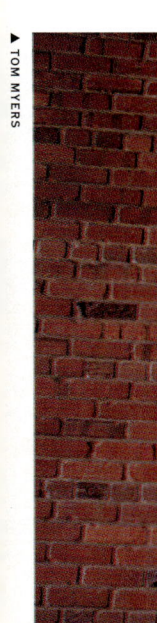

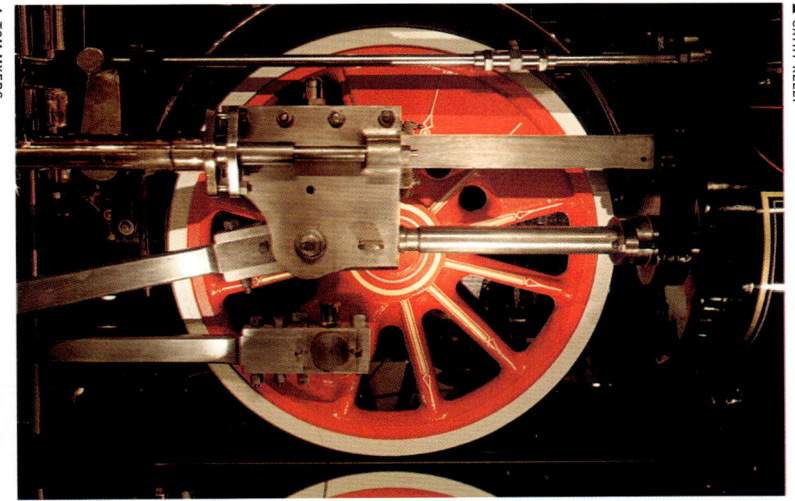

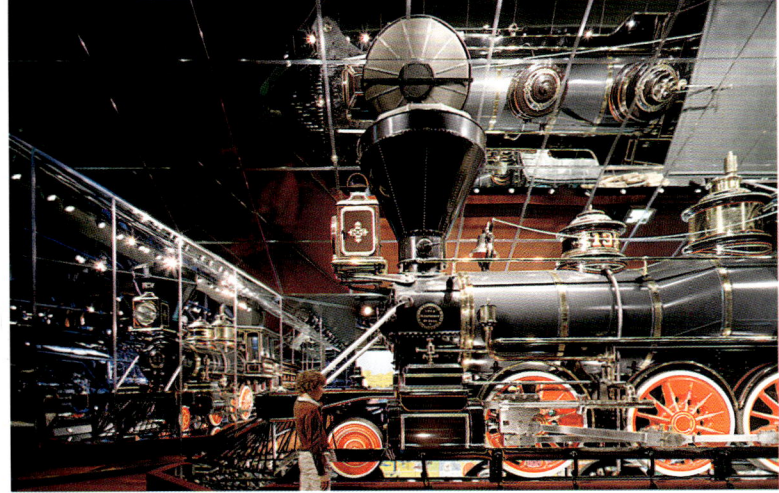

The California State Railroad Museum covers 100,000 square feet and includes a full-scale train depot and a sleeper car that gently rocks to the rhythm of the rails. More than a train collection, the museum in Old Sacramento is a stirring tribute to a bygone time.

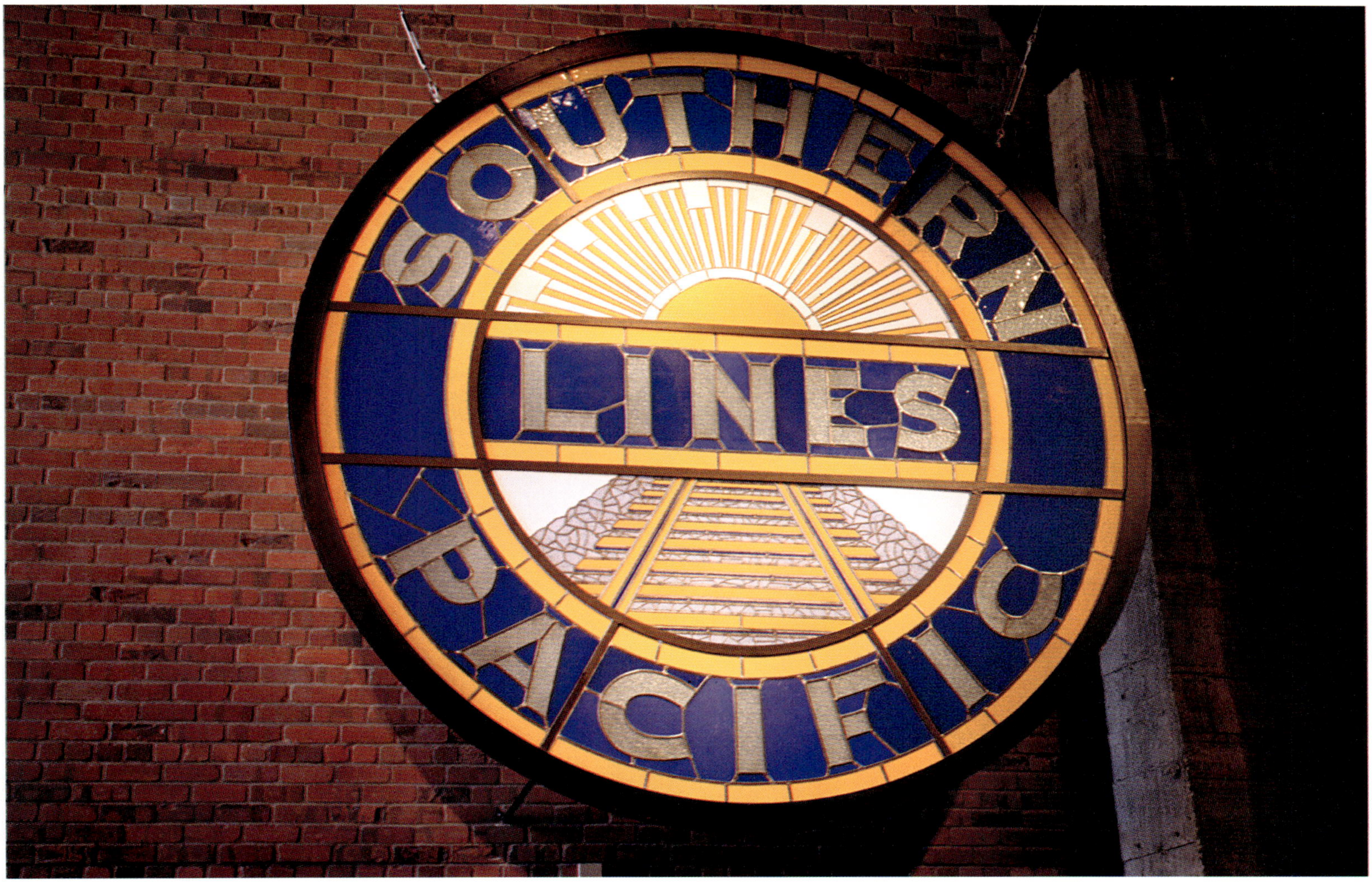

Page 86: Photo by Allen Quinn
Page 87: Photo by Tom Meyers

Despite a population of more than a million, the Sacramento area has a small-town feel that's accentuated by the presence of still-active railroad facilities in midtown locations like the Roseville train yard (top), or the tracks at 34th and R streets in artist Fred Dalkey's oil painting (bottom).

Whether it's reflected in the reality of a photograph or the art of William Allan, sunset in the Sacramento Delta is a stirring sight.

The Sacramento and San Joaquin rivers have carved the Delta region into 1,000 miles of navigable waterways with colorful names like Potato Slough, and islands with equally fanciful monikers like Rough and Ready. It's also home to every kind of watercraft, from sleek cruisers to ramshackle houseboats.

▲ JEFF BURKHOLDER / LIFE IMAGES
▲ JEFF BURKHOLDER / LIFE IMAGES

▼ TOM MYERS

▲ ALLEN QUINN

▲ TOM MYERS

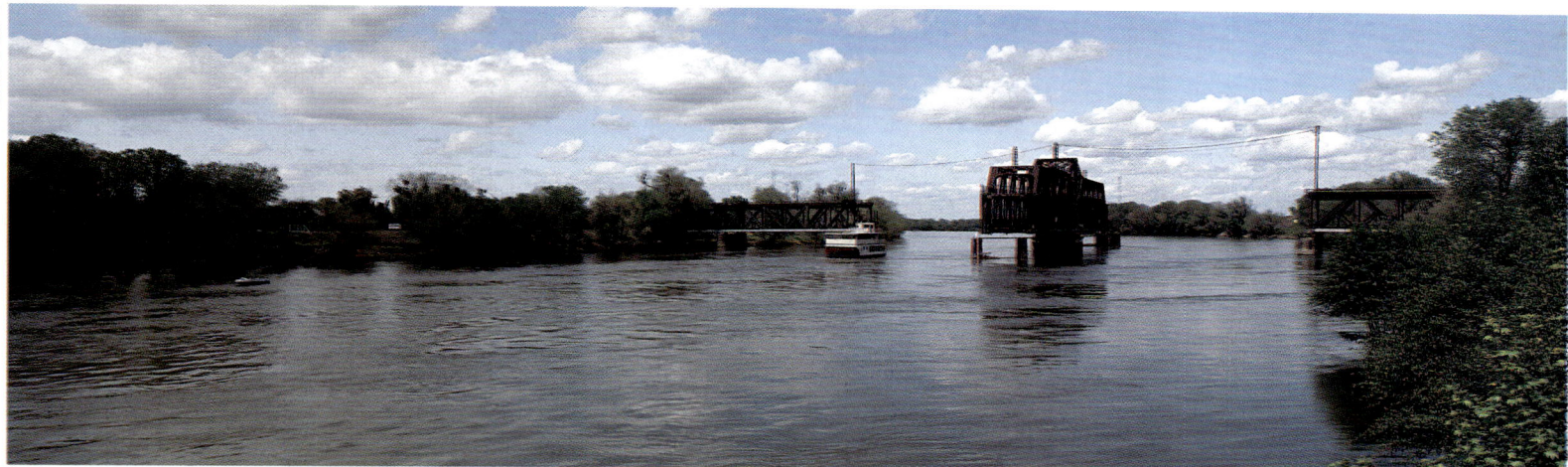

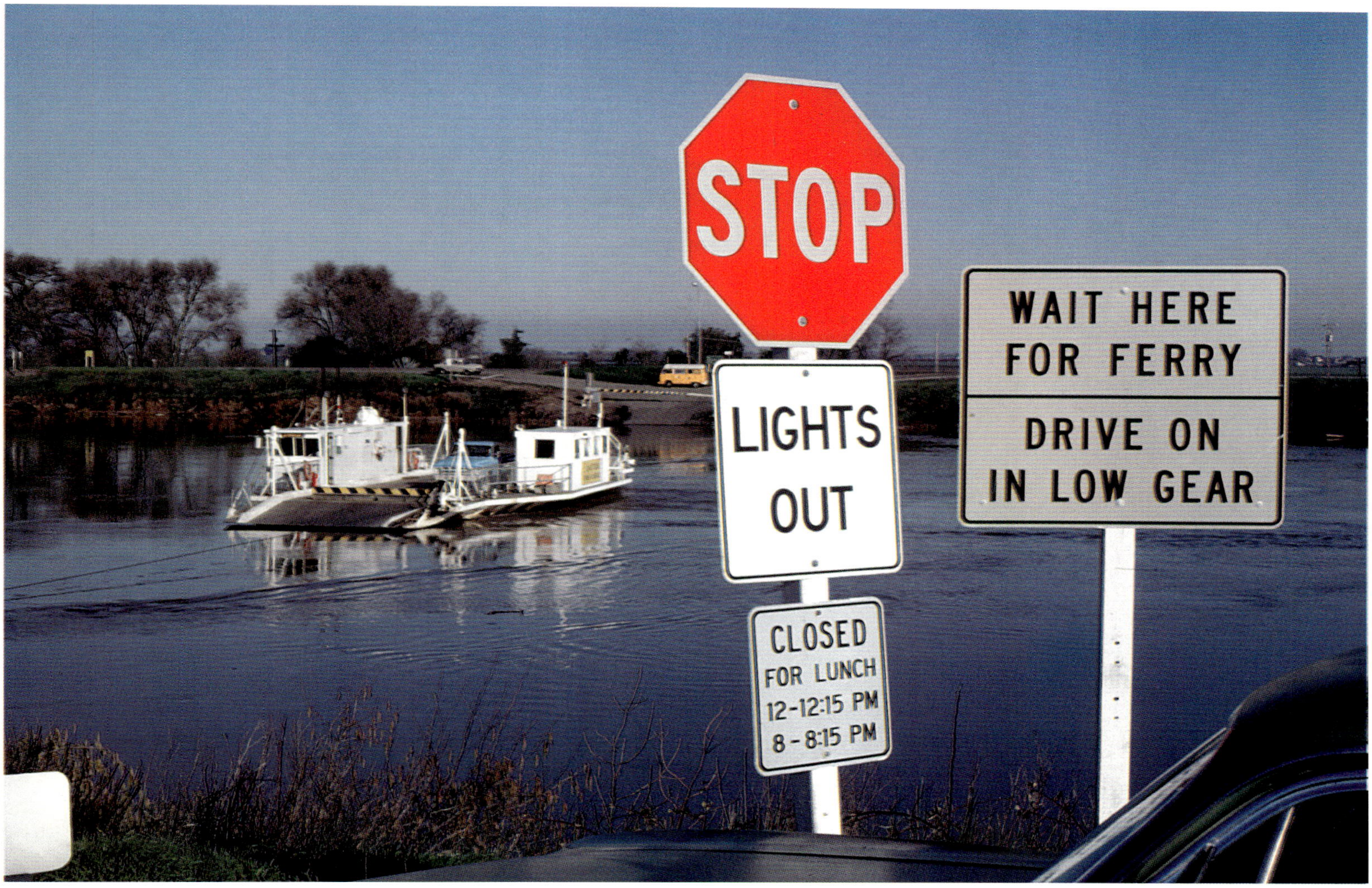

The Delta's watery maze creates special transportation problems that are handled in special ways, from movable bridges (top) to ferries (bottom).

The yuppie restaurants call them crayfish, but in the Delta community of Isleton, they're known as crawdads. And people gobble up more than six tons of them each year at the annual festival. The Delta is also home to catfish farms, the tule reed, and the ubiquitous pickup truck.

TAPESTRY 95

There's not much left of the Delta town of Locke, but at one time it was America's last real Chinatown. At its peak in the 1920s and 1930s, the town was home to 1,200 Chinese farm workers.

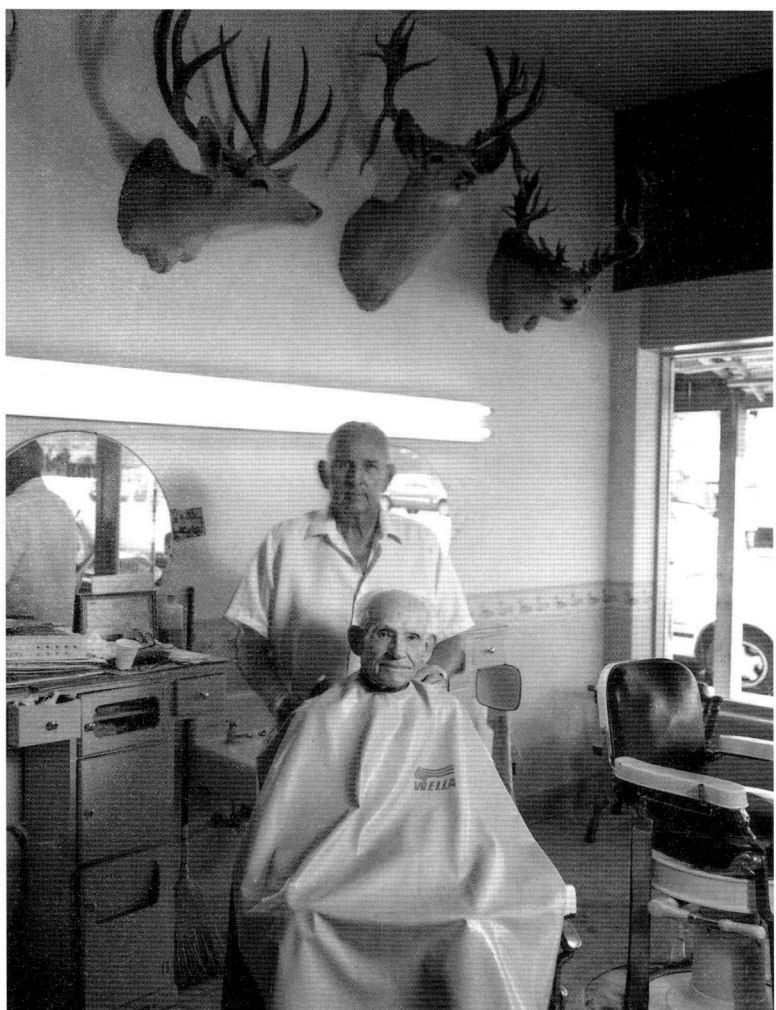

DELTA TOWNS LIKE COURTLAND AND CLARKSBURG ARE HOME TO FARMS AND FOLKS—AND PROBABLY MORE KEYS THAN THERE ARE LOCKS IN THE WHOLE REGION.

So prolific are the area's rice fields that more than 500,000 metric tons were sold to Japan alone in 1994. The grain pumps $1 billion-plus into the Valley's economy.

Rice isn't the only produce grown in these parts. The region also abounds in almonds, apricots, pears, and peaches.

Of course all that fruit has to go somewhere, and a lot of it ends up as prize-winning jam and jelly at the state fair.

▲ TOM MYERS

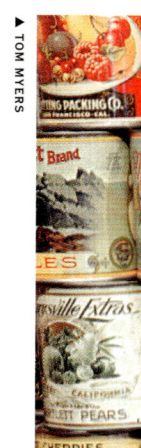

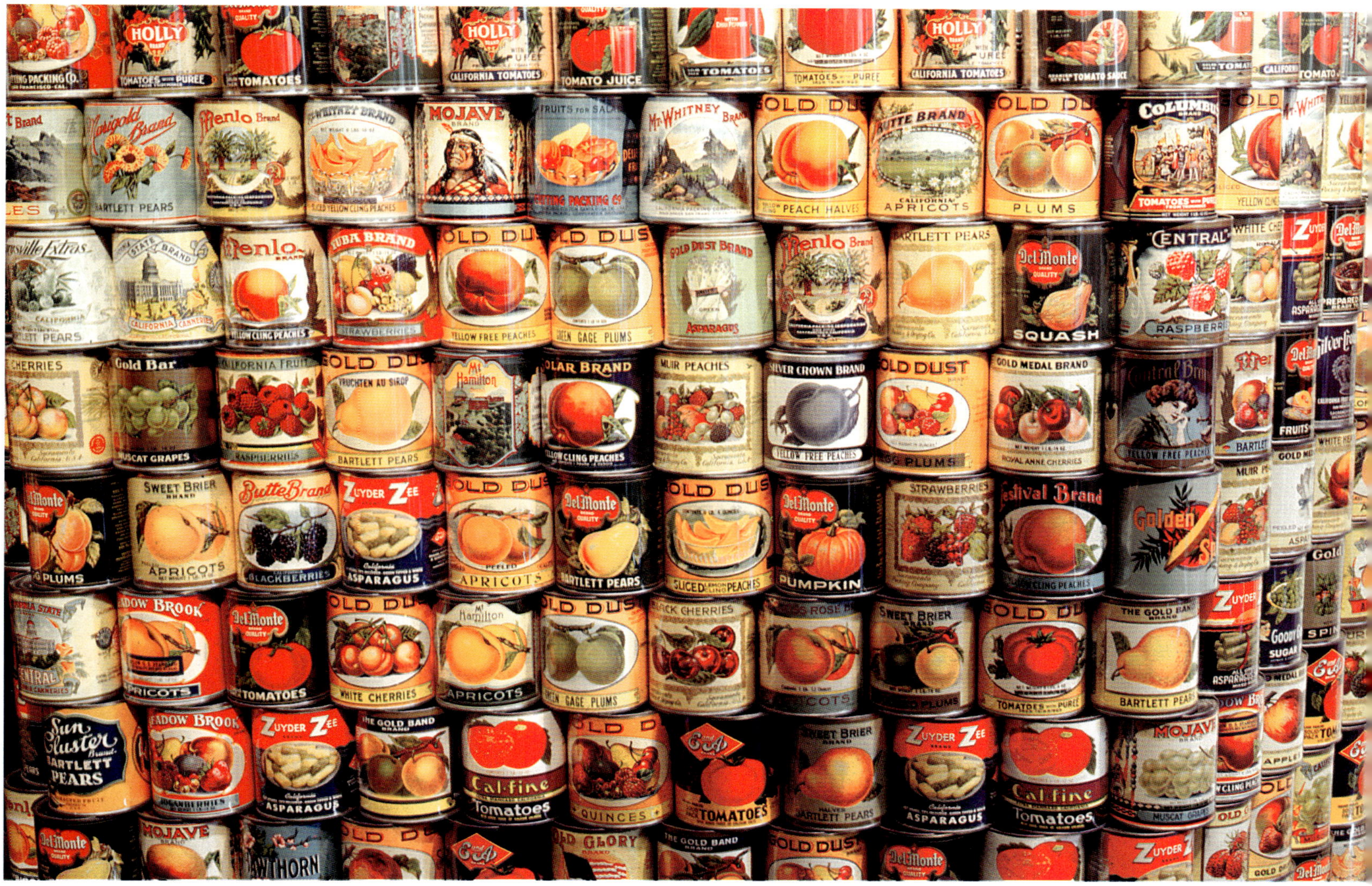

A visitor to the Sacramento Museum of History, Science, and Technology might conclude there's a label for every piece of fruit or vegetable the region produces.

In the foothills east of Sacramento, there's a place called Apple Hill. Every fall it becomes a magnet for folks with visions of "cider," "pie," and "fritter" floating in their heads.

Natives aren't particularly fond of Sacramento's "Big Tomato" nickname. But it does beat "Big Rice Hull."

There is an invasion taking place in Sacramento's farmlands, led by people who want a little bit of country with their lifestyle.

Scheduled for completion in spring 1995, the $80 million expansion of the Sacramento Community Convention Center will triple the size of the existing center and feature a new, 2,454-seat performing arts theater.

▲ SACRAMENTO CITY ARCHIVE

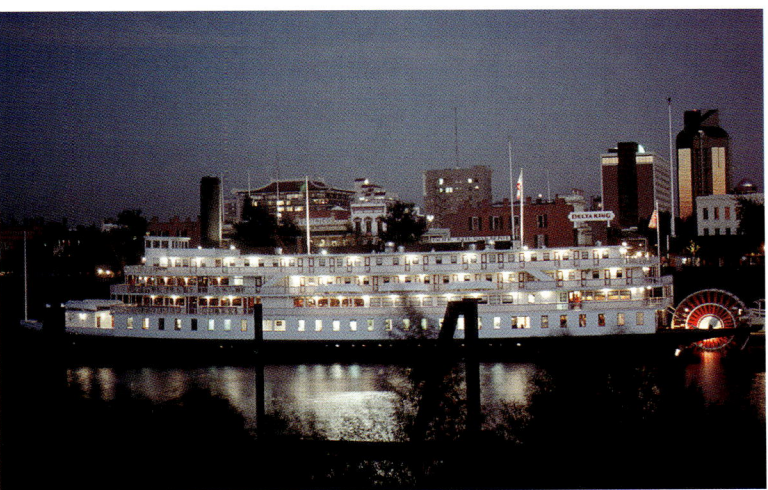

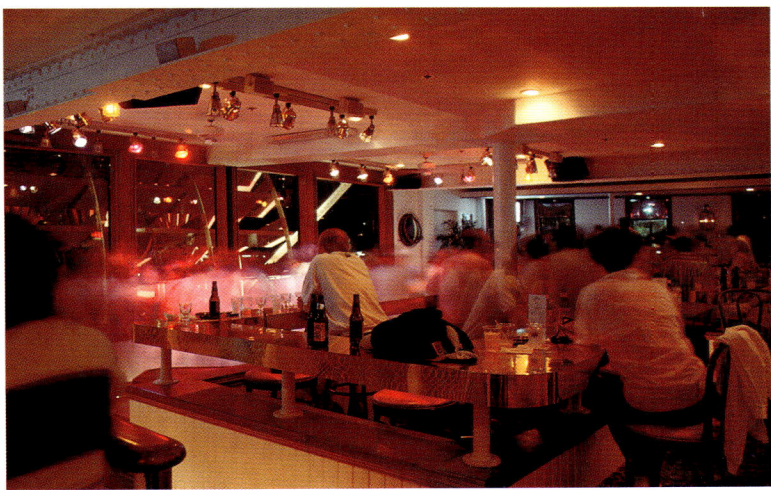

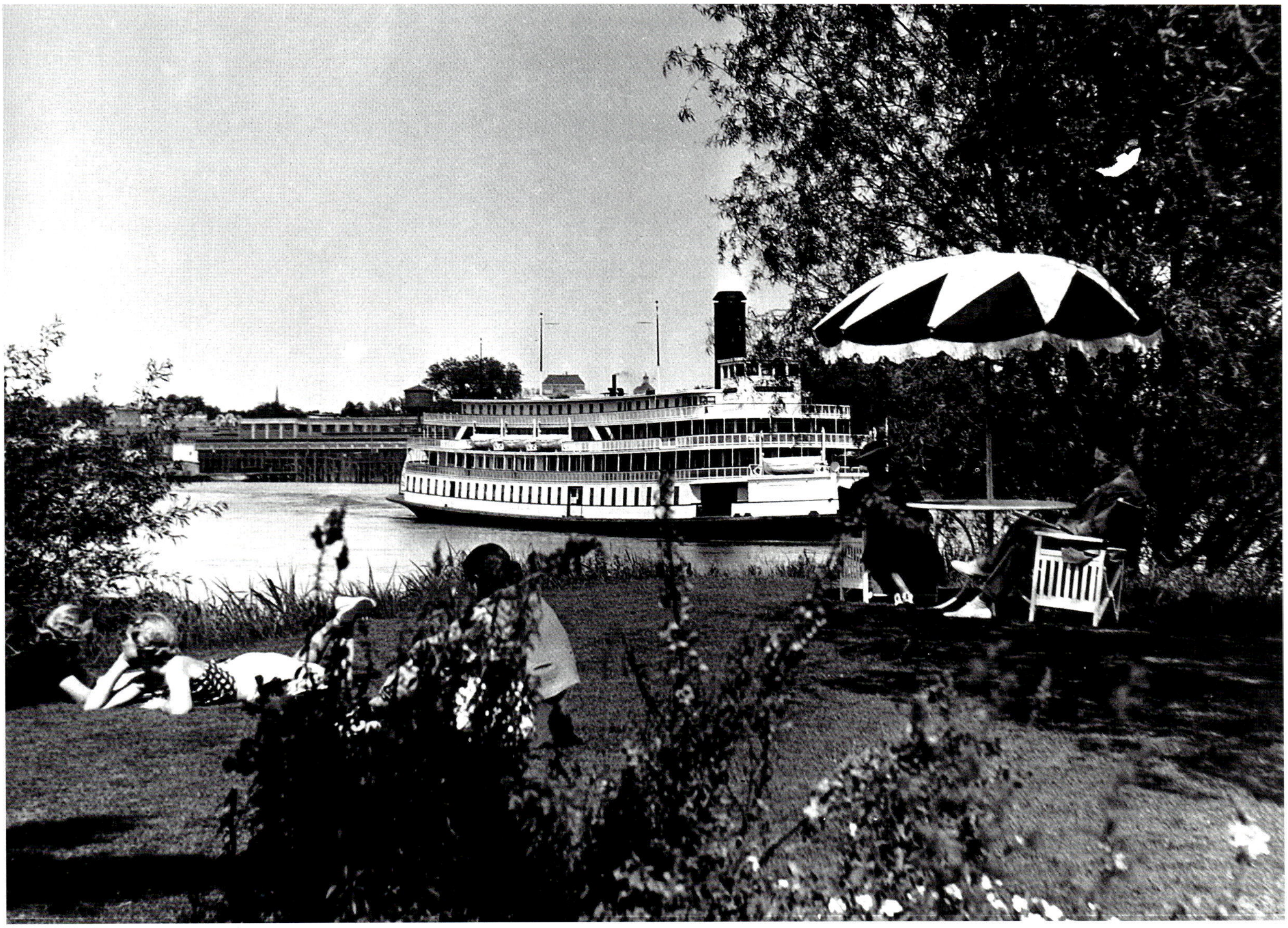

▲ TOM MYERS

▲ SALLY MYERS

ONCE UPON A TIME, IT PLIED THE WATERS BETWEEN SACRAMENTO AND SAN FRANCISCO. THEN IT LANGUISHED FOR YEARS, SUNK IN THE MUDFLATS. IN 1989 THE *DELTA KING* WAS RESTORED TO ITS FORMER GLORY AND OPENED AS A FLOATING RESTAURANT, HOTEL, AND CENTERPIECE OF OLD SACRAMENTO.

It's 90 miles to the Pacific, but Sacramento has its own bustling deepwater port, shipping agricultural and other products around the world.

It isn't exactly Broadway (that's 15 blocks away), but midtown's J Street nonetheless has its share of bright lights.

On fine summer nights, there's alfresco dining—1950s style.

In a state with more registered vehicles than people, it's natural that Sacramentans have long had a love affair with the automobile. Of course not all of them love cars as much as vintage auto collector Dick Bertolucci (opposite, top) or car dealer and pitchman extraordinaire Cal Worthington (bottom).

TAPESTRY 113

Originally opened in 1948, the Crest Theatre in the K Street Mall still shows classic films in an old-fashioned, full-size setting. Sacramentan Russ Solomon (bottom right) is founder of the Tower record, video, and book chain that started as a small section of a family pharmacy (top right).

There are different ways to lose the blues in Sacramento: a cocktail at a neighborhood saloon; a late-night dessert at Rick's; or if you're local bluesman Mick Martin, a few harmonica riffs.

▲ TOM MYERS

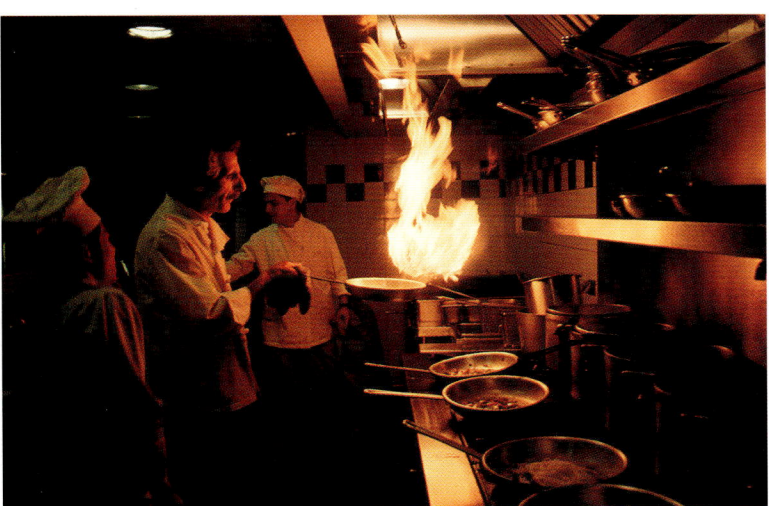

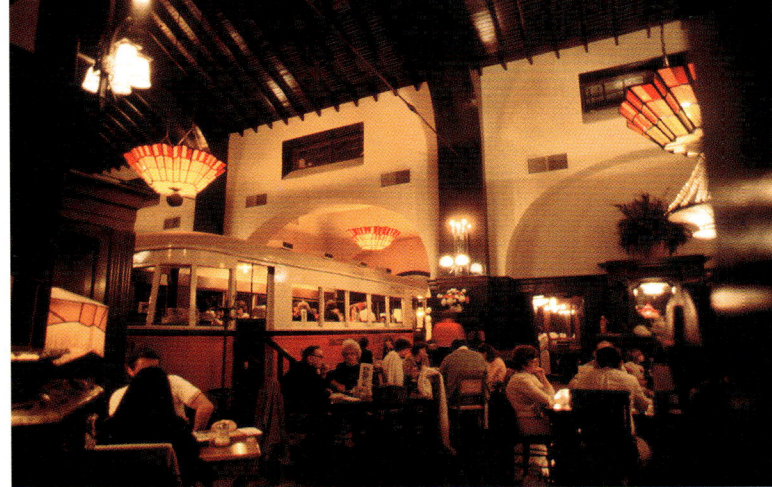

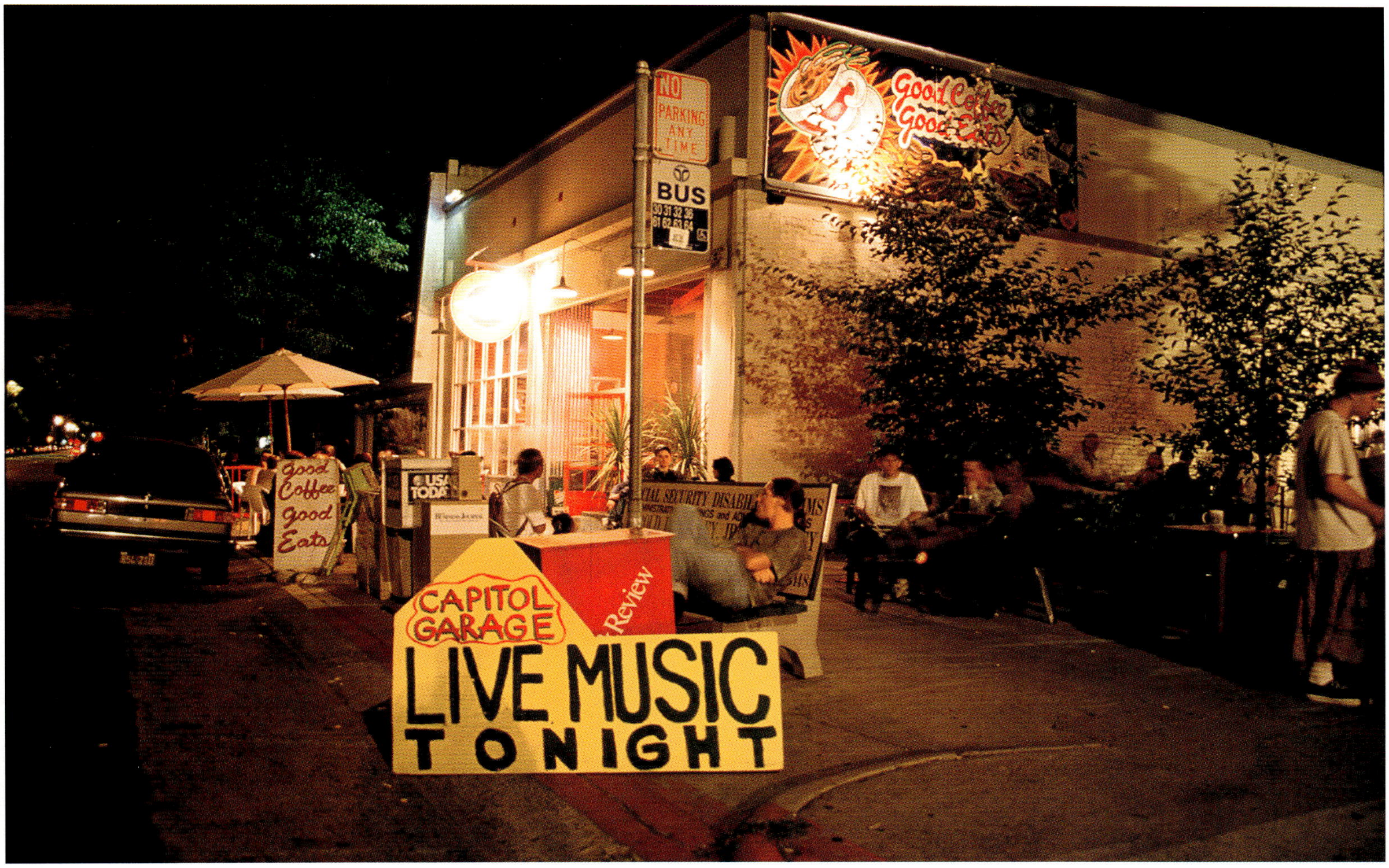

▲ TOM MYERS

▲ TOM MYERS

Befitting its multi-ethnic heritage, Sacramento offers a diverse collection of eateries, including Americo's (opposite), the Adesso Italian Bistro (bottom left), the Old Spaghetti Factory (bottom right), and the Capitol Garage Coffeeworks (top), located in—what else—an old garage.

"What's cooking?" is a question local chefs Steve Capanel (left) and Peter and Barbara Torza (right) never tire of answering.

Since Sacramento is just a long vine away from the world-famous wine country of the Napa and Sonoma valleys, why wouldn't local gourmet and wine connoisseur David Berkeley smile?

Sure it's an oil painting by Fred Dalkey (opposite), but 27th and P streets—and a lot of midtown—really look like this.

For 40 years, the pink Oak Park house behind Audrey Wilcox was Sacramento's most popular restaurant, run by her father, George Dunlap, a former railroad cook. It's been closed for 20 years, but on Sunday afternoons, you'd swear you can still smell chicken cooking.

Ray Tretheway is, quite simply, the "Tree Man of Sacramento." Through the Sacramento Tree Foundation, Tretheway has helped plant tens of thousands of trees, from ash to willow, giving the city a leafy ambience unmatched in the state.

▲ KENT LACIN ▲ TOM MYERS

▲ TOM MYERS

Since the city's future is in the hands of its children, it's fitting that Sacramento holds the Children's Festival in Old Sacramento each year. The event is designed to expose kids to the area's performing and visual arts as well as its cultural diversity.

A hundred years ago, Betsy Marchand's grandfather helped naturalist John Muir launch the environmental movement. Nowadays, Marchand (left) is a leader in the effort to shape and preserve the area's future. Frances Tidey (right) uses her years of educational experience to help the less-advantaged pursue the dream of a college degree.

Prodded by the "eggciting" presence of a thriving University of California campus, much of the city of Davis gets around without internal combustion.

Like many zoos around the country, the Sacramento Zoo is undergoing a transition from animals imprisoned in stark cages to more wide-open spaces. The "new" zoo will have a rivers-of-the-world theme.

The first phase of the zoo's renovation is a 200,000-gallon Lake Victoria replica. Coupled with popular programs such as Zoo Overnight (bottom), the zoo is becoming a place that teaches as well as entertains.

Thanks to a year-round calendar of festivals and events—like the Camellia Festival (left) and the Sacramento Conservation Fair (bottom right)—Sacramentans have grown accustomed to seeing the out-of-the-ordinary.

Other annual events, such as Earth Day (top left) and the Children's Festival in Old Sacramento (right), promote a positive message as well as provide entertainment for Sacramentans of all ages.

Sacramento's populace has many faces, from the ceremonial masks of the Pacific Rim to the finery of Central and South America.

The city's celebratory fetes are just as varied, from the Japanese Kite Festival to the Dia de los Muertos (Day of the Dead) celebration.

The individual efforts of players like Mitch Richmond (top left) and Walt Williams (bottom right), and the spectacle of the National Basketball Association have made Kings games a sellout event.

◀ ROCKY WIDNER

◀ JEFF BURKHOLDER / LIFE IMAGES

▼ ROCKY WIDNER

▼ ROCKY WIDNER

TAPESTRY 135

A RIVER, A RAFT, AND A KID. MULTIPLY BY A THOUSAND OR TWO, AND YOU HAVE THE YOUNG LIFE RAFT RACE—A RACE THAT EVERYBODY WINS (LEFT).

ED ASMUS

Local restaurateur and sportsman Eppie Johnson started it as a lark with about 350 entrants. Now, the "Great Race"—6.4 miles of kayaking, a 5.8-mile run, and a 12.5-mile bike ride—attracts more than 2,000 participants and thousands of spectators (right and middle).

Riches are where—and how—you find them. On the American River, where the California Gold Rush began, some pan, some dredge, and some get lucky.

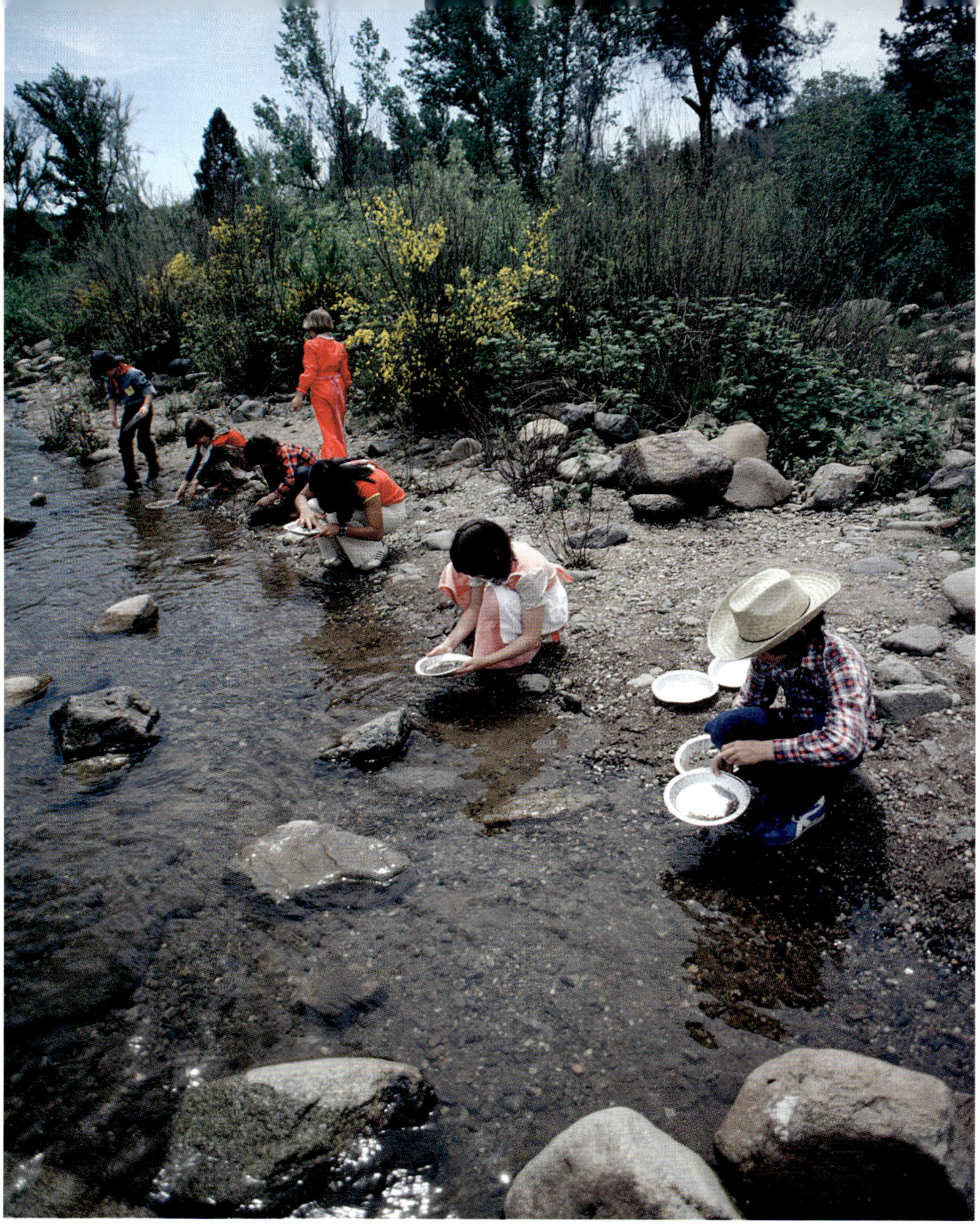

▼ TOM MYERS

▼ TOM MYERS

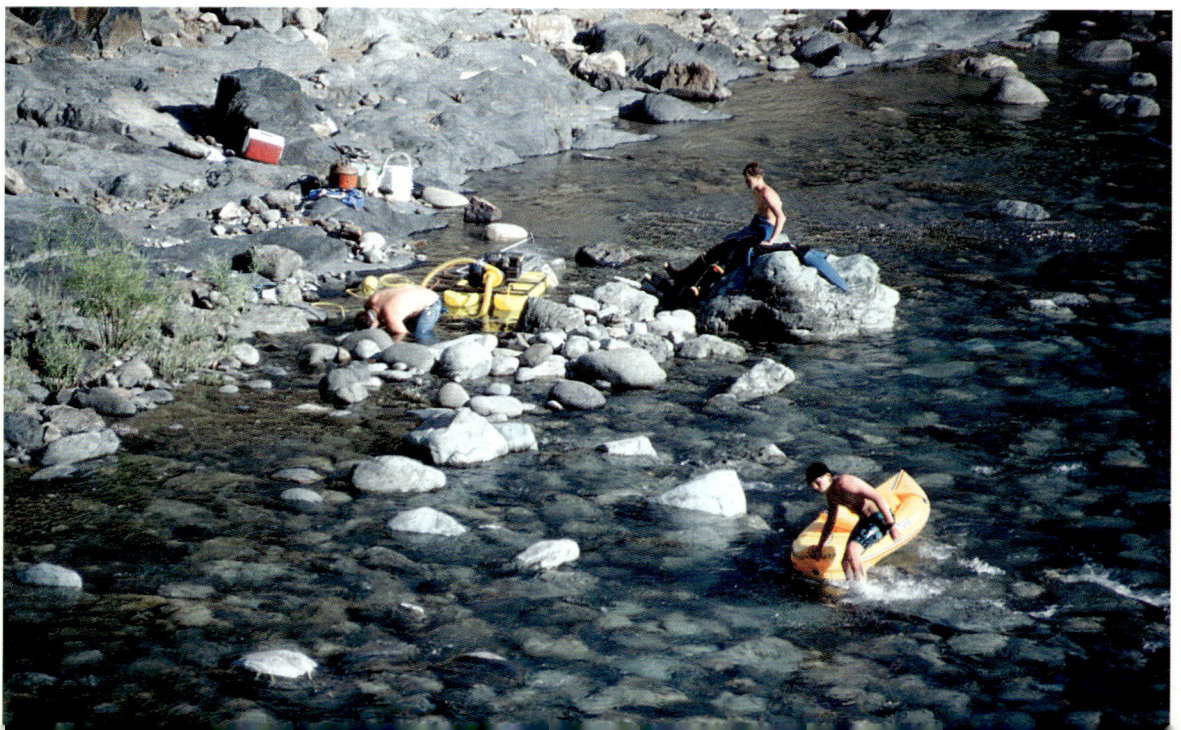

▲ TOM MYERS

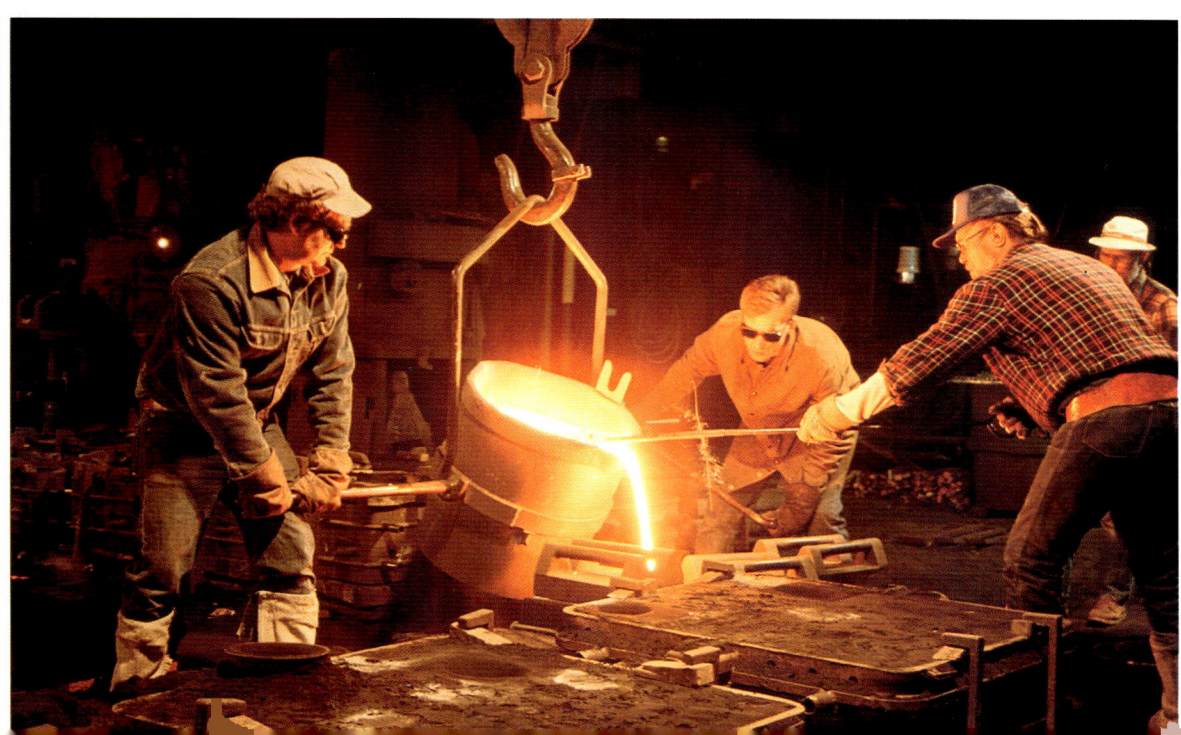

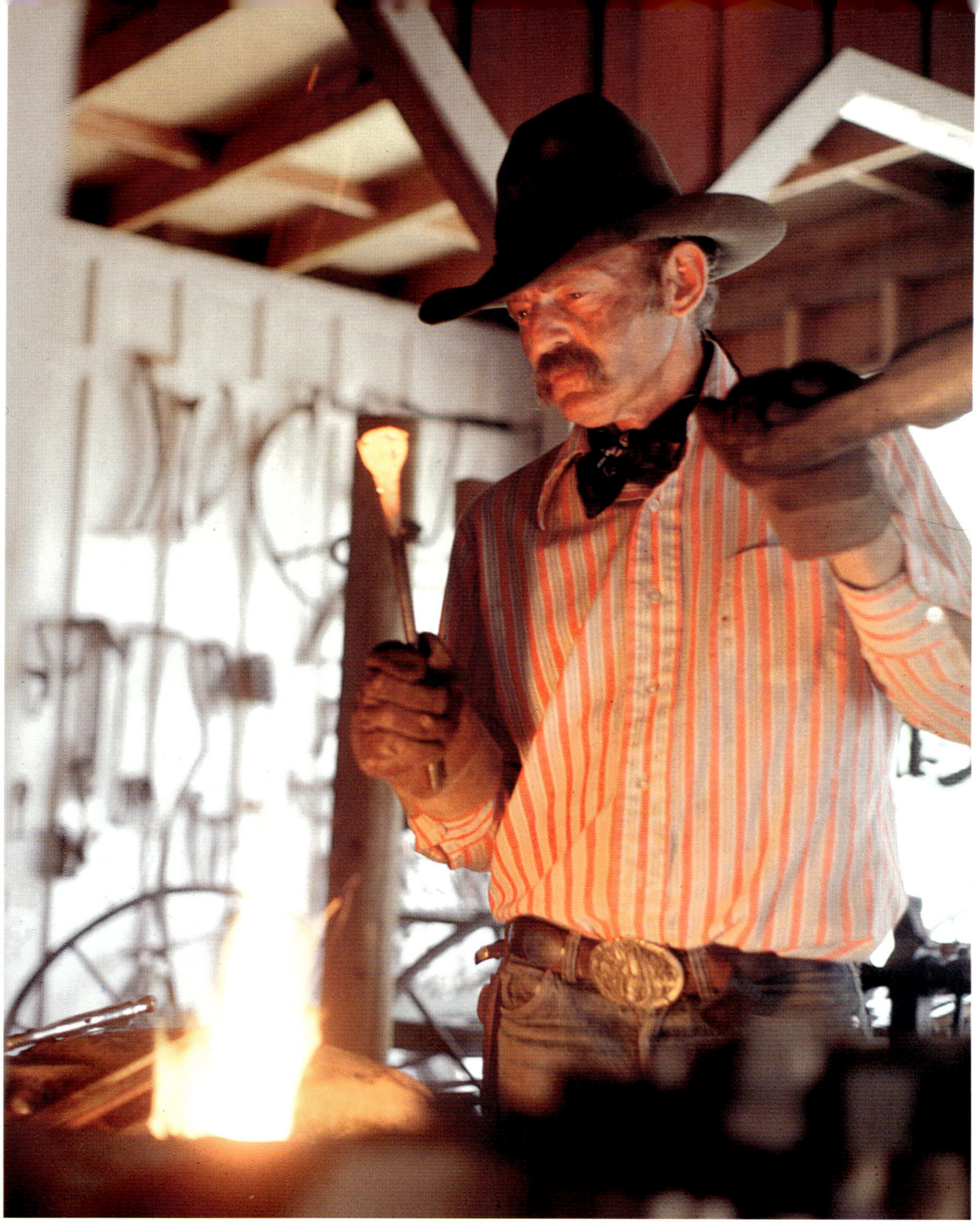

▲ SALLY MYERS

THE OLD-FASHIONED WAY IS STILL BEST IN SOME INSTANCES—LIKE WAGON MAKING BY FIDDLETOWN BLACKSMITH RON SCOFIELD (TOP) OR SMELTING GOLD AT THE SUTTER CREEK FOUNDRY (BOTTOM).

Sure, Sacramento is the "Camellia City," but other varieties of flowers thrive, from roses (top) to California poppies (bottom). That creates a smorgasbord for butterflies.

▲ PAT LIVINGSTON
▲ TOM MYERS

▲ KURT FISHBACK

In a region of mighty rivers and majestic Sierra lakes, a foothill pond can hold its own on a Sacramento spring morning.

A FOOTHILL ROAD LINKS SACRAMENTO'S PAST AND FUTURE, AND PASSES THROUGH A PRETTY GOOD-LOOKING PRESENT.

THE PAST IS

THE SACRAMENTO METROPOLITAN
CHAMBER OF COMMERCE
CELEBRATES ITS 100TH ANNIVERSARY

PROLOGUE:

INTRODUCTION

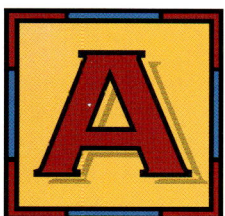

As the first booming outpost on the Gold Rush trail that held any semblance of permanence or civilization, Sacramento—established, by most good estimates, in 1839—has had plenty of opportunities to celebrate itself. A 50-year anniversary. A grand centennial. A sesquicentennial. ■ And it will only be another generation before people are forming bicentennial committees and setting out to throw a memorable bash.

Not only has Sacramento had plenty of *time* to celebrate, it's also had plenty of *reason* to celebrate. From the somber procession welcoming a dignitary to a raucous parade on a hot summer night, Sacramento is well versed in the fine art of commemorating those milestones that deserve recognition.

This year, the city has the opportunity to celebrate another of these anniversaries: the Centennial of the Sacramento Metropolitan Chamber of Commerce.

It's now been a solid 100 years since this organization went from being a dream in the minds of leading business and civic leaders, 15 of whom had served for some time as an organizing committee, to a reality. On September 27, 1895—with some 300 members signed up, at least 75 of whom attended the first organizational meeting—the Sacramento Chamber of Commerce was officially chartered. For those who belonged, the initiation fee was a whopping $5; monthly dues stood at $1 per month, payable quarterly, in advance.

When it was formed, the Chamber oversaw what was, by the standards of the day, already a prosperous and growing community. California had been a state since 1850. Sacramento had been the state capital since 1854. It had been the western terminus of the Pony Express for the short time it was in business (1860-61); although it took only eight days for Express riders to race their horses across the 2,000 miles of badlands, mountains, canyons, and deserts, all concerned discovered that the transcontinental telegraph that was completed in 1861 was a whole lot quicker, and considerably less taxing on man and beast.

Then, in short order, came the railroads, with Sacramento serving as a key stop for the Central Pacific and Union Pacific, which

"Placer Mining near Sacramento, 1849" by George Mattins

were joined to link the coasts with the driving of a golden spike in 1869.

But it was undeniably gold—nuggets and dust and mother lodes—that had fueled the city's ascent during its early years. John Augustus Sutter, who had pitched his tent on the American River near here, built a trading post and sawmill that changed history when, in 1848, Sutter's mill foreman, a fellow by the name of James Marshall, looked down into the water that was being sluiced out of the mill and saw . . . gold. The rush, as we know, was on. Sutter never became wildly rich from gold, but when he turned over his land holdings to his son, the young man decided that the green fields and rolling hills he surveyed alongside the Sacramento River were, in fact, gold of another sort. He laid out streets, planned buildings, and began assembling the rough-and-tumble collection of traders and prospectors into a community he called Sacramento.

Today, the mansions built by those who became fabulously wealthy from gold pried or panned or blown out of "them thar hills" around Sacramento can still be seen. A hundred years ago, when the Chamber of Commerce was

founded, they fairly dominated the city, lending it a sophistication and sense of itself that most young cities take centuries to acquire. Sacramento had, by 1895, all the comforts of the "civilized" burgs of the East Coast. An opera, grand hotels, newspapers, several orchestras, dramatic societies, social societies, churches, and all manner of mercantile and manufacturing activity were in abundance. What's more, thanks to the area's climate—plenty of warm days, heavy on the sunshine—it's easy to see how city leaders would need an organization to help channel all this business activity in productive directions. Thus the rationale for, and mission of, the Sacramento Metropolitan Chamber of Commerce.

WITHIN FIVE YEARS THE CHAMBER had become an active participant in the daily business of the city. By 1900, when it moved to permanent offices at 214 J Street, the Chamber had concerned itself with such issues as flood control, irrigation, the dredging of a deepwater channel, water purity and sewage matters, education, transportation, agriculture, and a street fair and show. These latter activities were introduced in 1900, the same year that the Chamber went about the business of helping to organize California's 50th birthday party (we told you it was a city of celebrations), as well as the increasingly popular California

State Fair. It was, by anyone's standards, a busy time. What's remarkable, however, is that many of the same issues that the Chamber dealt with then are still paramount today. Not that there hasn't been tremendous progress on every front. But the methods, the strategies, and many of the issues have, it's obvious, always been important to those of us who live and work here.

The following year the Chamber was feeling a bit prosperous itself, so it bestowed a pay raise on the janitor who kept its offices clean, granting him $20 a month rather than the $12 he was receiving. Soon he would have even grander quarters to maintain, as the Chamber purchased land (in 1905) on 7th Street between I and J for $9,625 to house its own building.

The same year brought curious tidings for all who lived in Sacramento. First, the Chamber brought a blimp to town—the first ever seen in Northern California—and instructed its stalwart pilot to keep flying it over the city for the delight of those below. And, perhaps even more shocking in that day and age, the Women's Council was allowed to begin holding their meetings at the Chamber's new building. Both events transpired with no lingering side effects registered by the populace.

Within its first decade—a mere 10 years!—the Sacramento Metropolitan Chamber of Commerce had more than surpassed its early goal of seeing to it that the business interests of the city were well represented. It had become an active participant in the economic vitality of the community. Its lobbying efforts, programs, and missions were all tied toward making Sacramento a better place for all to live.

The following section is designed to help you see just *how* active the Chamber has been in helping to mold the future of Sacramento. Pick any decade, any point on the time line of the past century, and you will see the Chamber vigorously working for change, betterment, and prosperity. As the Chamber has evolved into the effective, progressive institution that it now is, many milestones have been surpassed. Herewith, we cast a long look back at the many accomplishments of the Sacramento Metropolitan Chamber of Commerce.

Sacramento Centennial Celebration, 1939.

THE PAST IS PROLOGUE

1839	1848	1850	1854
Settlement begins at present-day Sacramento. 	Gold is discovered in the American River by the foreman at a mill owned by John Augustus Sutter. The Gold Rush begins. Mexico cedes the province of California to the United States.	California enters the Union.	Sacramento is chosen to become California's capital. 

1900	1901	1902	1907
The Chamber locates its offices at 214 J Street, and helps organize the city's first street fair and trade show. In addition, the Chamber helps pull together both the California State Fair and the 50th anniversary celebration of the state's admission to the Union.	The Chamber works to bring President William McKinley to town to address the citizens.	The Chamber adds a valuable resource by "scheduling" all of the land in the city, making information about individual properties immediately available to interested prospects.	The Chamber campaigns hard to prevent the state capital from being moved to another city.

1915	1916	1918	1919
A woman named Mrs. Carmichael is the only female on the Chamber's records holding membership.	The Chamber organizes the Patriotic Home Service League to take care of the families of those Sacramento men who took up arms and went to battle the infamous outlaw Pancho Villa in the wake of Villa's massacre of 18 American miners on the Mexican border.	The Chamber is successful in recruiting a major government warehousing project. 	Thanks in large measure to the efforts of the Chamber, the federal government announces a decision to purchase Mather Field, which is seen as one of the city's primary assets.

1869	1895	1896	1898
The Central Pacific and Union Pacific railroads are joined in Utah with the driving of a golden spike. Sacramento becomes one of the key western stops on the first transcontinental rail-road.	The Sacramento Chamber of Commerce is formed with some 300 members. Initial topics for concern include flood control, irrigation, the construction of a deep-water channel on the Sacramento River, and the condition of wharf facilities.	The Chamber offers a $250 bounty—quite a sum in those days—to the person who comes forward with the best plan for introducing a clean, clear water supply to the city.	The *Sacramento Bee* lauds the Chamber for its work in obtaining improvements to Northern California's navigable streams. The Chamber advocates measures to protect the interests of its members.

1908	1909	1912	1913
The Chamber sponsors a meeting with all civic bodies to form a comprehensive plan for railroads in Sacramento.	Fire destroys the Chamber's building on 7th Street. Nonetheless, the Chamber takes the lead in getting all relevant groups in Northern California together to decisively publicize industry.	The Chamber calls a statewide convention to acquaint all concerned with the various proposals being made regarding river improvement.	The Chamber inaugurates the year with a rally to fight against constructing state buildings in San Francisco. A Junior Chamber of Commerce is formed.

1921	1922	1923	1925
The Chamber helps to bring about the adoption of a new form of city government that includes a city manager, and endorses the formation of a junior college district as well as improvement of the city wharf.	Always ready to celebrate, the Chamber stages a "Days of '49" festival, and invites some 22,000 newspaper and magazine editors to come and partake freely of this commemoration of Sacramento, the Gold Rush, and the infinite progress that had been made since the first nuggets were found.	The completion of a new, $2.7 million filtration plant is among the Chamber's many achievements for the year.	The Chamber acquires a new communication tool—radio station KFBK. Established four years earlier, the station is one of the first in Northern California. The same year, regular airmail service to Sacramento is begun, in large part due to a number of Chamber initiatives paving the way. The Chamber also attracts a major cannery to the area and completes an industrial survey.

1926

To tap into the fertile farmlands and groves near Sacramento, the American Can Company constructs a $1.85 million plant in the city. The Chamber institutes three campaigns to promote business in the Sacramento region.

1927

The Chamber plays host to America's hero Charles Lindbergh, shortly after his historic transatlantic nonstop flight. Lindbergh's visit makes the city—and the Chamber—focus even greater attention on the value of air travel as a vital complement to the city's already strong series of roads, rivers, and rail lines.

1934

With the country in the throes of the Great Depression, the Chamber forges ahead with progressive plans and initiatives. Among the more successful is the Chamber's persistent advocacy of Mather Field as a military aviation hub. In return, President Franklin Roosevelt announces the following year that Mather will, indeed, be developed as an air defense headquarters, while the Chamber is asked to head a nationwide effort to support the national air defense program.

1935

The Chamber urges the California legislature to balance the state's budget and operate California on a "pay as you go" basis.

1942

With the Chamber as a sponsor, the "war effort" in Sacramento proceeds admirably with 30 small manufacturers and machine shop owners joining to form War Industries, Inc. The result: more military contracts for all concerned.

1944

The Chamber receives commendation for its ongoing wartime efforts and its postwar planning for the entire area.

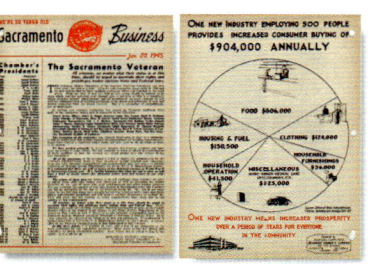

1945

The Chamber meets with officials from Oakland and San Francisco to continue discussions of the deepwater channel. In addition, the Chamber comes down firmly on the side of voluntary health insurance rather than a government-mandated policy. Mather Field becomes a permanent training base, after serving as an outstanding training facility throughout the war. And, the first steps are taken toward bringing professional sports to town, as the Chamber supports a plan to bring an amateur basketball team to the city.

1946

The deepwater channel takes one more step toward fruition as the Chamber supports the Sacramento Ship Channel Project (as it has become officially known) in a proposal before Congress. The channel, as mandated here, will be at least 30 feet deep at low water, will have a bottom width of 200 feet on the straight stretches and 300 feet on the curves, and is slated to run from Suisun Bay to Sacramento. The Chamber brings the Campbell Soup plant to Sacramento.

1952

The Chamber works toward a solution for traffic problems and urges the early completion of the American River levee.

1953

In the "Nice Ring to It" department, the Chamber takes out full-page ads in national magazines proclaiming that "Sacramento Is the Plum of America." The Chamber also vigorously opposes the relocation of the U.S. Geographical Survey Office from Sacramento.

1955

Sacramento Facts, a new Chamber publication highlighting business information on a monthly basis, makes its debut. The Chamber studies the merger of some city and county offices.

1956

The Chamber develops a nine-point state highway priority project list and an eight-point work program for Sacramento's aviation facilities.

1936

The construction of a deep-water channel remains a major goal for the Chamber as it seeks to develop and strengthen the city's transportation modes.

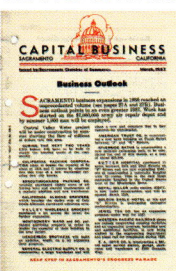

1939

Direct air and passenger service between Sacramento and Los Angeles is begun by United Air Lines as a result of Chamber efforts. The Chamber's vigorous efforts bring to fruition a new air logistics base to the city, McClellan Air Force Base.

1940

The Chamber asks the city engineering department to survey downtown parking problems and suggest solutions. If parking continues to be a problem, Chamber officials fear that businesses will rapidly relocate outside downtown's central business district.

1941

The Chamber's extensive efforts are successful in getting Mather Field reopened and expanded.

1947

The Chamber again strongly opposes moving state offices from Sacramento to San Francisco and begins work on an initiative to bring a four-year college to Sacramento.

1948

The Chamber forms the Sacramento Area Industrial Advisory Committee. In addition, the years of work on the Chamber's part pay off in the opening of Folsom Dam. Also, the Chamber pushes for an urban redevelopment survey.

1949

A Master Zoning Plan for the Sacramento metropolitan area is supported by the Chamber, which also emphasizes the joint planning actions of several nearby counties.

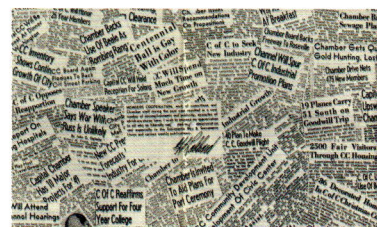

1950

The Chamber is responsible for implementing a "Made in Sacramento" program, a weeklong affair that showcases local manufacturers and artisans. This program proves so successful that it soon becomes an annual event. The Chamber also presents a seven-point industrial development plan.

1957

The guest speaker at the Chamber's monthly breakfast meeting is actor Ronald Reagan, who talks about "governmental controls on business." Also during this year, the Chamber medical affairs committee works with the City/County Health Department in arranging for the administration of adult polio inoculations in Sacramento County.

1958

In keeping with the times, the Chamber launches another local and national ad campaign. Gone is the "plum" image. This time the sloganeers declare Sacramento to be "America's Cool City." On a more practical note, the Chamber forms a committee to study taxation issues at all levels.

1960

The Chamber starts the Wholesale Trade Committee.

1963

The Chamber saves businessmen $800,000 through a reduction in tax assessments, and also holds the city's first foreign trade conference.

THE PAST IS PROLOGUE

1964

The Chamber supports efforts for a regional junior college district plan, and also endorses a general obligation bond to fund storm drainage improvements.

1966

The Chamber exerts its influence to try to keep the California Zephyr, one of the country's last fine passenger trains, from being taken out of service.

1967

With a name change to reflect its growing influence, the Chamber is now the Sacramento *Metropolitan* Chamber of Commerce. The year saw the final victory of the organization's efforts to have the state fair expanded when Governor Ronald Reagan announced his endorsement of the immediate construction of the California Exposition and Fair. This same year, a 12-point program is put forward, with specific targets, including metropolitan government; industrial development; business and community development; taxes; redevelopment of transportation resources; governmental affairs; education; equal opportunity in the workforce and elsewhere; military and government involvement; agricultural promotion; special promotion and development of the Port of Sacramento, the California Exposition, and the metropolitan and municipal airports; and Chamber reorganization.

1974

The Chamber moves to new quarters and sponsors an open house for its spacious new building. The Chamber also supports the Sacramento Metropolitan Master Plan as well as city and county consolidation.

1975

The Chamber supports having a single agency to establish and administer a balanced-use water management program for Sacramento and opposes a resolution to significantly change the existing local government campaign laws.

1976

The Chamber takes a stand on a variety of transportation issues, including keeping options open for another American River Bridge. The Chamber opposes the Proposition 15 nuclear initiative.

1977

In a potpourri of concerns, the Chamber supports the prevention of unfair County Health Inspection Fees from being imposed on businesses; the Civil-Military Forum; the Sacramento Small Business Center (initiated by the Chamber); the relocation of the California Farm Bureau; the Quality of Life Task Force (another Cham-

Chamber opposes utility tax hike

1981

The Chamber works closely with Sutter Community Hospitals and endorses its physical planning for the 1990s.

1982

Among the concerns facing the Chamber are hazardous materials ordinances, Ride-sharing, and opposition to the Street Level Commercial Ordinance, which specifies that new developments in the Central Business District must have retail tenants or owners on the first floor of their buildings. The Chamber also opposes the mandatory five-cent deposit on beverage containers, and supports various governmental meas-ures banning the possession, sale, and manufacturing of drug paraphernalia in California.

1983

The Chamber helps pass a bill addressing small-business development, as well as initiating a state capitol building lobbying effort fashioned after the Capitol-to-Capitol trip.

1984

The Chamber is instrumental in bringing the NBA Sacramento Kings to town. At long last, Sacramento has a professional sports franchise. The Chamber establishes CAPAC, a political action committee.

1968	**1970**	**1971**	**1973**
The Chamber's new Metropolitan Development Department becomes the first U.S. Chamber organization to deal with urbanization. The Chamber inaugurates the "Earn and Learn" program for young people, resulting in over 2,000 job openings for participants.	The Chamber, long a proponent of strong education as a vital element in a community's success, supports various proposals calling for equity in support of school districts. The Chamber supports the Director of Airports in his recommendation of Air California's application to service Sacramento.	The Chamber takes its first lobbying delegation to Washington, D.C., on a "Capitol to Capitol" trip. Among the issues supported is one that will continue the missions at Sacramento's area military installations.	The Chamber kicks off a new Citizens Crime Alert program. Looking well beyond the horizon, the Chamber forms the new International Business Committee to help promote international trade in the metro Sacramento area. The Chamber cosponsors the World Affairs Conference.

	1978	**1979**	**1980**
ber initiative); and the endorsement of the Alaskan Arctic Gas Pipeline Company, as the most feasible approach to bringing badly needed supplies of natural gas to the area. The Chamber conducts an in-depth review of the Sacramento County budget.	The Chamber publishes its first "Sacramento Job Guide." The Chamber also studies the Sacramento Air Quality Maintenance Plan.	The Chamber supports abolition of the property tax on business inventories.	The Chamber supports the Highway 65 byway to ensure that Hewlett-Packard remains in the area, and advocates for a $3 million GTE regional data processing center. The Chamber cosponsors the Sacramento Area Energy Conference.

1985	**1986**		**1987**
The Chamber's efforts help KVIE Channel 6 receive a federal grant. The Chamber also scores a victory for securing funding to keep Stone Lock open to boating traffic.	The first Leadership Sacramento class graduates. Other concerns during this period are Adopt-A-School programs (the Chamber helps initiate 26), the light-rail starter line, the hiring of new police officers, solar energy, more professional sports, and new construction at McClellan and Mather Air Force bases. The Chamber holds	its first Small Business Roundtable, which becomes a prototype for the state. The Chamber attracts two additional airlines to Sacramento Metro Airport and convinces existing airlines to increase service. The Chamber also conducts an S.O.S campaign to benefit the financially struggling Sacramento Symphony.	The Chamber and the American Lung Association join forces to form the Cleaner Air Partnership. Business Volunteers for the Arts (BVA) gets its beginnings at the Chamber.

LEADERSHIP SACRAMENTO

1988

The Chamber seeks to improve air service by assisting United Air Lines in establishing minihub service to Sacramento. The Chamber also conducts a "March on Baseball" to San Francisco to demonstrate the city's continuing high level of interest in sports. The Chamber works closely with the City Council and County Board of Supervisors to improve the services and efficiency of government.

1989

The Chamber leads the effort to save one of the last, great natural marshlands in the country from being ruined. The Chamber also serves as a key organization in the study of management of the American River water and the achievement of a 200-year flood protection plan.

1990

The Chamber strongly promotes full use of McClellan Air Force Base and Sacramento Army Depot, as well as actively participating in the Sacramento Area Commission on Mather Air Force Base Conversion. The Chamber studies the Stone Lakes Wildlife Refuge proposal because of its possible encroachment on farmlands.

1991

Among the Chamber's education initiatives is a "Teachers of Tomorrow" service aimed at reducing the shortage of minority teachers in the metropolitan area. Water availability remains one of the Chamber's top issues, as does the threat of military base closures and their possible reuse by private enterprise. In addition, the Chamber hosts delegates from Europe, the Soviet Union, and the Pacific Rim countries. The Chamber's Capitol-to-Capitol visit group

1992

Another busy year brings another array of issues to the Chamber's calendar. Among them: The Chamber strongly supports the efforts to bring the Department of Defense Finance and Accounting service to Sacramento. The Chamber is active in the draft of the Sacramento County General Plan. Efforts to save Mather Air Force Base are a primary concern. The Chamber is active in the draft of the Sacramento County General Plan. The Chamber's Business Against Drugs Committee creates a model drug- and alcohol-free workplace policy that is the first of its kind on the West Coast. And, the Chamber holds the first-ever business summit, inviting 22 area chamber of commerce and other business-oriented organizations to come together to discuss mutual areas of concern, such as mandated health care and the so-called "Job Terminator" bill. The Chamber launches LEEDS (Linking Education with Economic Development in Sacramento).

1993

As the years become more and more busy, the Chamber finds itself endorsing an ever more diverse array of initiatives. Among them: NAFTA; the Japan-America Conference of Mayors and Presidents of Chambers of Commerce (a weeklong Chamber-sponsored event); and the County Red Tape Committee, designed to streamline the permitting and regulatory processes faced by businesses. The Chamber leads a success- ment of position recommendation. For the first time, the Chamber petitions to be permitted to enter the lawsuit to file a brief in defense of Sacramento Metro Airport. The Chamber starts a multimedia public relations campaign, "The Chamber Means Business."

1994

The Chamber supports a broad-based riverfront planning approach to help guide future development of the Sacramento riverfront. The 24th "Cap to Cap" trip is deemed one of the most successful to date. The Chamber opposes the placement of any sales tax increase initiatives on the November ballot, and opposes other tax increase measures being proposed. The Chamber participates in the County Water Plan Forum and unveils a Quad Modal Transportation Vision. In keeping with previous efforts, the Chamber opposes single-payer health care controls. And, amidst the flurry of activity, the Chamber plans its 100th anniversary celebration, set to occur in 1995. The Chamber's International Expo features new technologies and speakers from around the globe. The Chamber's new crime task force gears up to develop strategies to improve the crime situation in the city and county.

RETURNS WITH A FIRM PROMISE OF MORE THAN $21 MILLION IN FEDERAL FUNDS TO REPAIR AND STRENGTHEN SACRAMENTO RIVER LEVEES. THE CHAMBER CHALKS UP A PARTIAL SUCCESS WHEN THE PENTAGON AGREES TO PUT ALL FIVE OF THE NATION'S STRATEGIC AIR COMMAND BASES ON EQUAL FOOTING WHEN FUTURE BUDGET CUTS ARE CONSIDERED. THE CHAMBER PROMOTES MATHER AIR FORCE BASE AS A MAJOR AVIATION FACILITY THAT IS EQUIPPED FOR A VARIETY OF AVIATION-RELATED USES.

FUL EFFORT TO KEEP MCCLELLAN AFB OFF THE BASE CLOSURE LIST. THE CHAMBER EARNS 20-YEAR REACCREDITATION FROM THE U.S. CHAMBER—ONLY 10 PERCENT OF THE CHAMBERS ACROSS THE NATION EARN THIS HONOR. THE CHAMBER INSTITUTES AN ISSUE MANAGEMENT TEAM TO IDENTIFY, SELECT, AND ASSIGN ISSUES FOR ANALYSIS AND THE DEVELOP-

CONCLUSION

AS MENTIONED, IT HAS BEEN AN ACTIVE CENTURY INDEED. THERE HAVE BEEN COUNTLESS ISSUES, INITIATIVES, PLANS, PARTIES, LOBBYING EFFORTS, AND CAMPAIGNS SPONSORED, FORMED, HELD, AND HOSTED BY THE CHAMBER. THE PRECEDING LIST IS JUST A BRIEF SAMPLE DESIGNED TO GIVE YOU AN IDEA OF HOW BROAD THE CHAMBER'S INTERESTS ARE AND HOW STEADFAST ITS COMMITMENTS HAVE REMAINED. ■ IF ANY CONCLUSION CAN BE DRAWN FROM THIS EXERCISE IN DEFINING THE PREVIOUS CENTURY'S ACCOMPLISHMENTS, PERHAPS IT LIES IN THE COMMON ELEMENTS THAT PERVADE THE CHAMBER'S WORK. TRANSPORTATION, WATER QUALITY, EDUCATION, BUSINESS DEVELOPMENT, AND THE QUALITY OF LIFE FOR ALL WHO LIVE IN THE SACRAMENTO METRO AREA ARE BUT A FEW OF THE COMMON THREADS THAT BIND THE PREVIOUS CENTURY INTO SOMETHING OF A COHESIVE WHOLE. ■ NOW, WITHOUT LOSING SIGHT OF ANY OF THESE GOALS, MISSIONS, OR VALUES, IT'S TIME TO LET FLY THE BALLOONS, POP THE CORKS, AND ALLOW THE CELEBRATION TO BEGIN. HERE'S TO THE NEXT 100 YEARS. MAY THEY BE AS PRODUCTIVE—AS GOLDEN, IF YOU WILL—AS THE ONES THE CHAMBER HAS BEEN BLESSED TO ENJOY THUS FAR.

PROFILES IN EXCELLENCE

A LOOK AT THE CORPORATIONS, BUSINESSES, PROFESSIONAL GROUPS, AND COMMUNITY SERVICE ORGANIZATIONS THAT HAVE MADE THIS BOOK POSSIBLE.

THEIR STORIES—OFFERING AN INFORMAL CHRONICAL OF THE LOCAL BUSINESS COMMUNITY—ARE ARRANGED ACCORDING TO THE DATE THEY WERE ESTABLISHED IN THE SACRAMENTO AREA.

1 8 5 7

1857 Mercy Healthcare Sacramento
1895 Sacramento Metropolitan Chamber of Commerce
1903 Pacific Gas and Electric Company
1909 Lionakis-Beaumont Design Group
1920 Adams Group
1921 Rice Growers Association of California
1923 Sutter Health
1926 The Spink Corporation
1929 Tenco Tractor, Inc.
1935 Raley's
1935 Sacramento Credit Union
1947 CSUS School of Business Administration
1947 Sacramento Municipal Utility District
1950 Aerojet
1951 Sacramento Light Opera Association
1953 Mather Federal Credit Union
1954 KOVR Channel 13
1954 McDonald's Corporation
1959 Giselle's Travel Bureau
1959 Graphic Center
1959 KVIE Channel 6
1963 Port of Sacramento
1965 U.S. Computer Services

◆ TOM MYERS

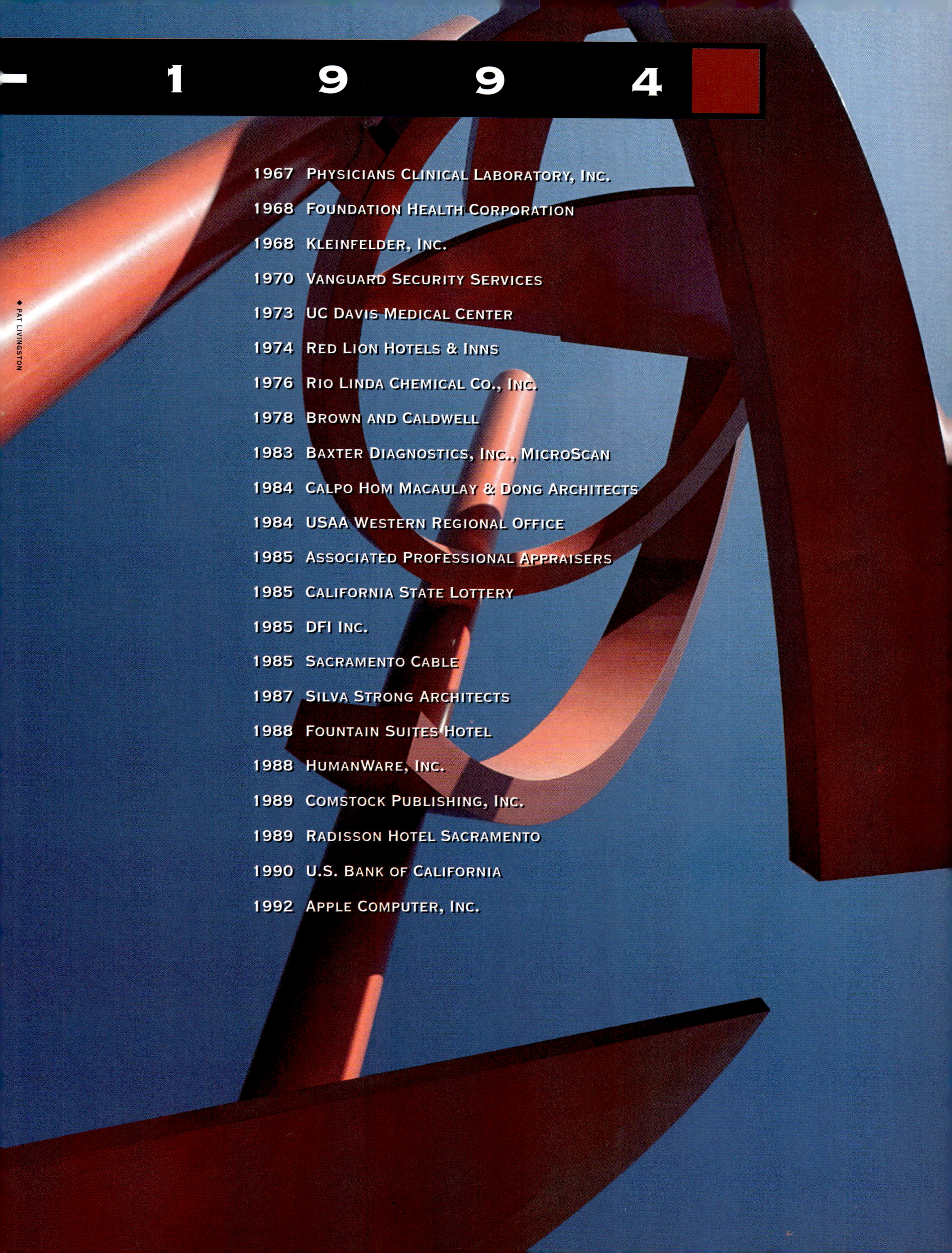

1994

1967	Physicians Clinical Laboratory, Inc.
1968	Foundation Health Corporation
1968	Kleinfelder, Inc.
1970	Vanguard Security Services
1973	UC Davis Medical Center
1974	Red Lion Hotels & Inns
1976	Rio Linda Chemical Co., Inc.
1978	Brown and Caldwell
1983	Baxter Diagnostics, Inc., MicroScan
1984	Calpo Hom Macaulay & Dong Architects
1984	USAA Western Regional Office
1985	Associated Professional Appraisers
1985	California State Lottery
1985	DFI Inc.
1985	Sacramento Cable
1987	Silva Strong Architects
1988	Fountain Suites Hotel
1988	HumanWare, Inc.
1989	Comstock Publishing, Inc.
1989	Radisson Hotel Sacramento
1990	U.S. Bank of California
1992	Apple Computer, Inc.

◆ PAT LIVINGSTON

Mercy Healthcare Sacramento

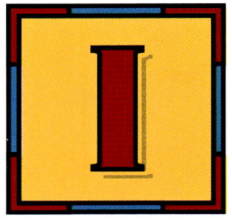

IN SACRAMENTO DURING THE LATE 1850S, THE SISTERS OF MERCY WERE NOTED FOR THE TIRELESS MANNER IN WHICH THEY WALKED THE MUDDY STREETS BRINGING FOOD AND MEDICINE TO THE RESIDENTS OF THE CITY, WHOSE POPULATION HAD SWELLED DRAMATICALLY AS A RESULT OF THE GOLD RUSH OF 1849. AS THEY HELPED SCORES OF PEOPLE SUFFERING FROM MALARIA, SCURVY, DYSENTERY, AND TYPHOID fever, the Sisters became known as the "Walking Nuns."

Originally from Dublin, Ireland, they cared for orphans and families abandoned by the gold miners who had pursued their dreams in the Sierra Nevada. Focusing on education and health care, the Sisters established an orphanage and schools, and provided health care services as visiting nurses. Their mission of caring, established in Sacramento in 1857 by eight young women, is now carried out by more than 6,000 employees of Mercy Healthcare Sacramento in partnership with 1,500 physicians and 1,000 volunteers.

Today, Mercy is a regional system focused on providing a full range of health care services with the goal of improving the total health of the community. "While Sacramento is a far different city today than it was in 1857, the health needs remain great," comments Sister Bridget McCarthy, president. "And we at Mercy Healthcare Sacramento maintain a strong commitment to respond to these needs."

Planning for Change

As America's health care industry faces increasingly complex challenges, many experts believe that groups of affiliated hospitals have the best chance for future success. Mercy Healthcare Sacramento is making significant contributions toward pioneering that concept in Northern California.

Its four Sacramento hospitals (in downtown Sacramento, Carmichael, Folsom, and the South County area), along with a complete range of ambulatory, subacute, and nonacute services, form an integrated regional system. This system is designed to provide access to quality health care services for residents throughout the greater Sacramento area and to link services so there is a smooth transition from one type of health care to the next.

The Sisters' philosophy of care is to look at the whole person—to assist individuals in managing their physical, mental, and spiritual health. They are committed to maintaining and improving health through education and counseling, and they strive to provide care in an environment that encourages healing, recovery, independence, and a positive sense of well-being.

Mercy offers a complete range of services to meet the community's needs and is recognized as a leader in several areas.

Cardiovascular Services

Mercy has a national reputation for leadership in cardiovascular medicine. With cardiac surgery programs at two hospitals (Mercy General and Mercy San Juan), Mercy performs more open-heart procedures than any other local provider, and its mortality rates are consistently among the lowest in the nation.

Mercy also offers a full range of nonsurgical cardiac capabilities, including cardiac catheterization and cardiac diagnostic imaging. In

keeping with its commitment to restoration of health, Mercy offers heart patients cardiac conditioning programs at Mercy General and Mercy San Juan.

Obstetric Services

With five childbirth facilities in the Sacramento area, Mercy brings more than 7,500 new lives into the world each year. The system also operates a regional neonatal intensive care unit (NICU) on the Mercy San Juan campus. This Level III unit offers state-of-the-art services for premature and low-birth-weight infants. Babies who are delivered at other Mercy hospitals and require

BUILDING ON A LONG HISTORY OF IMPROVING THE TOTAL HEALTH OF THE SACRAMENTO COMMUNITY (ABOVE), MERCY IS TODAY AT THE FOREFRONT OF THE DIAGNOSIS, TREATMENT, AND PREVENTION OF STROKES (RIGHT).

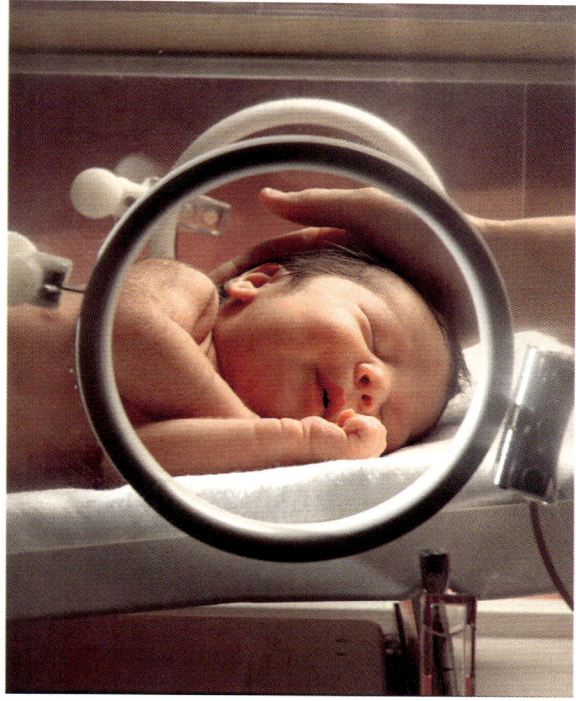

CLOCKWISE FROM FAR LEFT: COMMITTED TO PROVIDING A FULL RANGE OF SERVICES, MERCY HEALTHCARE CONTINUES ITS MISSION TO ADDRESS THE HEALTH NEEDS OF THE COMMUNITY.

THE LEVEL III NEONATAL INTENSIVE CARE UNIT AT MERCY SAN JUAN HOSPITAL OFFERS STATE-OF-THE-ART SERVICES FOR PREMATURE INFANTS.

MERCY IS A RECOGNIZED LEADER IN LASER CAPABILITIES IN THE SACRAMENTO AREA.

intensive care are transferred safely and quickly to the NICU via a neonatal transport system.

Diabetes Management

Diabetes is one of the most prevalent and often undiagnosed chronic illnesses in the adult population. Yet if it is identified in its early stages, diabetes can be managed, and many of the severe health effects can be prevented. As part of its commitment to the health of the community, Mercy Healthcare established the Mercy Diabetes Center. Offering comprehensive diabetes screenings and extensive diabetes management programs, the center helps hundreds of Sacramento-area residents identify and control their condition. The result: healthier people who can maintain their health and reduce the potential for serious illness.

Laser Capabilities

Mercy is recognized as the area leader in laser capabilities, maintaining the broadest array of laser technology available to local physicians. Laser procedures now play a large role in outpatient medicine, replacing costly and time-consuming methods of diagnosis and treatment.

At its outpatient centers, located throughout the Sacramento area, Mercy provides laser capabilities to diagnose and treat conditions from head to toe. Procedures pioneered at Mercy facilities include gynecological, prostate, urological, ophthalmological, ear, nose, and throat surgeries.

Neuroscience Services

Mercy has been at the forefront of the diagnosis and treatment of stroke. As a participant in breakthrough research for stroke treatment sponsored by the National Institutes of Health, Mercy established the area's only acute stroke intervention program. Located at Mercy General Hospital, this program is leading the way toward improved outcomes for stroke patients by allowing physicians to administer and evaluate various drugs for stroke treatment.

Room at the Inn

As president of a thriving regional health care system that provides millions of dollars each year in charity care and community benefits to the poor and needy, Sister Bridget says Mercy Healthcare Sacramento will embrace the challenges of the future the same way the Sisters of Mercy have for more than a century. "With our commitment to respond to the needs of the vulnerable in our community," she emphasizes, "my prayer is that fewer people will hear the message 'there is no room at the inn' because we have made a difference."

SACRAMENTO METROPOLITAN CHAMBER OF COMMERCE

REPRESENTING THE INTERESTS OF BUSINESS IN THE SACRAMENTO REGION IS A BROADER RESPONSIBILITY THAN IT WAS WHEN THE SACRAMENTO METROPOLITAN CHAMBER OF COMMERCE WAS CHARTERED A CENTURY AGO. BUT EVEN THOUGH COMPLEX MODERN ISSUES SUCH AS AIR QUALITY, RIVERFRONT DEVELOPMENT, SMALL-BUSINESS DEVELOPMENT, AND REGIONAL CONCERNS HAVE REPLACED TURN-OF-

the-century issues, the Chamber continues to provide progressive leadership to its members and the Sacramento region.

"We are the only broad-based organization that represents and serves the interests of business throughout the Sacramento region," says CEO Russell J. "Rusty" Hammer, "and that's critical in terms of the region's future. Because it is here that we bring all of the business interests in the region together to ensure the growth and development of small and large businesses and to promote a diverse economy."

Now beginning its second century of service, just what sort of results does the 2,000-member organization expect? "Sacramento needs to fulfill its potential as an international city," Hammer says. "As the capital city of the state of California—the sixth-largest economy in the world—Sacramento is perfectly positioned to become an international magnet for companies who want to tap into that economy. When people think of California, we want them to think of Sacramento. The Chamber is committed to making that happen."

REGIONAL ECONOMIC DEVELOPMENT

In the bid to create such a reality, the Chamber has become one of the Sacramento region's most forceful advocates of a regional approach to economic development. According to 1994 President Thomas W. Eres, the Chamber—representing over 2,000 businesses employing more than 150,000 people—is uniquely suited to impact the Sacramento region in a positive way. "Leadership and coordination for regional development need to come from a coalition that has a broader scope than a single jurisdiction," Eres says. "They need to come from resources that aren't hamstrung by political or governmental affiliations or funding which hinder an organization's ability to have a truly regional focus. We

CLOCKWISE FROM TOP RIGHT: THE CHAMBER'S HISTORY IN SACRAMENTO DATES BACK TO 1895. ITS OFFICES ARE STILL LOCATED AT 917 7TH STREET.

ARDEN FAIR SHOPPING CENTER AND THE WELLS FARGO CENTER ARE WELCOME SYMBOLS OF THE REGION'S MODERN IMAGE.

THE CHAMBER'S LEADERSHIP (FROM LEFT) INCLUDES CEO RUSSELL J. "RUSTY" HAMMER, 1994 PRESIDENT THOMAS W. ERES, AND 1995 PRESIDENT ROGER NIELLO.

truly have this regional focus."

Economic development, Eres insists, should focus on the long term and lay a foundation for the future. "With its 100 years of support of business in the Sacramento region," he says, "the Chamber has the capacity to provide leadership and positive forums, and to support specific tasks focused on getting that job done."

Indeed, the organization has demonstrated time and time again its ability to encourage regional economic development. Late in the 1980s, for instance, the Chamber served as a key contributor in a major study of the management of the American River and achievement of a 200-year flood protection plan. Also during the 1980s, the organization helped Sacramento's Regional Transit secure $95 million for its light-rail commuter train line, led efforts to recruit and hire 50 new city police officers, helped the Sacramento Municipal Utility District secure $9.5 million for the operation of a photovoltaic power plant, and advocated local governmental approval of more than $31 million in new construction projects at McClellan and Mather Air Force bases.

In the 1990s, decisive leadership continued to be a key component in the Chamber's diverse activities. When Mather Air Force Base was closed, for instance, it was the Chamber that brought four airfreight carriers together to discuss plans to perpetuate Mather's use as an aviation facility. When another Sacramento military installation—McClellan Air Force Base—was also targeted for closure, the Chamber stepped forward again, helping to prevent the loss of this main regional and strategic national asset.

BUILDING A BETTER FUTURE

Innovation is also a hallmark of the Metropolitan Chamber. In 1992 the organization debuted its Business Against Drugs committee, which implemented the first drug- and alcohol-free workplace policy on the West Coast. The organization also played a central role in the drafting of Sacramento County's General Plan and in securing more than $21 million in federal funds to repair and strengthen levees along the Sacramento River. An informed, potent advocate on a variety of issues—including workers' compensation reform, water use in the year 2030, and federal prison expansion into Sacramento—the Chamber also helped host the Japan-America Conference of Mayors and Presidents of Chambers of Commerce, and organized the area's first business summit, a gathering of 22 regional chambers of commerce and related business groups that met to discuss matters of mutual interest.

Hammer says the Metropolitan Chamber is justifiably proud of the many contributions it has made toward stimulating the business and economic climate of the Sacramento region. But, as a dedicated steward of Sacramento's budding international future, the organization is well aware of the risks involved in spending too much time celebrating past accomplishments. "You can look back and celebrate," Hammer says, "but you also have to look forward and plan."

As the Sacramento Metropolitan Chamber of Commerce enters its second century of serving community and business needs, Roger Niello, president for 1995, looks forward to the challenge of seeing Sacramento become an international city. "We have the people, the climate, the perseverance, and the attitude needed to achieve world-class status," says Niello. "The key to tomorrow's success is today's planning, and I'm certain Sacramento will continue to grow and prosper well into the 21st century."

Adams Group

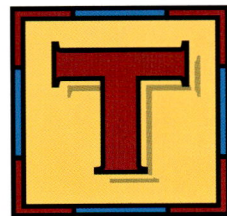

THE LONG HISTORY OF THE ADAMS GROUP BEGAN IN WOODLAND ALMOST 150 YEARS AGO. MOST OF THE COMMUNITY'S EARLY RESIDENTS WERE GOLD MINERS WHO, HAVING FAILED TO HIT IT BIG IN THE MINES, CAME DOWN OUT OF THE HILLS IN THE 1850S TO TRY THEIR HAND AT FARMING IN THE VALLEY. ONE OF WOODLAND'S EARLY SETTLERS, HENRY WYCKOFF, BUILT "YOLO CITY," A GENERAL STORE THAT served the needs of the growing number of farmers in Woodland, 19 miles from Sacramento.

Yolo City might have remained a trading post had it not been for Missouri native Frank Freeman, who arrived in Woodland in 1857, bought Wyckoff's store and 160 acres of land, and began developing a town he dreamed would someday be a trading center for one of the richest grain-growing counties in the United States. To accomplish the feat, Freeman needed a lot of help, and pioneer David Adams stepped forward.

Adams, also from Missouri, had packed up his family and headed west on the overland wagon trail for California. He settled on a large tract of Freeman's land west of Yolo City, where he built a home and a ranch on the north bank of Cache Creek. Like Freeman, Adams knew that crops would thrive in the rich adobe soil. Deciding to farm tobacco and alfalfa, Adams constructed the first irrigation canal in California and quickly built a 3,000-acre farming operation.

By the completion of the transcontinental railroad in 1869, the dream of Woodland as a nationwide farming hub had begun to take shape.

During harvest time, trains arrived in and departed from Woodland constantly, transporting fruit, vegetables, and grains to the rest of California and, later, overseas. By the 1920s, the Adams family business had evolved into a grain company specializing in the acquisition, drying, and storage of feed grains and malting barley. The company continues operations today as a part of the Adams Group.

A Tradition of Innovation and Service

Even a visionary like David Adams probably never imagined how far his family's business would go. Still headquartered in the heart of some of the richest agricultural land in the world, the Adams Group has matured into an $80 million entity with two international affiliates. But even though business is clearly different today than it was in the 1920s, the core values established by the company's forefathers have remained intact.

"My great-grandfather, great-uncle, and father worked very hard to establish a reputation for exceptional work performance," says Bill Adams. "Today, even though the company has diversified into commodities hauling and food processing, we're still setting high standards of excellence. In fact, the Adams Group's history of prosperity since the 1920s is a direct result of continuing the single-minded dedication to combining progressive and innovative techniques with strict attention to customer service."

The Adams family operates businesses in four major categories: grain merchandising and warehousing, agricultural hauling, specialty oil processing, and air cargo transportation.

The grain company started in the early 1900s by David Adams' sons blossomed under the leadership of grandson David Adams. Now the largest privately held grain company headquartered in California, the company operates Northern California's most expansive grain-drying operation, as well as seven warehouse facilities that translate into 200,000 tons of covered storage.

Early in the 1960s, Bill Adams founded Adams Trucking to complement the company's grain merchandising and warehousing activities. Adams Trucking has evolved from two tractors and two sets of trailers into the largest agricultural hauler in California. The trucks now haul bulk grain, peaches, pears, and tomatoes all over California from a prime headquarters location served by four major freeway systems (Interstate 5 and U.S. 99 for north/south travel and Interstate 80 and U.S. 50 for east/west travel), deepwater ship channels in Sacramento and Stockton,

AS ONE OF THE COMPANY'S FOUR MAJOR BUSINESSES, ADAMS TRUCKING HAS EVOLVED FROM TWO TRACTORS AND TWO SETS OF TRAILERS INTO THE LARGEST AGRICULTURAL HAULER IN CALIFORNIA (BELOW).

ADAMS AIR CARGO HAS SPECIALIZED EQUIPMENT FOR HAULING AIR CARGO CONTAINERS TO AND FROM ALL MAJOR AIRPORTS IN THE WESTERN UNITED STATES (BOTTOM).

BY THE 1920S, THE ADAMS FAMILY BUSINESS HAD EVOLVED INTO A GRAIN COMPANY SPECIALIZING IN THE ACQUISITION, DRYING, AND STORAGE OF FEED GRAINS AND MALTING BARLEY (LEFT).

and ocean container terminals in San Francisco and Oakland. The versatile equipment operation includes grain hoppers, convertible trailers, fruit and freight flatbeds, and tomato tubs. The fleet is monitored by a computerized dispatching and radio communications system.

In 1980, Bill Adams expanded upon his family's foundation in the grain business by extending its expertise into the field of food processing. This $20 million-a-year export business features the custom processing of specialty oils with emphasis on products produced in California, such as safflower, walnuts, and almonds. The oils are sold in quantities ranging from bulk ship parcels to half-liter bottles throughout the United States, the Far East, and Europe.

Bill Adams recently purchased a small air cargo company and, through his unique management style, has built it into a thriving transportation service. The company has loading docks in airports in Phoenix, Los Angeles, San Francisco, Portland, and Seattle, and has specialized equipment for hauling air cargo containers to and from all major airports in the western United States. At its loading docks, Adams Air Cargo can include a customer's cargo in regularly scheduled shipments to other airports, or can provide dedicated equipment to deliver cargo directly to an air freighter at a prearranged time.

With sons Mike and David actively involved in operating the companies, Bill Adams says the future of the Adams Group is a bright one. "Continuing the single-minded dedication to excellence my family established," he says, "the Adams Group has the resources, experience, and depth of employee commitment to confront the challenges and to capitalize on the opportunities that lie ahead."

LIONAKIS-BEAUMONT DESIGN GROUP

AS SACRAMENTO IS GROWING IN NATIONAL PROMINENCE AND SOPHISTICATION, SO IS LIONAKIS-BEAUMONT DESIGN GROUP, THE AREA'S LARGEST ARCHITECTURAL FIRM. NOW IN ITS THIRD GENERATION OF LEADERSHIP, SACRAMENTO'S OLDEST CONTINUOUSLY OPERATING ARCHITECTURAL FIRM HAS CHOSEN NOT TO REST ON ITS IMPRESSIVE LAURELS, BUT INSTEAD TO CHART A BOLD NEW FUTURE.

PARTNERS JOSHUA REYNEVELD, BRUCE STARKWEATHER, AND TIMOTHY FRY (BELOW RIGHT) ARE PROUD OF THE FIRM'S COMMITMENT TO ENERGY EFFICIENCY AND THE ENVIRONMENT.

LIONAKIS-BEAUMONT DESIGN GROUP HAS MADE ITS MARK ON SACRAMENTO WITH SUCH PROJECTS AS 926 J STREET (BELOW MIDDLE) AND KAISER PERMANENTE SOUTH SACRAMENTO OFFICE BUILDING (BELOW LEFT).

The long list of "laurels," however, was not easily contained. The seeds were planted back in 1909, when George Sellon, a Chicago-trained architect, founded the firm. Fresh from a two-year term as California's first state architect, Sellon quickly became known as a pioneer, designing Sacramento's first steel-reinforced building and the city's first high-rise office structure. Soon, Sacramentans became accustomed to attending school, holding church services, and doing business in buildings designed by the firm.

When Sellon died in 1954, a new generation of management took over. For the next 30 years, Whitson Cox, J.R. Liske, George Lionakis, Klyne Beaumont, and Howard Engberg indelibly stamped the firm's thumbprint on the Sacramento region. The firm cemented long-standing relationships with a small collection of blue-ribbon clients, such as the *Sacramento Bee*, Sacramento County, Pacific Gas & Electric Company, Sacramento Municipal Utility District, Cosumnes River College, and various health care clients and school districts.

The hallmark of Lionakis-Beaumont Design Group's second generation was commitment to providing high-quality, timeless building designs and outstanding customer service. Their legacy was a base of loyal clients and a cadre of multidisciplined professionals who successfully served a geographic region that was fast becoming a major metropolitan area.

Joshua Reyneveld, today's managing partner, knew that Lionakis-Beaumont Design Group had the credentials necessary to become one of the leading architectural firms in Northern California. That knowledge came from his six years of experience as a client of the firm. "When I first joined the firm in 1986," he says, "I wanted to maintain the extraordinary level of service I had been receiving as a client. I also wanted to position Lionakis-Beaumont Design Group as the preeminent full-service architect of the Sacramento/Central Valley area."

Reyneveld crafted an innovative and daring vision for the firm's third generation. Together with partners Bruce Starkweather and Timothy Fry, Reyneveld is actualizing a simple, yet revolutionary vision: to transform the business of architecture from designing buildings to designing futures. The transformation thus far has involved the addition of new services, including a wide range of planning, facilities management, and interior design services; it also has involved a focus on responsiveness and being the "single point of contact" for all facility needs.

Between 1987 and 1993, the firm has grown in size at an average rate of 20 percent per year. To Reyneveld, such growth is positive proof that Northern California has

STEVE SIMMONS

SCOT ZIMMERMAN

incorporated Lionakis-Beaumont Design Group into the region's architectural and engineering future.

A Bold Step into the Future

With such sustained growth, Reyneveld, Starkweather, and Fry were faced with a problem. The firm's existing office space was too small, and the lease was due to expire in nine months. "We could have leased a building in the foothills or the suburbs," Reyneveld says, "but we decided that if we are going to be a firm of the future, we ought to do our part toward urban revitalization and buy a building in the city. We wanted to do our part to improve air quality and traffic congestion. By rehabilitating an existing building, we are continuing our commitment to make the Sacramento region a better place to live."

The firm renovated a 1940s brick warehouse that was once home to an industrial glass company, and paid special attention to energy efficiency and the environment. The building itself is located near light-rail public transit lines, so employees can leave their cars at home or ride into work together. In addition, the design features a recycling room and a storage area for three special commuter bicycles Reyneveld purchased in Holland. Perhaps the most important design feature is that most of the office utilizes natural light. With input from the entire staff of architects, engineers, and interior designers, Lionakis-Beaumont Design Group created a unique and elegant corporate environment.

Building on the Base

The firm's headquarters isn't the only unique project in its award-winning portfolio. Other recent successes include $14.5 million in growth projects at the *Sacramento Bee*, the $37 million Fairfield Data Center, $27 million in major expansion projects for Kaiser Permanente's South Sacramento Medical Center, and a $7 million fine arts complex at Cosumnes River College. The firm also designed and engineered a $9.9 million aircraft maintenance facility at McClellan Air Force Base, a $13.6 million junior high school in Turlock, and approximately $21.3 million in new facilities and renovations at California State University, Chico.

Reyneveld says Lionakis-Beaumont Design Group is continuing to build on the base of excellence established in decades past. He believes that the critical factor in the firm's bright outlook is its ability to listen to the client and provide superior service with a multidisciplined approach within a "single point of contact" environment.

Put it all together, Reyneveld adds, and the end result is worth much more than laurels. "It's all about history and commitment and quality of life," he says. "In designing futures with our clients, we are putting a new face on the business and the buildings of architecture in the Central Valley. We are the Lionakis-Beaumont Design Group."

THE FIRM'S CURRENT HEADQUARTERS, A RENOVATED 1940S BRICK WAREHOUSE, WAS AN ADAPTIVE-REUSE PROJECT THAT PAID SPECIAL ATTENTION TO ENERGY EFFICIENCY AND THE ENVIRONMENT (TOP RIGHT AND LEFT).

OTHER PROJECTS DESIGNED BY THE FIRM INCLUDE THE KAISER PERMANENTE SOUTH SACRAMENTO MEDICAL OFFICE BUILDING (BOTTOM RIGHT) AND FAIRFIELD DATA CENTER (BOTTOM LEFT).

Rice Growers Association of California

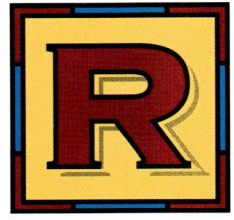

RICE WAS FIRST PRODUCED IN CALIFORNIA ON A COMMERCIAL BASIS IN 1912. EIGHT YEARS LATER, THOUGH, THE STATE'S FLEDGLING RICE INDUSTRY WAS STILL UNSTEADY. THE MOST LIKELY BUYERS OF CALIFORNIA RICE—A POWERFUL, TIGHT-KNIT GROUP REPRESENTING THE STATE'S PRIVATELY OWNED MILLS—WERE UNCOOPERATIVE, LEAVING CALIFORNIA RICE GROWERS WITH UNDERFUNDED CURRENT CROPS

and the previous year's crop sitting in warehouses unsold. In October of 1921, in an effort to create a public forum available to all member growers, the Rice Growers Association (RGA) of California was incorporated.

Led by Ralph Merritt, an important figure in California's agricultural industry, RGA opened a paddy exchange on the second floor of the Capitol National Bank Building in downtown Sacramento. From these quarters, the new cooperative quickly established itself as a pioneer in California's rice industry.

Helping Growers Ensure Quality

One of the first precedents RGA established was to offer its members an advance payment at harvest against the final return. This allowed growers to market their rice crops in an orderly manner while repaying short-term production loans to commercial banks as they came due. RGA also began providing its members with an overview of changes in market demand through a weekly newsletter based on information collected by the U.S. Department of Commerce from American embassies around the world.

By the mid-1920s, RGA had established itself as the leader in the processing and marketing of California rice for bulk shipments to domestic industrial processors and export buyers. The cooperative, for example, had shipped one of California's largest early export orders to Japan. RGA had also been instrumental in filling Japanese orders to cover the shortage of rice in that country caused by a major earthquake in 1924. In 1930 RGA expanded operations by investing in a rice mill and becoming directly involved in marketing and milling rice.

Tragedy struck that same year when the mill caught fire and was completely destroyed. The cooperative was plunged into a financial crisis that was exacerbated by the Great Depression. Determined to overcome the challenge, RGA members rebuilt the mill within 18 months, and the organization slowly recovered from the debt created by the fire.

Between 1945 and 1960, RGA concentrated on building retail markets for its members' rice in Hawaii, Puerto Rico, and the western United States. Highlighting these efforts was the introduction of the well-known HINODE label, which was first used in Hawaii

IN A TYPICAL YEAR, RGA HANDLES 5 TO 10 PERCENT OF THE STATE'S AVERAGE RICE PRODUCTION, MARKETING PRODUCTS FOR THE BENEFIT OF THOSE MEMBERS WHO USE THE COOPERATIVE.

during the early 1940s on 10-pound packages of medium grain rice.

At the time, each Hawaiian grocery store employed dozens of workers, who repackaged the rice from 100-pound bags shipped by RGA and wrote the HINODE name in crayon on each smaller bag they filled. Today, labeling and packaging are much more sophisticated operations handled by RGA Products, Inc., one of three wholly owned subsidiaries of the Rice Growers Association. And the medium grain rice introduced into the Hawaiian islands has evolved into an array of HINODE products marketed in some 4,000 grocery stores across the United States, as well as in military installations around the globe.

Headquartered today in West Sacramento, the Rice Growers Association of California serves the milling and marketing needs of some 250 California rice growers. In a typical year, RGA handles 5 to 10 percent of the state's average rice production, marketing products for the benefit of those members who use the cooperative.

Setting the Stage for New Growth

As the largest rice milling firm in California in terms of capacity, RGA once had the ability to mill 26 million hundredweight of paddy rice annually. But in a bid to diversify its production beyond milled table rice products, the organization recently left the rice drying and storage arenas, and has sold three of its four mills.

Both RGA and the rice industry have shifted emphasis from milling and marketing bulk exports to completely fulfilling increasing domestic demands for rice. According to President and CEO Bill Ludwig, this move is securing the future of California's rice growers. "Our objective," he says, "is to generate stable income streams for our members from premium returns for food products in markets that offer opportunities for consistent growth over the long term."

Ludwig points out that this opportunity for growth is certainly available in the domestic market, where annual per capita consumption of rice rose from nine pounds in 1978 to more than 20 pounds in 1991 as consumers became more interested in ethnic foods and the nutritional value of carbohydrates. This trend has continued, and RGA has responded with several innovative products and services, including a new line of HINODE products packaged in resealable, ZIP-PAK bags (an industry first) and HINODE blended rices, the cooperative's newest "value-added" product.

With still other innovative products and services in development, Ludwig says RGA is perfectly positioned to help another generation of California rice growers earn a better future. "In recent years we have reorganized the cooperative and adjusted our direction," Ludwig says. "But one thing remains the same as when the cooperative was formed. We are here to provide a stable base of revenues for our members. That is our ongoing objective."

TODAY, THE HINODE PRODUCT LINE IS MARKETED IN SOME 4,000 GROCERY STORES ACROSS THE UNITED STATES, AS WELL AS IN MILITARY INSTALLATIONS AROUND THE GLOBE.

SUTTER HEALTH

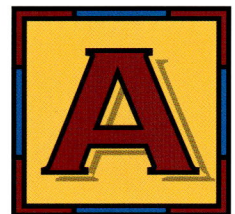

AMID THE DEADLY INFLUENZA EPIDEMIC OF 1918, PATIENTS FILLED SACRAMENTO'S FOUR ANTIQUATED, WOOD-FRAMED HOSPITALS. DRIVEN BY THE OBVIOUS NEED FOR BETTER MEDICAL FACILITIES, 17 LOCAL DOCTORS TOOK ON THE CHALLENGE OF BUILDING A NEW HOSPITAL. TODAY, THAT PIONEERING HOSPITAL HAS EVOLVED INTO SUTTER HEALTH, A NOT-FOR-PROFIT REGIONAL HEALTH CARE SYSTEM WITH 14 HOSPITALS, four skilled nursing facilities, a home care unit, medical groups, and various other health care services reaching more than 50 Northern California communities.

A HISTORY OF COMMUNITY COMMITMENT

While change has been steady since Sutter's founding in 1923, the organization's commitment to excellence, innovation, and cost-effective service has remained unchanged. "Whether it's technical innovations such as ROBODOC™ (a robotic arm that provides precision drilling in hip replacement surgery) or customer service-focused improvements such as new family-centered home health services, the name Sutter has come to mean quality," says Van Johnson, president and CEO of Sutter Community Hospitals, a division of Sutter Health.

Sutter Community Hospitals today offers many areas of clinical focus organized as centers of excellence under one administrative umbrella.

The Sutter Cancer Center is a regional oncology center serving more than 2 million Northern Californians. Longtime leaders in the fight against cancer, the center's physicians and researchers have pioneered such treatments as intra-operative radiation therapy, in which radiation is focused directly on a tumor while sparing surrounding tissue.

The Cancer Center is also renowned for its Tumor Registry program (begun in 1942) and for its management of the Cancer Surveillance Program for the State of California. Acting as one of 10 regional cancer registries, Sutter monitors some 10,000 cases at 40 facilities in 13 counties surrounding Sacramento. New projects at the Cancer Center include a 155,000-square-foot radiation/oncology facility scheduled to open in 1996 and a state-of-the-art, inpatient bone-marrow transplant unit.

Since the 1930s, when Sutter Maternity Hospital became the nation's first facility devoted exclusively to labor, delivery, and postpartum care, Sutter has strived to take a fresh approach to childbirth. The Sutter Center for Women's and Children's Services welcomes more than 6,800 babies annually, making it one of California's highest-volume obstetrical facilities.

From a unique teen clinic assisting young mothers to informative women's forums, childbearing classes, and follow-up procedures, the center has established a reputation for excellence. UNICEF recently recognized it as one of the nation's few "baby-friendly" hospitals.

The Sutter Heart Institute has consistently positioned itself at the forefront of coronary care, treating more than 100,000 patients since 1958. Sutter physicians performed Sacramento's first successful adult open-heart surgery in 1959 and the first successful pediatric open-heart procedure in 1962. In 1989 the Heart Institute hosted the region's first successful heart transplant. The facility is today one of the nation's highest-volume heart transplant centers, performing more than 1,100 surgeries annually.

A NETWORK FOR THE FUTURE

Sutter Health has worked diligently to create a network of care—gathering diverse health services under one corporate entity. According to Johnson, the resulting integrated health organization "will become the principal care delivery system in the next millennium because of its ability to maintain and strengthen care quality while cutting costs and improving access."

But improving access is more than a goal. Early in 1992, Sutter initiated Project TEACH, which provides a number of social and medical services to homeless children. A collaborative effort between Sutter Community Hospitals, the Sacramento County Office of

CLOCKWISE FROM TOP LEFT:

THE OAK PARK MULTISERVICE NEIGHBORHOOD PROJECT MEETS THE HEALTH AND HUMAN SERVICES NEEDS OF AREA RESIDENTS.

SUTTER'S RANGE OF SERVICES OFFERS A LIFETIME OF CARE.

SUTTER CENTER FOR PSYCHIATRY PARTNERED WITH THE UC DAVIS SCHOOL OF MEDICINE TO OFFER RESIDENCY TRAINING.

THE CHILDREN'S BEREAVEMENT ART GROUP USES ART THERAPY TO HELP YOUNGSTERS WHO HAVE LOST A LOVED ONE.

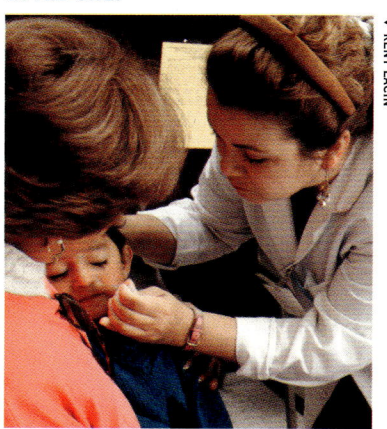

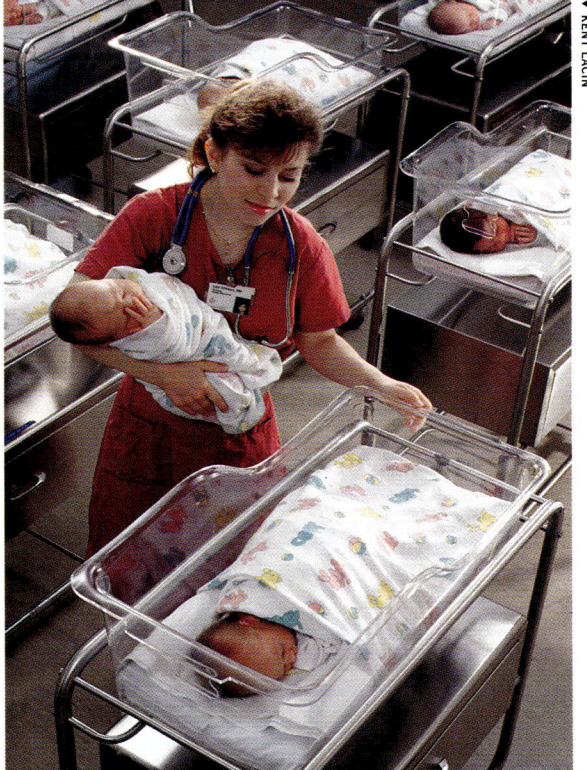

SUTTER CENTER FOR WOMEN'S AND CHILDREN'S SERVICES, LOCATED AT SUTTER MEMORIAL HOSPITAL, WELCOMES MORE THAN 6,800 BABIES ANNUALLY, MAKING IT ONE OF CALIFORNIA'S HIGHEST-VOLUME OBSTETRICAL FACILITIES (NEAR LEFT).

HUNDREDS OF HIGH SCHOOL AND COLLEGE STUDENTS ARE HELPING OTHERS WHILE HELPING THEMSELVES THROUGH A VARIETY OF YOUTH VOLUNTEER PROGRAMS AT SUTTER HOSPITALS (FAR LEFT).

Education, the Sacramento County Task Force for the Education of Homeless Children, the Sacramento City Unified School District, and the California Department of Education, Project TEACH offers services ranging from tutoring, counseling, and immunizations to school registration, enrollment, and records transfer.

Sutter continues to expand services to Sacramento's neighborhoods through medical plazas. A major strategy for the future, medical plazas gather a variety of health care services—from physician offices to ambulatory services—in one convenient location. Sutter Medical Plaza/Orangevale opened in the fall of 1994, and Sutter Medical Plaza/Laguna opened in 1993.

Roseville Hospital, a Sutter Health affiliate that has served south Placer and north Sacramento counties since 1952, plans to open a Level II trauma center—the first in the five-county Sierra region. Known as the Sacramento Valley Emergency Medical Services Agency, the center is scheduled for completion early in 1995. The hospital also broke ground in October 1994 on a new health care campus to be completed in 1997.

Big things are also under way at Sutter Davis Hospital, a 100,000-square-foot facility that opened in the fall of 1994. This facility is designed as a "one-stop shop" where patients take advantage of numerous services, including a self-contained Birthing Center and an adjacent medical office building.

Auburn Faith Community Hospital, located northeast of Sacramento, has been a Sutter affiliate since 1989. The 108-bed hospital offers a variety of services, such as a 24-hour emergency department, family-centered maternity care, laser technology, and a comprehensive cardiac rehabilitation program.

Another important affiliate is the Sutter Center for Psychiatry. Founded in 1958, the center was the first in the Sacramento area to offer community-based inpatient programs for adults, children, and adolescents. Its specialized clinical services include the Sutter Outpatient Drug and Alcohol Program, a perinatal substance abuse program, and electroconvulsive therapy.

To complement these community-based facilities, Sutter Medical Group was formed in 1990. This group of more than 100 physicians represents a broad spectrum of primary care and specialist physicians. Additionally, Sutter Health has fully affiliated with Omni Health Plan, a rapidly growing HMO that serves more than 100,000 people in Northern California.

Building on more than seven decades of compassion and high-quality care, Sutter Health has its eye clearly focused on the future of health care in Northern California.

Pacific Gas and Electric Company

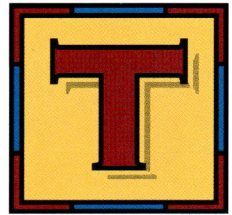

THE LARGEST INVESTOR-OWNED UTILITY IN THE UNITED STATES, PACIFIC GAS AND ELECTRIC COMPANY WAS INCORPORATED IN 1905 AND TODAY SERVES 48 OF CALIFORNIA'S 58 COUNTIES—A SERVICE TERRITORY OF OVER 94,000 SQUARE MILES IN NORTHERN AND CENTRAL CALIFORNIA WITH A POPULATION OF 11.8 MILLION. THIS SERVICE TERRITORY RANKS AS THE 15TH-LARGEST ECONOMY IN THE WORLD.

PG&E emerged from a rough-and-ready collection of pioneer gas and electric companies over a century ago. The population boom fueled by the Gold Rush turned into steady growth for the area, and as mission towns transformed into metropolises, electrical power became necessary to heat, light, and run homes. PG&E stepped forward to meet the growing demand and today has over 170 power-generating units, ranging from natural gas power plants to the world's largest geothermal facility.

PG&E was established in Sacramento in 1903. Its predecessor, San Francisco Gas Company, was founded in 1852. PG&E has built a reputation for providing safe, reliable, low-cost electric and natural gas service. Today, its electric business annually provides gas and electricity to a diversified market.

Fueling Progress Toward a Clean Environment

In recent times, however, PG&E's contribution to Sacramento has gone beyond solely providing natural gas. The utility has also become an industry leader in the development of clean air transportation and the marketing and promotion of natural gas vehicles. PG&E began experimenting with natural gas vehicles early in the 1970s. Today, the utility's vision has produced the fastest-growing utility-operated natural gas vehicle program in the United States. There are currently more than 650 natural gas vehicles in PG&E's own fleet and 32 natural gas fueling stations in the company's service territory.

In a bid to extend its expertise with natural gas vehicles beyond its own fleet, PG&E is collaborating with Aerojet, a Sacramento aerospace manufacturer, to develop a low-cost, lightweight, mobile natural gas storage module that will soon be used to supply natural gas fuel to companies operating entire fleets of vehicles. PG&E plans to have 125,000 vehicles operating on natural gas in Northern and Central California by the year 2000 through partnerships like the one with the Sacramento Regional Transit District.

Pacific Gas and Electric Company has fueled California's growth for almost a century. The utility remains on the leading edge of available technology and continues to lead the way, helping to develop and implement technologically advanced energy systems to further serve its growing California customer base.

PACIFIC GAS AND ELECTRIC HAS BECOME AN INDUSTRY LEADER IN THE DEVELOPMENT OF CLEAN-AIR TRANSPORTATION AND THE MARKETING AND PROMOTION OF NATURAL GAS VEHICLES.

The Spink Corporation

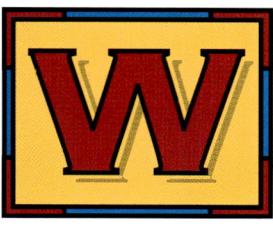

When he opened his first office in 1926, civil engineer Joseph E. Spink defined success in simple terms. Start with tireless energy, add vision, and mix thoroughly with the highest standards of quality and performance. ■ Following that formula, Spink's Sacramento-based engineering firm grew with its hometown, maturing from a small business into today's multidisciplinary firm. The Spink Corporation now provides a comprehensive array of professional services, ranging from civil, electrical, mechanical, and structural engineering to architecture, land planning, landscape architecture, surveying, mapping, and photogrammetry.

Nearly Seven Decades of Growth

The company's growth process began late in the 1920s, when Joseph Spink designed Sacramento's first modern subdivision. Later, the company performed preliminary work on the Port of Sacramento, the region's deepwater ship channel. Following World War II, Spink turned his attention to helping meet the city's growing demand for housing. During the 1950s, as Sacramentans began a steady migration to the suburbs, the firm provided complete engineering and planning services for the development of up to 11,000 lots a year.

In the 1960s, despite the death of its founder, The Spink Corporation designed a host of award-winning projects, including subdivisions in Folsom, Freeport, Roseville, and El Dorado Hills. The firm also designed the 1,200-foot Guy West Suspension Bridge, linking California State University, Sacramento, with Campus Commons, a Spink-designed, mixed-use residential development still recognized for its innovative cluster design. Ultimately, Spink was responsible for design and engineering of over half of the Sacramento metropolitan area.

As Sacramento's growth gained momentum in the 1970s, The Spink Corporation added an architectural and building design group, incorporating structural, mechanical, and electrical engineering into the mix of in-house services. That move gave the firm the in-house capability to design a diverse range of building projects, from medical facilities and multifamily housing projects to commercial and retail space, warehouses, and historical renovations. The firm also expanded its planning and landscape design departments, which have since been responsible for major residential developments such as Gold River, Laguna West, and Northern Natomas, in addition to golf courses, parks, and commercial centers.

Looking to the Future

After decades of involvement with the planning and design of a significant portion of Sacramento's urban landscape, The Spink Corporation continues to shape the region. Recent projects include the Interstate 5/Laguna Boulevard interchange, the Pastoral Center for the Catholic Diocese of Sacramento, levee work for the Sacramento Area Flood Control Agency, and planning and infrastructure design for the Broadstone mixed-use development in Folsom.

With an eye on the future, how does Sacramento's largest engineering and architecture firm plan to sharpen its winning edge? "Since the 1960s, our mission has been to expand our capabilities, broaden our field of service, and bring all the different teams in-house," says Chairman Theodore D'Amico, adding that this ambitious goal has presented unique challenges over the years. "In the past, we've had to compete with specialists. It's difficult to be a multidisciplinary firm—a generalist—and develop the expertise and quality of a specialist. But we've done it. Where is the future? It's where we've been for years: total service."

Clockwise from top left: The Spink Corporation's headquarters represents the firm's comprehensive design capabilities in architecture, engineering, planning, and landscape architecture.

The award-winning Guy West Suspension Bridge at California State University, Sacramento has become an enduring campus landmark.

The new Riverlake development is the latest in a long history of projects in Sacramento's Pocket area for which Spink has provided planning and engineering services.

Tenco Tractor, Inc.

For more than 60 years, Northern Californians have turned to Tenco Tractor, Inc., for high-quality farm and construction equipment. The company has grown from a small, Depression-era tractor shop in Marysville to a multimillion-dollar dealership with eight facilities serving 34 Northern California counties. ■ Tenco today provides service and equipment for a wide range of industries including logging, site construction and heavy construction, paving and compacting, land leveling, power generation, trucking, industrial materials handling, and agriculture. In addition to equipment sales and service, the company offers rentals and leases.

The company's founder, Daniel W. Beatie, began setting the pace for progress back in 1931 when he risked everything he owned to found Marysville Tractor and Equipment. Beatie had grown up on a farm, worked on a railroad, and then entered the banking business, so he knew firsthand what the struggle for survival was all about. Thanks to his skills and hard work, Marysville Tractor and Equipment not only survived the Great Depression, but emerged as a solid and productive enterprise that continues to thrive decades later. The burgeoning business grew quickly and solidly under Beatie's leadership, and by 1962 it served customers in 10 counties. The company subsequently changed its name to Tenco Tractor, Inc.

Ken Beatie, who succeeded his father as president in 1955 at age 39, moved the firm's corporate headquarters in 1969 to a 160-acre site in south Sutter County near Sacramento Metro Airport. With a location suited to accommodate even more growth in the future, the company was geared for long-term success.

Investing in Sacramento

Today, Tenco Tractor is committed to making a difference in the community like never before. Ken Beatie, for instance, has played a key role in Sacramento organizations such as the Boy Scouts, while his son Dan manages the family-owned Donner Mine Camp that serves area nonprofit organizations. Elsewhere in the Sacramento region, the company expends time and resources on a host of community organizations and causes. Highlighting these efforts is Tenco's annual scholarship program in which nine regional community colleges receive $1,500 each to help a deserving student pursue his or her education at a four-year university.

Tenco is also committed to developing programs aimed at offsetting the shortage of well-trained heavy equipment diesel mechanics. To that end, the company is collaborating with Delta College in San Joaquin County to develop a new training facility offering students hands-on experience in addition to classroom instruction.

Why spend valuable time and money on something Sacramento educators could worry about? According to Gordon K. Beatie, grandson of the founder, and president since 1976, the company's commitment to preparing skilled workers for tomorrow has created a win-win situation for both Sacramento and Tenco. "In order to ensure an adequate employee base for our company," he says, "we need to be actively involved in the regional educational process. These days, skilled labor is a vital and rare resource. By working to provide this resource,

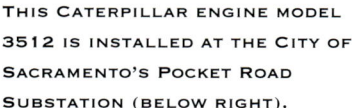

This Caterpillar engine model 3512 is installed at the City of Sacramento's Pocket Road Substation (below right).

The Caterpillar Challenge 65 agricultural tractor is shown at Scheidel Ranch in Sutter County (below).

IN ROSEVILLE, TWO CATERPILLAR MODEL D10 TRACTORS PUSH A MODEL 651 WHEEL SCRAPER AT PETER KIEWIT PACIFIC DIVISION, ROCKY RIDGE.

we're helping ourselves, and we're helping our community."

Along with cultivating skilled labor for Sacramento's future, Tenco is equally committed to providing for the people who currently work for the firm. "Our goal is to maintain a productive work environment where all employees have the opportunity to develop their potential and be recognized for their contributions and performance," says Beatie. "Our success is built upon a philosophy of uncompromising ethics, teamwork, and professionalism."

Building a Solid Future on Quality Products and Service

As Northern California continues to be one of the fastest-growing areas in the United States, Beatie says Tenco has plans to augment its already active market base. In a complex and rapidly changing economic climate, Tenco's mission for the future is a simple one: to provide quality products and services that meet—or exceed—customer expectations.

Even as the company works to expand its already diverse and extensive product lines and inventories, Beatie emphasizes that customer service will remain Tenco's highest priority. With more than 300,000 square feet of state-of-the-art facilities, a parts inventory worth more than $8 million, and a large fleet of service vehicles and factory-trained technicians, it's clear why Tenco is regarded as an industry leader in service.

"As Northern California continues to grow, Tenco is committed to meeting the increasing needs of our customers with the best possible equipment and service," Beatie says. "Our goal is to achieve another 65 years of customer satisfaction."

For Beatie, the challenge is a formidable one. After all, there aren't many businesses around that can boast a past as colorful and successful as Tenco Tractor's. Beatie, however, is confident that the company's highly trained, professional staff can meet the challenge. "We're understandably proud of the company my grandfather started in the midst of the Depression," he says. "Tenco has survived and succeeded because of its ability to be progressive and innovative, and to aggressively change with the times."

A CATERPILLAR LIFT TRUCK MODEL V80E IS HARD AT WORK AT BERCO REDWOOD IN SACRAMENTO.

175

RALEY'S

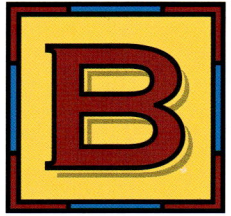

BRILLIANT RED RALEY'S SIGNS DOMINATE THE SUPERMARKET LANDSCAPE IN NORTHERN CALIFORNIA AND NEVADA. HEADQUARTERED IN WEST SACRAMENTO, ACROSS THE SACRAMENTO RIVER FROM CALIFORNIA'S GOLDEN-DOMED CAPITOL, RALEY'S SUPERSTORES GREW OUT OF THE DREAMS OF A YOUNG MAN WHO CAME WEST TO CALIFORNIA LOOKING FOR A GOLDEN OPPORTUNITY.

The young man was Thomas P. Raley, a bold, innovative dynamo who dreamed of building his own grocery business. He located his first market in Placerville, California, a Gold Country town in the foothills east of Sacramento. It was 1935, amid the Great Depression, but Tom Raley's dreams were not dimmed by a slow economy. He believed in hard work and generous service applied with enthusiasm.

A SUPERMARKET PIONEER

In the first of what would become a lifetime of marketing innovations, Raley took advantage of an open area adjacent to his new store. He put in a parking lot, inviting customers to park close to the store. Then he advertised Raley's as "the nation's first drive-in market."

ALWAYS AN INNOVATOR, COMPANY FOUNDER TOM RALEY (TOP) CREATED "THE NATION'S FIRST DRIVE-IN MARKET" IN THE 1930S.

JOYCE RALEY TEEL, OWNER AND COCHAIRMAN OF THE BOARD (RIGHT).

Tom Raley's enterprising spirit made him a pioneer in the grocery business. He was the first to market precut, packaged, self-service meat. It wasn't a hit right away, but customers learned to trust Raley's high standard of quality—prepackaged or not.

"I'll never sacrifice quality for low prices," Raley often declared. And he never did. Fine quality meat and produce remain a signature of Raley's Superstores.

In 1958 Raley opened his first side-by-side supermarket/drug center, creating the one-stop shopping concept. The two stores, which offered groceries, drugs, and household items under one roof, were divided by a wall. In 1973 the wall came down, and Raley's Superstores were born.

In the same year, Raley's became a regional operation when it purchased the Eagle Thrifty chain of stores based in Reno, Nevada. Their combined volume exceeded $100 million.

In 1980 Raley's made its first venture into processing and manufacturing. To purchase dairy products competitively, Raley's joined with Bel Air Supermarkets and Save Mart Supermarkets to form Mid-Valley Dairy, located in California's Central Valley. The joint venture today operates the most sophisticated computerized milk processing plant in the United States. An ice cream and culture products manufacturing facility was added to the enterprise, followed by WestPac Foods, a 700,000-square-foot grocery warehouse. These facilities enable Raley's to buy directly from manufacturers at the lowest prices available.

Innovation at Raley's continually demonstrates a high regard for customers. The first to institute independent testing of produce for pesticide residues, the company is known nationally for pioneering the NutriClean testing program. Customers can look for "NutriClean Certified" signs in the produce department, assuring that no detectable pesticide residue is found on the product.

In 1990 Raley's became the first grocery in the nation to establish a comprehensive program of food safety and sanitation practices in its stores. Raley's was also the first to have a grocery bag recycling policy, offering cloth bags for sale and a five-cent rebate for each reused paper bag.

A GROWING FAMILY ENTERPRISE

When Tom Raley died in 1991, his dream had developed into the 10th-largest privately held company in California. With the 1992 purchase of the Bel Air supermarket chain, Raley's/Bel Air now employs over 10,000 people in 81 stores. Company revenues are approaching the $2 billion mark, and Raley's/Bel Air is the 22nd-largest supermarket chain in the country.

Raley's is still a family enterprise. Tom Raley's only child, Joyce Raley Teel, is now the owner, serving as cochairman of the board with her husband, Jim Teel. President and CEO Chuck Collings and Jim Teel worked side by side with Tom Raley for decades, helping guide the business through

RALEY'S/BEL AIR IS TODAY THE 22ND-LARGEST SUPERMARKET CHAIN IN THE COUNTRY. AT LEFT IS THE EL DORADO HILLS, CALIFORNIA, RALEY'S SUPERSTORE.

changing economic conditions and challenging business ventures. Now Michael Teel, Joyce and Jim's son, is emerging as a dynamic leader of the company.

Always involved in the communities in which it does business, Raley's is an active sponsor of many arts, education, and service activities. One of its most significant programs, founded by Joyce Raley Teel, is Food for Families, a nonprofit agency that brings together many local organizations and the media to help feed the hungry in the communities served by Raley's. Since its inception in 1986, Food for Families has raised more than $3 million in cash from customers, suppliers, and donations from Raley's. Nearly 2 million pounds of food has been given to feed hungry families in Northern California and Nevada.

"My goal is to fulfill and expand the vision of my father," said Joyce Raley Teel when she assumed the position of cochairman of the company. "His dream for Raley's was of a constantly growing company—where customers are serviced as friends and neighbors, where employees are thought of as members of an extended family and given the opportunity to grow with the company, and whose owner would receive a fair return on the investment of resources and energy."

Stretching from Yreka in Northern California to Oakhurst near Yosemite, from San Francisco's East Bay to Elko, Nevada, Raley's/Bel Air continues to fulfill that vision.

EMPLOYEES FOLLOW THE FOUNDER'S PHILOSOPHY OF HARD WORK AND GENEROUS SERVICE APPLIED WITH ENTHUSIASM (ABOVE).

FROM LEFT:
JAMES E. TEEL, COCHAIRMAN OF THE BOARD; MICHAEL J. TEEL, ASSISTANT TO THE PRESIDENT; AND CHARLES L. COLLINGS, PRESIDENT AND CEO.

Sacramento Credit Union

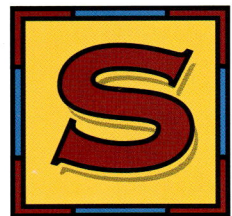

Sacramento Credit Union has a rich history comprising over 60 years' dedication to providing the best quality financial products and services to credit union members, eligible member groups, and the communities in which it does business. ■ The traditional credit union concept of people helping people, as applied to modern-day financial business practices, originated in 1849 when widespread crop failures in Germany caused farmers to lose their land to unscrupulous money lenders. The mayor of a small German town, Frederick Raiffeisen, suggested the farmers pool their money and make loans to each other at low interest rates. Once implemented, his idea saved the village farmers from financial ruin and launched a business practice that eventually led the United States Congress to pass the Federal Credit Union Act in 1934.

Sacramento Credit Union, founded in March of 1935, became one of the earliest local institutions to open for business under this federal legislation. Originally known as the Sacramento County Employees' Credit Union, the state-chartered credit union opened its doors with a volunteer staff of only three—one manager, one teller, and one bookkeeper. Working out of shared office space located at 715 7th Street in Sacramento, the credit union began taking savings deposits and making personal loans to county employees.

Today, the Sacramento Credit Union has progressed well beyond those early years. Celebrating its 60th year of serving members in 1995, the credit union has grown into a financial enterprise with over $95 million in assets and more than 26,000 members.

THE MAIN OFFICE OF SACRAMENTO CREDIT UNION IS LOCATED AT 8TH AND H STREETS IN DOWNTOWN SACRAMENTO (FAR RIGHT). FIREWORKS LIGHT UP THE SKY OVER SACRAMENTO'S LANDMARK TOWER BRIDGE, THE CREDIT UNION'S LOGO IMAGE.

PHOTOS BY CATHY KELLY

Not for Profit, Not for Charity, But for Service

From its inception, Sacramento Credit Union has acted according to the lesson learned by those pioneering farmers—helping one another can help all succeed. "We are fortunate to have a staff that believes in the purpose the credit union was formed to fulfill: not for profit, not for charity, but for service," says President and CEO Jerrold A. Kinlock. "Our staff works on a daily basis to improve service to our members, who are the real owners of the credit union."

As part owners and shareholders, members have benefited from the innovative service orientation of their credit union since it was founded. In 1958 the organization was among the first credit unions in Northern California to expand lending services to include real estate, home improvement, and auto loans. Additional products and services followed, with travelers checks and money orders being offered in the mid-1970s. Individual retirement accounts were added in the 1980s, as well as a VISA card with worldwide acceptance and one of the lowest interest rates available. Since 1991, Sacramento Credit Union has also offered customized financial planning services. Whether a member is planning for a secure retirement, saving for a college education, or learning about tax-advantaged investments, a certified financial planner is available to provide financial guidance.

For these and other efforts on behalf of its members, the credit union has received a number of honors. In 1993, for instance, three independent rating services—including the National Credit Union Administration, created to regulate the credit union industry and insure member deposits up to $100,000—recognized Sacramento Credit Union as having the highest overall performance for a credit union. "We are pleased to be ranked among the best in our industry," Kinlock says. "Our success and continued growth are most important because that makes it possible to do even more for the people we're here to serve—our members."

SIX DECADES OF SOLID, CONSISTENT GROWTH

Over its 60-year history, Sacramento Credit Union has focused on growth at a prudent pace, building a strong foundation for a solid and dynamic future. By the late 1960s and early 1970s, membership increased significantly and new branch offices were opened, including the current Bradshaw Road location, south of Highway 50. In 1971 land was acquired in downtown Sacramento for the credit union's current main office at 8th and H streets. In 1986 the organization selected a logo consistent with its early roots and strong foundations—a rendition of Sacramento's landmark Tower Bridge, which was erected in 1935, the same year the credit union was founded.

Sacramento Credit Union clearly paved the way for its current prominence in Sacramento.

The credit union extends membership privileges to all relatives of credit union members, as well as to approved employer groups throughout the Sacramento area and the state. This has meant that new member groups, such as the Sacramento Metropolitan Chamber of Commerce and its participating businesses, are eligible to take advantage of Sacramento Credit Union membership. The credit union is well positioned to offer new membership benefits into the next decade and beyond.

The future brings the possibility of new branch locations, making access more convenient; new financial service technologies that streamline the process of conducting financial business; and new products and services to better serve the wide range of members' financial needs. All such innovations will focus on the goals of helping members meet their financial needs today and achieve greater financial success in the future, while continuing the sound, consistent growth practices that have made Sacramento Credit Union successful in its first 60 years of delivering the best financial service possible.

THE TOWER BRIDGE, ERECTED IN 1935, THE SAME YEAR THE CREDIT UNION WAS FOUNDED, SPANS THE SACRAMENTO RIVER TO DOWNTOWN IN THE EARLY EVENING TWILIGHT.

CATHY KELLY

Sacramento Municipal Utility District

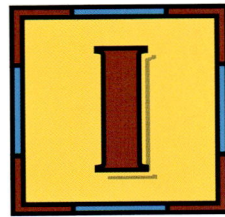

IN 1989 THE SACRAMENTO MUNICIPAL UTILITY DISTRICT FACED ITS BIGGEST CHALLENGE SINCE THE ELECTRIC UTILITY WAS CREATED NEARLY HALF A CENTURY BEFORE. OVERNIGHT, SMUD LOST NEARLY HALF ITS GENERATING CAPACITY WHEN CITIZENS VOTED TO CLOSE THE RANCHO SECO NUCLEAR PLANT, THE SACRAMENTO AREA'S LARGEST POWER PLANT.

In the wake of that decision, the district knew it would be forced to replace the lost nuclear power by purchasing electricity from outside utilities. SMUD also knew that purchasing power from other sources for its 468,000 customers would eventually send rates skyrocketing. After some brainstorming and an extensive public dialogue, the leadership at SMUD found an answer.

With the same progressive vision that has helped the organization evolve from a small water utility in the 1920s into one of the nation's leading electric utilities, the SMUD board and staff steered the district in a new direction. SMUD's plan for the future is to move from dependence on a large central station plant towards a diverse energy approach that relies on cleaner, more reliable, and less expensive sources of power.

Pioneering a Cleaner Tomorrow

Today, renewable energy projects produce a good portion of the power SMUD delivers to its 900-square-mile service area. The Upper American River Project is the cornerstone of SMUD's renewable energy mix, providing 660 megawatts of power. Two geothermal plants in Sonoma County contributed another 480,000 kilowatt-hours in 1992.

Another SMUD renewable resource is the world's first utility-owned and -operated photovoltaic power plant, which began operating in 1984 on a 20-acre field near the closed Rancho Seco. Known as PV1, the innovative facility utilizes rows and rows of metal panels that turn sunlight into electricity without the need of a turbine or generator. Two years after it opened, with a second component on line, the 2-megawatt plant began its current level of production, supplying power for nearly 1,000 Sacramento homes.

Another of SMUD's innovative projects is a 50-megawatt wind farm in nearby Solano County. By 1996 dozens of huge wind turbines should be generating enough energy for 17,000 Sacramento homes.

SMUD is also developing a group of four cogeneration plants that will use natural gas to produce electricity, as well as steam for industry. By replacing existing steam boilers and acquiring air pollution offsets, the cogeneration plants are expected to help improve Sacramento's air quality, create more than 200 private-sector jobs, and generate more than $1 million in tax revenues for Sacramento County.

In addition to these programs

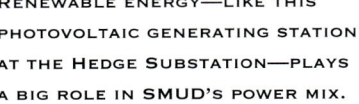

RENEWABLE ENERGY—LIKE THIS PHOTOVOLTAIC GENERATING STATION AT THE HEDGE SUBSTATION—PLAYS A BIG ROLE IN SMUD'S POWER MIX.

▼ RUDY MYERS

SOLAR HOT WATER HEATERS ARE A PART OF SMUD'S AWARD-WINNING ENERGY EFFICIENCY PROGRAM.

already under way, research continues at California State University, Sacramento, and the University of California, Davis, in search of economically feasible and environmentally sound solar thermal and biomass technology. SMUD is leading the development of a solar thermal plant that will generate electricity for up to four hours after sunset. SMUD engineers are also examining the possibility of a 100-megawatt solar thermal plant, which would be the world's first commercial, solar thermal central receiver. Current estimates indicate that, in Sacramento's hot, sunny climate, such a plant would generate enough electricity to power 35,000 homes.

ELECTRIFYING SACRAMENTO

For SMUD, being committed to a clean and efficient future means more than upgrading its power sources. The district has been instrumental in developing technologies that will benefit everyone. The most notable of these is the electric vehicle; in 1992 SMUD built the first solar-powered, electric-vehicle charging stations in the western United States. Today, dozens of charging outlets are located throughout the Sacramento area, making it convenient for drivers to recharge their vehicles while they are at work or running errands. Largely because of SMUD's expertise in this field, the U.S. Congress appropriated funds for projects at McClellan Air Force Base aimed at advancing electric vehicle technologies.

In conjunction with Sacramento Regional Transit, the area's mass transit authority, SMUD is also working to secure federal funding for an electric trolley system that would replace diesel buses. In addition, to help meet federal laws mandating that 2 percent of all cars sold in California be "zero emission" by 1998, SMUD is leading local efforts to establish an electric-vehicle manufacturing industry for Sacramento.

These efforts have not gone unnoticed. In 1992, for instance, the American Public Power Association bestowed upon SMUD its highest honor, the E.F. Scattergood Award, for sustained achievement and customer service by a publicly owned utility. Also in 1992, the California Municipal Utilities Association honored SMUD with its Resource Conservation Award.

SMUD offers customers one of the most ambitious arrays of energy-efficient options in the nation. These include a refrigerator recycling program for area residents, and Sacramento Shade, a tree-planting program launched in 1990. Recognized by the National Arbor Day Foundation, Sacramento Shade is well on its way to accomplishing the goal of planting 500,000 shade trees in the area by the year 2000.

As it has for nearly five decades, the Sacramento Municipal Utility District is applying characteristic determination to the Sacramento Shade project. Always striving to provide top service and create a better tomorrow for its customers, SMUD will continue to utilize its most important resources: vision and teamwork.

Aerojet

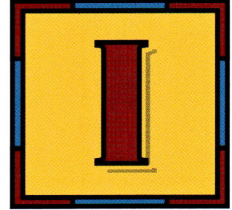

N 1936 A TEACHER, TWO STUDENTS, AND SOME ROCKET HOBBYISTS GATHERED IN A LIVING ROOM IN PASADENA, CALIFORNIA. AT THE TIME, MOST OF THEIR COLLEAGUES THOUGHT THE MEN WERE CRAZY. AFTER ALL, SENDING ROCKETS INTO OUTER SPACE WAS PURE NONSENSE. OR WAS IT? THEODORE VON KARMAN, THE ACCLAIMED AERODYNAMICS PROFESSOR FROM THE CALIFORNIA INSTITUTE OF TECHNOLOGY, KNEW there was something to rocket technology—something big.

Von Karman was right. In March of 1942, the Hungarian-born scientist and four associates borrowed $250 each from a friend and formed Aerojet Engineering Corporation. Over the next several years, Aerojet led America into the rocket age.

In its early years, Aerojet was a single-product company, producing Jet Assist Take Off (JATO) rocket motors, which provided extra boost for heavy airplanes faced with short runways and even shorter aircraft carrier decks. During World War II, Aerojet supplied the U.S. armed forces with thousands of JATO units from its headquarters in Azusa, California.

By 1950, with the Korean War creating renewed demand for JATOs, and entry into other forms of rocketry creating still more business, Aerojet had outgrown its facility in Azusa. But where does a company turn to find the thousands of acres needed to design, produce, and test the most advanced rocket propulsion systems in the world? East of downtown Sacramento, Von Karman found just what he needed.

Launch from Sacramento

Aerojet acquired 7,200 acres of barren Sacramento land laid to waste by years of gold dredging. Although the endless furrows of rocks looked worthless to the rest of the world, Aerojet soon built the world's largest facility for rocket engine design, development, production, and testing.

During its first decade in Sacramento, Aerojet skyrocketed to success. Between 1952 and 1962, employment mushroomed from 2,798 to 33,615, while sales soared from $21 million to $605 million. With America working to close the missile gap with Russia as declared by President Eisenhower, Aerojet responded to the challenge by developing and building propulsion systems for the Titan, Minuteman, and Polaris ballistic missiles. In 1958 the world got a glimpse at the company's expertise when Aerojet's second-stage engine powered a lunar probe—the first successful launch of the National Aeronautics and Space Administration.

In the 1960s, Aerojet played a crucial role in sending American astronauts to the moon. In fact, three out of every four rockets launched from Cape Canaveral in 1966 were powered by Aerojet propulsion systems.

As the first major American company with expertise in both liquid and solid rocket propulsion systems, Aerojet continued its leadership role in the country's defense and space programs during the 1970s. In 1975 Aerojet's liquid propellant Titan rocket engines launched the Viking spacecraft on its 500 million-mile voyage to Mars. At the same time, the company developed and produced an advanced second-stage solid propellant rocket motor for the Peacekeeper Missile, as well as the Orbital Maneuvering System engine used since the first flight of the Space Shuttle in 1981. Such technologies later led to development of the lateral thruster, a rocket engine the size of a bread box that produces as much thrust as an F-16 jet engine.

First stage rocket engines for the Air Force Titan space launch vehicle are prepared for delivery (below left).

Aerojet is applying space technology to more earthly pursuits by developing lightweight composite tanks for compressed natural gas storage and transportation (below right).

The company's Orbital Maneuvering System engines place the Space Shuttle into and out of its proper orbit (LEFT).

FOCUS ON THE FUTURE

Today, Aerojet's five founders would have difficulty recognizing the company they launched in that living room in Pasadena. Aerojet is owned by GenCorp, an Ohio-based Fortune 500 technology firm with strong positions in aerospace, automotive, and related polymer products. Headquartered in Sacramento—where the facility now totals 13,300 acres—Aerojet maintains additional operations in Azusa, and in Tennessee, Mississippi, Florida, and New Mexico.

In a time when defense industry cutbacks have challenged the bottom line, Aerojet is preparing for the future with vision and innovation. "We are now setting the stage for carrying out our vision over the next 50 years," says President Roger Ramseier. "Our plan is to take the skills and technologies we have developed over the years and look at them with new eyes to see if mixing, matching, and applying them in new ways will create new products and markets."

In keeping with this approach, Aerojet has developed the Resource Recovery System, which reuses ingredients in rocket propellant and provides an environmentally attractive alternative to the practice of open burning.

Aerojet is also working with Pacific Gas & Electric Company, the nation's largest investor-owned energy utility, to apply its aerospace and defense expertise to clean-air transportation. Using technologies honed on advanced composite rocket motor cases, fuel tanks, and high-performance spacecraft pressure vessels, Aerojet is developing a low-cost, lightweight mobile natural gas storage module that can be used to supply natural gas fuel to companies operating fleets of vehicles.

Aerojet also recognizes the need to do more than succeed on the bottom line. Through the GenCorp Foundation, the company invests more than $350,000 in the Sacramento community annually. Highlighting these efforts is Adventures in Aerospace, aimed at helping children in grades four through eight learn about math and science. Since 1983 more than 100,000 elementary schoolchildren have participated in the program.

Though Aerojet's next half century will hold its share of uncertainties, Ramseier is confident one thing will remain fixed. "We are dedicated to being a technology-based, high-quality, and low-cost innovator and producer," he says. "We are dedicated to delivering what we promise."

Volunteers reach out to youngsters in the community through the Adventures in Aerospace program (ABOVE RIGHT).

Jet Assist Take Off rockets "launched" the Aerojet name by providing the boost for a quick ascent from short runways and aircraft carriers during World War II (ABOVE LEFT).

Sacramento Light Opera Association

SACRAMENTO LIGHT OPERA ASSOCIATION—THE CAPITAL CITY'S OLDEST PROFESSIONAL PERFORMING ARTS ORGANIZATION AND CALIFORNIA'S LARGEST NONPROFIT MUSICAL THEATER COMPANY—WAS BORN IN A PARKING LOT, THE PRODUCT OF A FORTUNATE CONVERGENCE OF LOCAL BOOSTERISM AND BROADWAY KNOW-HOW, PRUDENT BUSINESS PRACTICES AND THEATRICAL ARTISTRY, COMPATIBLE

OVER THE YEARS MORE THAN 300 PRODUCTIONS OF SOME 150 DIFFERENT MUSICALS HAVE GRACED THE ROUND MUSIC CIRCUS STAGE, INCLUDING THIS 1990 PRODUCTION OF *CHESS* (RIGHT).

THE MUSIC CIRCUS TENT ON A LATE SUMMER EVENING (BELOW).

personalities and simple good luck.

In 1949 theatrical innovator St. John Terrell set up a circus tent in an empty New Jersey field and began producing musical plays. The Music Circus, as Terrell's hybrid was called, mixed familiar but disparate elements of theater in a combination no one had ever tried before: the informality of the circus; the arena layout that afforded everyone a good seat; the summer-camp, Chautauqua-style ambience; and the musicals themselves, then, as now, the first choice with theatergoers. It took the Eastern Seaboard by storm. From their headquarters in Los Angeles, Russell Lewis and Howard Young were watching closely.

Lewis and Young had produced eight shows on Broadway and 27 for national tours before heading west after their World War II service. They were considering setting up a music circus on the West Coast when they got a call from Eleanor McClatchy, president of the *Sacramento Bee* and the city's foremost theatrical "angel." The founder of the Civic Repertory Theater, one of the city's leading amateur troupes, she was determined to bring professional quality theater—in particular, musical theater—to Sacramento. McClatchy invited Lewis and Young up for a look around. The three hit it off from the start.

After two meetings and a few phone calls, the deal was done: Lewis and Young Productions launched Sacramento Music Circus—the first of the new "tune-tents" west of the Mississippi and only the fourth in the entire country—in the Civic Repertory Theater parking lot. It was an instant success, the "in" thing to do on a summer evening.

"A Lovely, Quiet Thing to Do"

Under Lewis and Young's direction, Music Circus, formally incorporated as the Sacramento Light Opera Association (SLOA), put its hometown on the theatrical map. With Lewis overseeing artistic details and Young tending to the business side of the enterprise, the partners quickly impressed professional actors across the country by bringing Broadway production values to the tent.

Over the years, Sacramento Music Circus became known as one of America's most fertile acting nurseries. "It would be impossible," Young once said, "to recall all the people who have used Music Circus as a training ground—a stepping stone to Broadway, film, and television." Among the unknowns who later made the trip to the big time are Madeline Kahn, a rather comic Magnolia in *Show Boat* (1969); Joel Grey, an impish Huck Finn in *Tom Sawyer* (1960); and Eileen Brennan, an earthy Queen Guinevere in *Camelot* (1967).

Established stars also took their turns under the big blue-and-green tent, thanks to the producers' Broadway connections. The mix of seasoned performers and enthusiastic newcomers, familiar shows with innovative stagings, and the outdoor, casual ambience added to the distinctive Music Circus experience. As Lewis once said, "There's something about the tent and the courtyard. There's something about people strolling in the half-light to their seats. It's a lovely, quiet thing to do."

Those half-lit summer nights have ushered thousands of Sacramentans to their first experience with live theater. Over the years more than 300 productions of some 150 different musicals have graced the round Music Circus stage, with the classics of the genre—*Show Boat, The King and I, Man of La Mancha, Oklahoma!* and the like—always well represented.

On the Cutting Edge

To survive, however, every theater must learn to adapt, to offer something beyond the expected. Always on the cutting edge, SLOA introduced the Broadway Series in 1989 as a wintertime companion to Music Circus. An indoor series at the Sacramento Community Center's proscenium theater, the Broadway Series offers newer works—many still playing on the Great White Way—and major revivals of established musicals.

But fate has a way of writing changes to the script. In December 1992 Lewis died at age 84. Young, his partner for over half a century, died the following spring at age 81, less than a year after receiving the Founders' Award from the National Alliance of Musical Theatre Producers for his decades of leadership in American stagecraft.

Today, SLOA is under the direction of Leland Ball, who brings 30 years of professional theatrical experience to his job. According to Ball, the company—now a $6.5 million enterprise with annual attendance in excess of 200,000—has a future even brighter than its star-studded past. "We remain committed to bringing our audiences the best professional theater and to challenging ourselves to become better than we have been," he says.

Indeed, Ball has already led his company to another first. In February 1994 SLOA's production of *West Side Story* was selected for presentation at the United Nations Center in Vienna in six performances to benefit the UN High Commissioner for Refugees. It was the first time an American nonprofit musical theater company had seen one of its productions transferred directly from its home stage to an overseas locale.

For Ball, the Austria trip meant more than just success for the Sacramento Light Opera Association. "Naturally we think we do good work here," he says, "but recognition from international arts professionals is icing on the cake. It's a coup not only for us, but for Sacramento as well."

Michael Gruber performed in the 1993 Broadway Series production of *Singin' in the Rain* (left).

In February 1994 SLOA's production of *West Side Story* was selected for presentation at the United Nations Center in Vienna in six performances to benefit the UN High Commissioner for Refugees (below).

Mather Federal Credit Union

MATHER FEDERAL CREDIT UNION CAME INTO EXISTENCE OVER 40 YEARS AGO WHEN SEVEN CIVILIANS WORKING ON MATHER AIR FORCE BASE RECOGNIZED A NEED FOR BETTER FINANCIAL SERVICES ON BASE. EACH OF THESE ORIGINAL MEMBERS CONTRIBUTED $5 TO FORM WHAT WAS THEN CALLED MATHER CIVILIAN CREDIT UNION. IN 1955, A MILITARY CREDIT UNION WAS ESTABLISHED TO SERVE THE NEEDS OF the active-duty personnel on base. Both organizations operated out of a two-story barracks until August 1962, when they merged operations to form Mather Federal Credit Union.

Mather Federal is a cooperative owned and governed by its members. Its purpose is to provide members with a safe place to save, while offering them low-cost loans and other convenient services. Mather Federal is governed by its voluntary Board of Directors and a supervisory committee. These individuals serve without compensation at the will of the membership. Each credit union member has one vote to elect officials who will represent their interests before the Board of Directors.

Currently, Mather Federal is the fourth-largest credit union in Sacramento, with assets of over $140 million. Branch operations are located throughout the Sacramento metropolitan area, providing convenient access for members. Automated teller machines are also available for after-hours access. Mather

Federal is actively involved in the community it serves, including the Base Reuse Commission, Rancho Cordova Development Committee, area chambers of commerce, and numerous charitable and civic organizations.

In January 1989, the Department of Defense announced the 1993 closure of Mather Air Force Base. The Board of Directors, management, and staff of Mather Federal were quick to reassure members that their credit union would remain open. Mather Federal's strong retired military membership, the creation of Heritage Club (which enables persons 50 and older to join), and the addition of associations and businesses such as health care clinics, law firms, hotels, restaurants, construction companies, and nonprofit organizations from throughout the Sacramento community provide a strong foundation for continued operations and future growth.

Sacramento employers are beginning to realize the value of linking their employees with the convenient, low-cost financial expertise available at Mather Federal Credit Union. "If an employer offers credit union benefits to his employees, then he wins, his employees win, and the credit

union wins," says President and CEO Allan S. Irwin.

Not all of Mather Federal's membership groups are employer based. One unique partnership was formed with a group of Russian immigrants. In 1990, several thousand Russian families immigrated to the Sacramento region. Unfamiliar with their new culture, the newcomers needed assistance in understanding the fundamentals of checking accounts, how interest is earned, what credit cards are, and how to plan for a sound financial future. The credit union held evening classes to teach these basics. A Russian translator was also provided. An individual from within this community was hired by the credit union to assist Russian-speaking members. For Irwin, Mather

CLOCKWISE FROM BELOW: PRESIDENT AND CEO ALLAN S. IRWIN (LEFT) JOINS BOARD OF DIRECTORS MEMBER LT. COL. SCOTT E. GERHART.

MATHER FEDERAL'S BILINGUAL EMPLOYEES HELP SERVICE ITS DIVERSE MEMBERSHIP.

MATHER FINANCIAL SERVICES, INC. PROVIDES INVESTMENT SERVICES SUCH AS ANNUITIES, LIFE INSURANCE, AND MUTUAL FUNDS TO MATHER FEDERAL MEMBERS.

PHOTOS BY PHIL ROBBINS PHOTOGRAPHY

Federal's extra efforts on behalf of these immigrants transcends the new member relationships created. "It was unique, but the overriding philosophy of the credit union industry is 'People Helping People.' We try to put that into practice every day."

The continued operations of the credit union's facility, located on what was formerly Mather Air Force Base, was assured in December 1991 when President Bush signed into law the National Defense Authorization Act for fiscal years 1992 and 1993. This law enables credit unions to recover at no cost the buildings they constructed on military installations slated for closure. As a result, Mather Federal continues to operate out of its Mather Air Force Base location.

In July 1992, Irwin received a special achievement award from the National Association of Federal Credit Unions for his tremendous efforts in the law's successful passage. He has served as president and CEO since June 1990. Prior to joining Mather Federal, Irwin served as a colonel with the United States Army and as CEO and manager of Signal Federal Credit Union.

Mather Federal realizes the importance of meeting the ever-changing needs of its diverse membership. As Irwin states, "Our purpose is to understand members' financial needs and then provide quality financial products and services that meet those needs." As a result of comments and suggestions from members, Mather Federal has opened additional branches, extended branch hours to include Saturdays, reduced the rate offered on its credit card, and installed a telephone loan application service—Loan By Phone.

In addition to these innovations, Mather Federal has joined a lending program that links auto dealers to the credit union for fast and convenient loan approval right at the dealership. Mather Federal also participates in Point-of-Sale, which enables members to make purchases with their ATM card at grocery stores, gas stations, and numerous other businesses. For access to accounts after hours, Mather Federal installed Priority Line, a telephone audio response system that allows members to perform a variety of transactions from the comfort and privacy of their home or office. With these advancements in technology, Mather Federal looks forward to providing members with the latest in convenience and access.

As for the future, with an unswerving dedication to fulfilling the needs of over 34,000 members worldwide, Irwin believes that Mather Federal Credit Union is poised for success in the decades ahead. "The most important ingredient in our success is our members," he says. "We aren't here to make money; we're here to help people."

CLOCKWISE FROM LEFT: MEMBERS CAN ACCESS THEIR MATHER FEDERAL ACCOUNTS AT OVER 32,000 ATM LOCATIONS WORLDWIDE THROUGH STAR, PLUS, EXCHANGE, CIRRUS, AMERICAN EXPRESS, MASTERCARD, AND THE ARMED FORCES FINANCIAL NETWORK.

ALPHAGRAPHICS PRINTSHOPS OF THE FUTURE IS AMONG OVER 100 SELECT EMPLOYEE GROUPS THAT MAKE UP THE CREDIT UNION'S EXPANDING FIELD OF MEMBERSHIP.

IN AN EFFORT TO ACCOMMODATE ITS LARGE RUSSIAN MEMBERSHIP, MATHER FEDERAL PROVIDES RUSSIAN-SPEAKING EMPLOYEES AT ITS RANCHO CORDOVA LOCATION.

PHOTOS BY PHIL ROBBINS PHOTOGRAPHY

KOVR CHANNEL 13

Much has changed since September 6, 1954, the night KOVR Channel 13 broadcast Sacramento's first television pictures from a talent show at the California State Fair. As the city has matured into a major metropolitan region, and the 21st-largest television market in the United States, KOVR 13 has grown up, too—from a small, independent station in nearby Stockton to a multimillion-dollar, award-winning operation.

Meeting the Needs of a Growing Sacramento

Initially, KOVR 13 didn't even have a studio in Sacramento. Channel 13 first operated as an independent station and broadcast into Sacramento from studios in Stockton and San Francisco. In 1957, however, the Gannett Company bought the station and moved it into Sacramento studios in 1960.

Through the years, KOVR 13 has invested in the technology to keep pace with a growing Sacramento. KOVR, for example, was the first Sacramento television station to videotape events at remote locations and play them back later on news broadcasts. More recently, the station debuted NewSat 13, a satellite truck that can broadcast live from anywhere, and Chopper 13, the station's helicopter.

Chopper 13 is the only television helicopter in the city that is able to land and take off from a helipad on the station's roof. This unique advantage means that KOVR's reporters can fly to and from breaking stories without having to first drive to a separate takeoff site. In turn, KOVR 13 is able to bring news and information to its viewers faster than any other station in the area. In fact, when KOVR's $8 million, state-of-the-art broadcast complex was designed early in the 1990s, architects created a unique double roof to shield the studios below from the high noise levels of Chopper 13's takeoffs and landings.

"Coverage You Count On"

KOVR 13, even with its access to news from across the nation and around the world, has not lost sight of its commitment to superior, in-depth coverage of local news. In all its efforts, the station strives to provide "Coverage You Count On."

KOVR's newsroom boasts a long list of journalistic accomplishments. For instance, in the mid-1970s the station secured the first television images of the SR-71, the Air Force's once-classified spy plane. A few years later, following the crash of a B-52 jet near Mather Air Force Base, it was KOVR 13

KOVR Channel 13 broadcasts from an $8 million, state-of-the-art facility (right).

Many of KOVR's programs in the 1950s originated live from its first studio in Stockton (above).

In the 1950s and 1960s, "Captain Delta" was one of Sacramento's most popular television programs for children (right).

again that probed into the incident and uncovered information Congress later used to strengthen pilot-training requirements.

For these and many other efforts, KOVR 13 News has been recognized by countless organizations: the Emmy Awards, the Associated Press, the Society of Professional Journalists, and the Radio and Television News Director's Association, to name a few.

Strengthening the Community

KOVR 13's commitment goes beyond just reporting the news. Over the years, the station has taken a leadership role in many community projects and events.

Early in the 1990s, as unemployment skyrocketed, KOVR 13 helped hundreds of Sacramentans find jobs at local businesses through its successful job fairs and through the popular "For Hire" segments on its newscasts. And when the Sacramento NAACP office burned in 1993, KOVR immediately responded by broadcasting a live "Telephone Town Meeting" and by donating office facilities so that NAACP volunteers could continue to accept calls.

Many Sacramentans are also familiar with the KOVR 13/ FamiliesFirst Foster Santa Project, which has provided thousands of shiny new bikes for local foster

children at Christmas. The highly respected and coveted Jefferson Award, which recognizes outstanding community service by local residents, is also sponsored by the station.

CHOPPER 13 CAN REPORT BREAKING NEWS FROM A DISTANT LOCATION WITHIN MINUTES.

THE NEWSAT 13 SATELLITE TRUCK SENT LIVE REPORTS BACK TO SACRAMENTO FROM THE OAKLAND HILLS FIRE IN 1991.

CSUS School of Business Administration

For more than four decades, the fundamental goal of the School of Business Administration at California State University, Sacramento has been to develop future leaders with an excellent management education and a broad understanding of their responsibilities in the business world and throughout the community. In consistently achieving this goal, the school has played a vital role in the economic development of the Sacramento region.

"For nearly 50 years, California State University, Sacramento has set a standard for academic distinction that has enhanced our graduates' abilities to influence economic development within our region, across the nation, and throughout the world," says CSUS President Donald R. Gerth.

Creating a Fertile Academic Environment

The business school started humbly in 1947 with two faculty members teaching classes in the garage of an apartment building at Ninth and Broadway; they held office hours upstairs, sharing the dinette and living room of one of the apartments. In 1953 the fledgling business school moved when classes began at the new college campus on J Street. Today, the faculty has grown to 135, while the curriculum has matured well beyond the original classes in accounting, personnel, marketing, and business education.

The CSUS business school currently offers undergraduate concentrations in accountancy, finance, human resources management, insurance, international business, management information systems, marketing, operations management, real estate and land-use affairs, and strategic management. Graduate degree programs include Master of Business Administration, Master of Science in Accountancy, and Master of Science in Management Information Systems.

As the only business school in the Sacramento metropolitan area with both undergraduate and graduate programs accredited by the American Assembly of Collegiate Schools of Business, the CSUS School of Business Administration provides a fertile academic environment. Top scholars and professors at the forefront of applied research and teaching innovation challenge students with a sophisticated, demanding curriculum.

Strong Demand for Graduates

Backed by the finest academic experience, graduates of the CSUS School of Business Administration are routinely in high demand among small businesses and large corporate recruiters representing firms as diverse as Arthur Andersen, Chevron, Hewlett-Packard, and JCPenney. And while many graduates secure positions in other cities and countries, more than 60 percent remain in the Sacramento area, playing key leadership roles at businesses such as Java City, a leading retail cafe chain in the greater Sacramento region. The success of Java City enhances Sacramento's reputation for providing fertile ground for small businesses where many graduates have been encouraged to launch entrepreneurial ventures of their own.

In the years ahead, Dean Josef D. Moorehead expects the school to continue to influence local economic development. "As the Sacramento region's economy matures," he says, "business leaders will continue to look to the CSUS School of Business Administration for outstanding graduates, programs, and services. My vision is to enhance the school's position as the premier source of management education, applied research and information, and services in the greater Sacramento region."

While the future in Sacramento, one of the nation's fastest-growing regions, clearly holds its share of uncertainties, Moorehead is quite sure of one thing: "At the CSUS School of Business Administration, we will maintain our dedication to excellence."

The school's location in the capital city affords faculty and students the opportunity to work with the State of California to improve economic development.

Business leaders look to the CSUS School of Business Administration for outstanding graduates and critical programs and services heightened by a commitment to the community and a dedication to excellence.

McDonald's Corporation

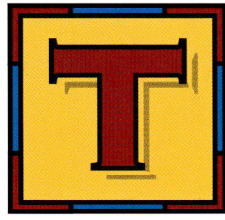

The idea came to Bob Olsen one morning in March of 1987. At the time, Olsen worked as a ranger for the Eagle Lake District of the Lassen National Forest, near Susanville in Northern California. Olsen saw a television advertisement for the worldwide network of 125 Ronald McDonald Houses—places where the families of critically ill children can stay while the children are in the hospital—and started to think. McDonald's Corporation's commitment to children would make the company a perfect partner in an effort to establish a camp for disabled and disadvantaged children. Olsen was right; McDonald's was eager to help.

McDonald's restaurants, founded by Ray Kroc in Illinois, have become a staple of family dining and entertainment in America and across the world. The Sacramento area's first McDonald's restaurant opened in 1954 in South Sacramento, and today the area's 85 franchises continue the company's commitment to community service. From innovative recycling programs to its efforts to recruit employees of all races and ages, McDonald's has displayed a special commitment to the communities in which it does business. Nowhere is that more true than in Sacramento, where the Northern California Golden Arches Association, a cooperative of Sacramento-area McDonald's owners, contributed the initial $600,000 donation necessary to get the $2.5 million Eagle Lake children's camp project under way.

A Special Place

Since opening in 1992, Camp Ronald McDonald at Eagle Lake has served more than 1,200 disabled and/or disadvantaged children. The unique camp is operated by Eagle Lake Children's Charities, a nonprofit organization formed in 1988 to guide the project to completion. Joined by other groups, including the Northern California Timber Association and the Telephone Pioneers of America, the McDonald's owners have made camp possible for children who could never go before.

"Unlike most camps," says Mary Tunison, executive director of Eagle Lake Children's Charities, "ours has been designed from the outset to be fully wheelchair accessible. In addition, we have staff trained to work with special-needs children, and all of our programs are specifically adapted to meet the needs of each group that's attending."

In the end, Tunison says the most significant benefit of Camp Ronald McDonald is the creation of an environment where disabled and disadvantaged children can experience success in their lives. "The camp offers an especially rich environment to conduct emotional and motivational activities for disadvantaged or at-risk youth," she says. "We are able to offer rewarding outdoor programs to a wide variety of young people who are often excluded from these important experiences."

But can a few days at camp really make a difference to a child with special needs? Tunison remembers a letter she got from one mother, who wrote, "I know my son won't be able to do many things in his life. At least now, after camp, he knows there are so many things he can do. Thank you for making my little boy into the fine young man I've dreamed he could be."

After years of making dining in a family atmosphere entertaining and affordable, Sacramento-area McDonald's franchises are building on their commitment to families by making Camp Ronald McDonald at Eagle Lake a reality.

SINCE OPENING IN 1992, CAMP RONALD MCDONALD AT EAGLE LAKE HAS SERVED MORE THAN 1,200 DISABLED AND/OR DISADVANTAGED CHILDREN.

Graphic Center

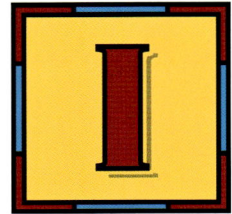

IN THE MID-1960S, TERRY GRIMES GRADUATED FROM COLLEGE WITH A BUSINESS DEGREE AND WENT TO WORK FOR A NORTHERN CALIFORNIA FREIGHT CARRIER. ONE OF HIS CLIENTS WAS GRAPHIC CENTER, A SACRAMENTO MANUFACTURER OF GREETING CARDS. IN 1969 GRIMES WAS HIRED BY GRAPHIC CENTER TO DEVELOP ITS PRINT DIVISION. A YEAR LATER, AT AGE 26, HE BOUGHT THE BUSINESS.

At the time, Grimes remembers, Graphic Center was struggling. "We had seven employees and five presses; one of the presses and two of the employees didn't work." But Grimes had already developed a keen business eye. With the vision to anticipate changes in the marketplace and the ability to respond to these shifts with advancements in technology and equipment, he has built Graphic Center into the largest solely owned printing company in Northern California. The company that once did $109,000 in sales in 1970 with a handful of employees has become one of the most successful printing firms in the region. In 1994 Graphic Center did $17 million in sales and posted a $4.5 million payroll for its 150 employees.

Shaping the Region's Printing Industry

From the beginning, Grimes knew Graphic Center's success hinged on finding a niche in the marketplace. Looking at the local printing industry, he saw that other printers were already serving Sacramento well. Grimes decided to take advantage of the city's location in the heart of California's business economy and structured the small company as a regional provider. He hired sales representatives in the San Francisco Bay area and began to call on businesses in the Napa Valley wine country, San Francisco, and San Jose. "We were small and flexible, and we could outgun the competition," Grimes says.

Today, more than two decades later, many of the successful client partnerships forged in those early years continue to flourish. Graphic Center's long list of distinguished clients includes Chevron, Sony, Bianchi Bicycles, Pacific Gas & Electric Company, Apple Computers, Foundation Health, Chiron, Bank of America, Kendall-Jackson, Gallo, Saudi Bank of Holland, Discovery Toys, Kikoman, Bay Area Rapid Transit, Amtrak, and artists such as Wayne Thiebaud and David Goines. In Sacramento, Graphic Center works with many of the capital city's top corporate entities, including Sutter Health, computer giant Intel, and the University of California, Davis.

Although vision and a commitment to high-quality printing and

FROM ITS INCEPTION, THE FIRM HAS BEEN AN INDUSTRY LEADER IN ADOPTING ADVANCED PRINTING TECHNOLOGIES.

ED ASMUS

customer service have played key roles in Graphic Center's growth, Grimes acknowledges that the company's rise to prominence has involved much more. From its inception, the firm has been an industry leader in adopting advanced printing technologies. Years ago, for instance, when other printers were buying 40-inch presses, Grimes bought 28-inch presses. His theory was that there were more $5,000 jobs than $10,000 jobs. The approach worked, Grimes says, adding that Graphic Center soon became the largest half-sheet printer on the West Coast. In the 1980s, when the demand for bigger job runs increased, Grimes traded his small presses for a web press and two 640 sheetfed presses.

More recently, Grimes has built on his commitment to advanced in-house technology. Along with three six-color presses, Graphic Center has added a Bobst die cutter, a second Mueller six-pocket stitcher, an Iris proofing system, an enhanced Scitex prepress system, and Macintosh imaging equipment. In addition, the firm is the only Sacramento printer to have its own in-house ink operation, Los Angeles-based Ink Systems, Inc.—which means consistent color matching and faster turnaround for clients. Ink Systems stocks a large variety of papers, and all colors are matched on the actual job stock by experienced, on-site technicians who are available around the clock.

Putting all of these technological capabilities together, Grimes believes that Graphic Center offers unique printing benefits to the Sacramento region. "We have a better mix of equipment under our roof than any other printer in Northern California. Consequently, we're able to do whatever it takes to produce the product our clients need," he says, adding that the company's shipping department operates a fleet of trucks that deliver throughout Northern California daily.

SETTING STANDARDS IN CORPORATE CITIZENSHIP

After 25 years as owner, president, chief operating officer, and sales manager, Grimes feels that Graphic Center's prosperity is due in large part to his ability to anticipate industry change. "I try to get a feel for market trends. In just this past year, we've invested close to $2 million in new equipment and expanded facilities," says Grimes.

As a Sacramento business leader, Grimes remains deeply committed to the community as well. A Sacramento native, he is active in numerous professional and charitable organizations, including past service on the board of directors for the Sacramento Entrepreneurship Academy and on the board of the Art Directors and Artists Club. Grimes currently serves on the board of directors at KVIE Channel 6 (Sacramento's public television station) and its Business Advisory Council. He is also an active supporter of the Student Buddy Program, an offshoot of The Mustard Seed.

With tremendous business responsibilities, why do Grimes and his wife, Graphic Center Marketing Director Katy Grimes, make time for the community? "We love it here," Terry Grimes says. "And we're proud to contribute to Sacramento's well-being."

CLOCKWISE FROM BOTTOM LEFT: IN 1970 TERRY GRIMES BOUGHT GRAPHIC CENTER, THEN A STRUGGLING COMPANY WITH ONLY SEVEN EMPLOYEES. TODAY, IT IS ONE OF THE MOST SUCCESSFUL PRINTING FIRMS IN NORTHERN CALIFORNIA.

COMPLEMENTING ITS COMMITMENT TO TECHNOLOGY IS GRAPHIC CENTER'S WORKFORCE OF 150 DEDICATED EMPLOYEES.

THE FIRM IS THE ONLY SACRAMENTO PRINTER TO HAVE ITS OWN IN-HOUSE INK OPERATION, WHICH MEANS CONSISTENT COLOR MATCHING AND FASTER TURNAROUND FOR CLIENTS.

GRAPHIC CENTER'S SHIPPING DEPARTMENT OPERATES A FLEET OF TRUCKS THAT DELIVER THROUGHOUT NORTHERN CALIFORNIA DAILY.

THE COMPANY'S COMMITMENT TO ADVANCED IN-HOUSE TECHNOLOGY INCLUDES AN ENHANCED SCITEX PREPRESS SYSTEM.

GISELLE'S TRAVEL BUREAU

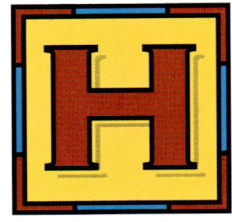

How does a travel agency with gross billings of $25 million triple its sales over a five-year period amid a struggling economy? For many of the 36,000 travel agencies in the United States, the easy answer would involve selling a lot of airline tickets. But at Giselle's Travel Bureau, the rise from a local business to the 47th-largest travel agency in the United States involves much more.

"Our methodology focuses not on goods but on services," says Cynthia A. Michalski, senior vice president of Giselle's Travel Bureau. "We maintain our competitive advantage by asking better questions. It's not 'How can we do what we do better?' but 'Why do we do what we do?' To our clients, the benefit of such an approach is the expansion of the horizon—removing limiting perspectives to allow innovation and new ways of doing things."

MAKING DREAMS COME TRUE

The philosophy came alive in 1991 when Giselle's Travel Bureau emerged from the consolidation of four established Sacramento agencies. The largest and oldest of the companies, Giselle's Travel, Inc., founded in Sacramento in 1959, boasted gross billings of $30 million. A second agency, Travel Bureau of Sacramento, had been operating in the capital city since 1969.

According to Michalski, the merger has strengthened Giselle's industry-renowned commitment to quality and service. In fact, with increased purchasing power, Giselle's has the strength to pioneer new services and programs while continuing to secure the best rates for clients. Growth has also allowed the firm to implement the newest technologies available to travel agencies, including remote automated ticketing. Similar to an automatic teller machine, an automated ticketing system allows travelers to call toll free, make reservations over the phone, and then pick up their tickets at a machine located conveniently nearby. Already serving the needs of large-volume clients across the United States, Giselle's is preparing to introduce its own national automated ticketing division.

But despite all kinds of high-tech innovations, it is the staff at Giselle's Travel Bureau that makes the difference to business travelers and vacationers alike. The agency offers complete travel management services for corporate clients. This includes group travel as well as meetings and conventions. Increasingly, businesses also are taking advantage of the agency's expertise in arranging travel packages, such as weekend outings or reasonably priced cruises as employee incentives.

Giselle's Travel Bureau is proud of its expert agents who deal one-on-one with vacation travelers, making sure that their needs are met to their complete satisfaction. "We're not just in the business of selling airline tickets," Michalski says. "We're here to make dreams come true." FIT (foreign independent travel) experts are on staff creating customized travel packages to fit clients' wishes. The same dedication to service applies to domestic travel as well.

As the year 2000 approaches, Giselle's Travel Bureau is working diligently to enhance its position as an aggressive, market-driven company and a leader in the transportation industry. By 1998 gross billings are projected to surge past the $140 million mark, Michalski predicts. Regardless of the company's size, however, Michalski avers that its success always will remain anchored in client service—to corporations, individuals, and organizations.

With roots dating back to 1959, Giselle's Travel Bureau has grown from a local business to the 47th-largest travel agency in the United States.

KVIE Channel 6

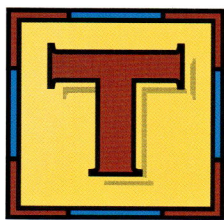

THIRTY-FIVE YEARS AFTER FIRST BROADCASTING ITS SIGNAL TO AN EAGER SACRAMENTO VALLEY AUDIENCE, KVIE CHANNEL 6 REMAINS COMMITTED TO PROVIDING THE FINEST IN EDUCATIONAL PUBLIC TELEVISION. "OUR MISSION HAS ALWAYS BEEN TO EDUCATE, ENRICH, ENLIGHTEN, AND INSPIRE OUR AUDIENCES THROUGH HIGH-QUALITY PROGRAMMING AND EDUCATIONAL OUTREACH SERVICES," SAYS ERIC Mandell, director of community relations and educational services. "The addition of Cable Channel 7 in 1985 has enabled us to double our program service to the community."

In addition to offering youngsters award-winning children's television programs that are known across the nation and the world, KVIE extends beyond the screen through educational outreach efforts. An example is the successful Sesame Street Preschool Educational Program. A training session for day care providers, parents, and educators, the program is designed to help participants use television as a learning tool and help children reach their full potential. KVIE's educational outreach is not limited to children, however. The station also serves Sacramento's corporate world, as staff members and volunteers travel to local businesses to educate professionals on how families can reap the benefits of public television.

Because two-thirds of KVIE's operating budget comes from membership contributions, the greater Sacramento community plays a critical role in Channel 6's success. Starting in 1959 with a first-year subscriber base of 8,000, KVIE today receives financial support from 65,000 members spread over 28 counties in and around Sacramento. In addition, the station boasts more than 5,000 volunteers who donate 55,000 hours each year.

AWARD-WINNING PROGRAMMING AND PRODUCTION

KVIE's on-air programming is reaching new levels of excellence. In addition to bringing such programs as "The Civil War" and "Nova" to Sacramento viewers, Channel 6 has in recent years produced a number of its own programs. Thanks to the enthusiastic support of the community, KVIE was able to construct a new, 69,000-square-foot production and broadcast center. The facility allows the station to greatly improve locally produced programs.

Evidence of its strong commitment to Sacramento, Channel 6 has won numerous awards for its production of innovative local programming. Among the programs produced at KVIE are arts, public affairs, and documentary specials, including "To Quench a Thirst: The California Water Crisis," which aired on all California public television stations, and "Grassroots Guide to Yard Care," a monthly series providing the latest techniques for successful gardening in the Central Valley.

"The new facility has put us in a different league in the eyes of the people who fund national programming," Mandell says, explaining that KVIE has been able to produce a host of national specials, including programs featuring Leo Buscaglia and Roger Whittaker. The station also masterminded "Covert Bailey's Fit or Fat," the popular health and fitness series seen on public television stations nationwide.

Mandell adds that KVIE recently became part of the "information superhighway" by linking up with the new Telstar 401 satellite. This will bring more than 40 channels of multimedia video and data services into the community to meet the needs of education and lifelong learning.

In the years ahead, these technologies will allow KVIE to reach even further into the Sacramento community. "We are eager to do more in the local community," says Mandell. "And we will fulfill that mission."

EVIDENCE OF ITS STRONG COMMITMENT TO SACRAMENTO, CHANNEL 6 HAS WON NUMEROUS AWARDS FOR ITS PRODUCTION OF INNOVATIVE LOCAL PROGRAMMING.

IN ADDITION TO ITS DEDICATED STAFF, KVIE RELIES ON THE GENEROSITY OF ITS 65,000 MEMBERS AND MORE THAN 5,000 VOLUNTEERS.

Port of Sacramento

PORT OF SACRAMENTO TRACES ITS HISTORY BACK TO 1916, WHEN THE SACRAMENTO CHAMBER OF COMMERCE ASKED THE STATE OF CALIFORNIA TO CONDUCT A SURVEY AIMED AT CREATING AN INLAND RIVER CHANNEL FOR OCEANGOING FREIGHTERS. THAT EARLY VISION WAS TO PROVIDE THE SACRAMENTO VALLEY'S RICH AGRICULTURAL FIELDS BETTER, MORE COST-EFFECTIVE ACCESS TO THE LARGE MARKETS ON the East Coast of the United States. As the world grew and changed, the vision evolved with it. An inland port could allow the region's growing businesses to seek international markets.

In 1963 that vision finally became a reality when Port of Sacramento opened for business. Today, the dream flourishes, as Port of Sacramento handles more than 1 million tons of cargo each year, with a value of more than $300 million. It is a valuable avenue of trade for shippers, manufacturers, agribusiness, forest managers, steamship agents, freight forwarders, and many others. More than 100 cargo vessels dock in the port each year, carrying everything from rice and grains to logs, wood chips, and clay. Port of Sacramento funds—directly and indirectly—2,500 jobs and personal income of more than $50 million per year.

Decades of Economic Contribution

Over its more than three decades of economic contribution, Port of Sacramento has demonstrated repeatedly that success in business requires adaptability. When the port was being planned back in the 1930s and 1940s, for instance, most observers agreed that the principal cargo would be canned fruits and vegetables produced at the host of canneries operating in the Sacramento region. By offering manufacturers an economical way to ship canned goods bound for the East Coast of the United States through the Panama Canal, Port of Sacramento officials expected business at the new deep-water ship channel to be brisk and long-term.

By the time the port opened, though, railroads had lowered freight rates, making it cheaper to transport canned goods by rail than by sea. But the port was able to adapt to this change. It recognized that the most economical way to ship many products was to load them, unbagged, into the cavernous holds of freighters. By building state-of-the-art loading and unloading conveyor systems, the port quickly became an important player in international bulk shipping.

Following 1963's maiden cargo of rice and logs, the port's volume grew quickly, reaching 1 million tons in 1967—years ahead of the early predictions. Bulk agricultural cargo such as rice, wheat, safflower, barley, and corn drove early growth. But by the late 1960s, forest products had become major export commodities as well. Cargo volume climbed steadily during the 1970s, due largely to increased demand for rice, wheat, fertilizer, and wood chips. Volume at the port peaked at nearly 3 million tons in 1980, as rice exports swelled to a record total of 1.1 million tons.

Vision and Innovative Leadership

In 1983 Port of Sacramento celebrated its 20th anniversary by reaching the 30 million-ton mark in total cargo volume—an achievement that had originally been predicted for 1997. But international markets changed again, and the port's export volumes of rice,

THROUGHOUT ITS HISTORY, THE PORT HAS HELPED ENSURE GROWTH BY INVESTING IN STATE-OF-THE-ART CARGO HANDLING EQUIPMENT.

More than 100 cargo vessels dock in the port each year, carrying everything from rice and grains to logs, wood chips, and clay.

wheat, and wood chips dropped dramatically.

Port officials responded to this challenge. Recognizing the increasing need to accommodate larger ships, Port of Sacramento pressed ahead with efforts to deepen its ship channel. In 1986 the port culminated 16 years of work by signing an agreement to deepen its ship channel from 30 feet to 35 feet. Upon completion, the additional depth will permit a high proportion of the world's bulk freight ships to navigate the 42-mile-long channel with full loads.

The port has been aggressively growing and diversifying its revenues. It has targeted bulk industrial commodities to add to its base of agricultural and forest products. The port also has been working to develop an inland barging business. Ultimately, it plans to use 500 acres of its currently undeveloped land for commercial and industrial development that will bring in new revenues and provide new growth for the community.

To make all this growth possible, the port is planning to invest millions of dollars to upgrade its infrastructure. A new generation of faster, more efficient cargo handling and storage facilities will enable the port to realize its vision of being a key player in the Sacramento-area economy.

Early on, Port of Sacramento recognized that the most economical way to ship many products was to load them, unbagged, into the cavernous holds of freighters.

Physicians Clinical Laboratory, Inc.

SINCE ITS FOUNDING, PHYSICIANS CLINICAL LABORATORY, INC. HAS ENJOYED AN EXPANDING AND EVOLVING RELATIONSHIP WITH SACRAMENTO—ITS HEADQUARTERS CITY—THAT REFLECTS ONGOING CORPORATE GROWTH. ■ THE COMPANY'S ROOTS IN THE CAPITAL REGION TRACE BACK TO 1986, WHEN PCL WAS ESTABLISHED AS A PARTNERSHIP OF THREE AREA HOSPITALS—SUTTER, MERCY, AND METHODIST—TO provide medical testing services for their acute care patients. At that time, annual revenues approximated $9 million, and the company had about 175 employees.

Much has changed since that inauspicious beginning. Under the aegis of a management team led by Chief Executive N.L. "Nate" Headley, who joined PCL in late 1989, the company has undergone a transformation widely praised by the clinical laboratory industry and Wall Street alike. Headley and his team set about retooling the company into a successful mixed-model, or "hybrid," medical-testing provider, capable of balancing the reference laboratory requirements of physicians with the needs of acute care hospitals.

PRESIDENT AND CEO NATE HEADLEY AT PCL'S CORPORATE HEADQUARTERS AT 2495 NATOMAS PARK DRIVE (NEAR RIGHT).

ATOMIC ABSORPTION ANALYSIS IS USED IN WHOLE BLOOD LEAD ASSAYS (FAR RIGHT).

Dynamic Growth and Progress

Today, as a result of a strategy that has focused on growth through a planned program of acquisitions and through internal means, PCL ranks as California's second-largest provider of clinical laboratory testing. The company has built a substantial market presence in four key geographic regions—Sacramento, San Francisco Bay Area, Central Valley, and Los Angeles—and blankets the state with more than 250 facilities, including three full-service laboratories, 28 STAT laboratories, and 231 patient service centers.

Central to the expansion strategy has been PCL's emphasis on two factors critical to success in the rapidly evolving clinical laboratory industry: market share and access. The company is the largest provider of medical testing in the Sacramento market, and it ranks either first or second in its other geographic regions.

With respect to access, PCL's ubiquitous presence provides patients with the convenience levels required to market the company's services to all segments of the health care community. Accessibility has been important in expanding PCL's base of business in the managed care sector, where the company has extensive experience and an outstanding record of performance.

To bring PCL's dynamic growth into perspective, in the past two years the company has recorded notable accomplishments that include tripling net revenues from about $40 million in fiscal 1993 to $120 million forecast for fiscal 1995; expansion of operations to markets outside Sacramento; completion of a public offering of common stock (PCL shares are listed on the NASDAQ national market system); and consummation of purchases for more than 25 independent California clinical laboratories, making PCL the fastest-growing company in its industry for two consecutive years.

Advanced Technology

Advances in information-system technology, too, have played an important role in spurring PCL's growth. The company has been an industry leader in using these breakthroughs to enhance operating efficiencies and client convenience. Among PCL's innovations has been LabTalk, a personal-computer-based system installed in physicians' offices. The LabTalk system has electronic message capabilities for ordering couriers and supplies, an on-line inquiry into laboratory information systems to access patient results, the ability to store and reprint patient reports for 60 days, and a test directory available to physicians and their staffs.

PCL also developed Lab Line, an automated telephone information network. This leading-edge communications system enables physicians to obtain test results and receive immediate fax transmittals of reports, virtually anywhere, using standard telephone or cellular equipment.

Commitment to the Sacramento Region

Even as PCL's operations have expanded beyond the Sacramento market, the company has continued to build its operations in this geographic area—part of a substantial, ongoing commitment to the local economy. The company currently operates more than 100 facilities in the capital region, which provide approximately 750 nonpolluting, service-sector jobs to area citizens. PCL's fiscal contribution to the local tax rolls is significant and expected to rise further along with corporate growth.

The company recently completed an expansion of its Sacramento "hub" laboratory to accommodate the testing volumes realized from its aggressive growth. The local facility now ranks among the largest clinical laboratories in the United States and is capable of serving 15,000 patients per day.

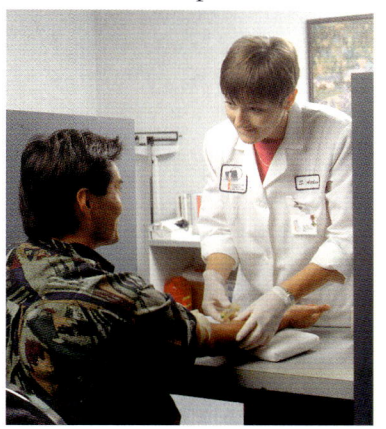
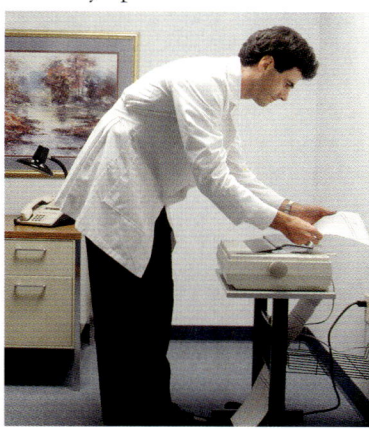

PCL recently relocated its management staff to corporate offices at 2495 Natomas Park Drive. As part of this move, the company is centralizing within its headquarters the billing function for all statewide operations—a formidable task given both PCL's size and the inherent complexities of health care payment processing.

As the leading clinical laboratory in Sacramento, an area of immense economic vitality, PCL realizes its growth is inextricably tied to the regional business community, to the health care professions, and to serving local citizens. The company anticipates playing an ever-growing role in the future.

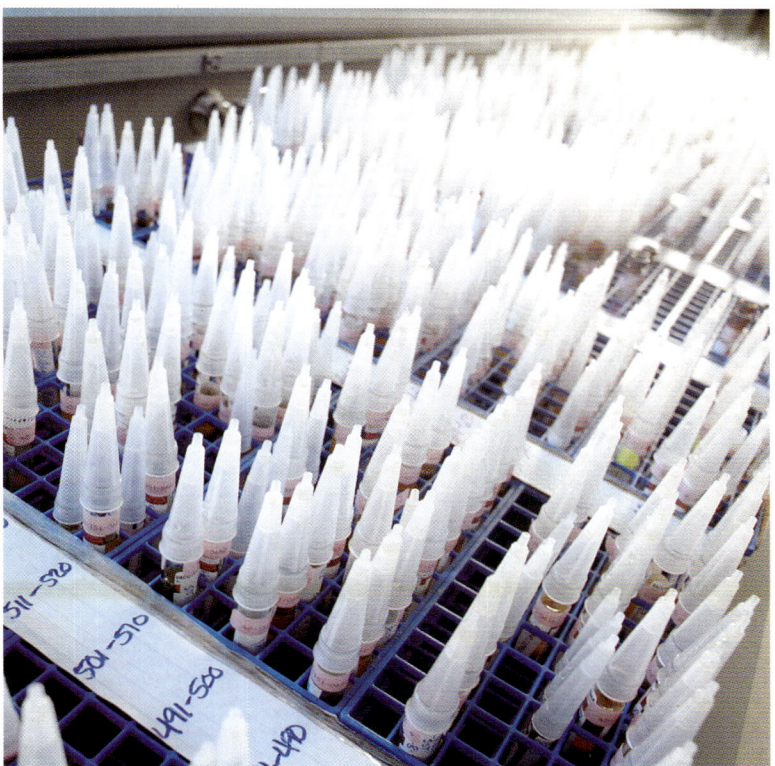

Clockwise from far left: A PCL phlebotomist draws a specimen for testing.

Physicians can receive test results quickly through PCL's communication system.

The company's fleet of over 150 courier cars helps ensure the fast turnaround of test results.

PCL performs approximately 400,000 tests per day.

Foundation Health Corporation

Sacramento's Foundation Health Corporation is a pioneer in the effort to make health care more efficient, convenient, and affordable. As rising health care costs lead to national reform, Foundation is positioned ahead of the pack, offering a variety of managed care programs that make quality care more accessible to a growing number of residents nationwide.

These plans include HMO, PPO, and point-of-service medical plans; dental, behavioral health, and vision plans; workers' compensation insurance; pharmaceutical programs; and group term life insurance. In addition, the company provides health coverage or administrative services under government-sponsored programs such as CHAMPUS, Medicare, and Medicaid.

Building a Solid Foundation

Today, Foundation Health Corporation is one of the nation's leading New York Stock Exchange-traded health care companies. But it has traveled a long road to get there.

President and Chief Executive Officer Daniel D. Crowley remembers contemplating the offer to join the company. It was April 1989, and he and a friend were sitting in a basement pizza parlor looking over records and discussing Foundation Health's marginal financial status.

Crowley decided to accept the offer to become CEO in 1989 and quickly rose to meet the challenge of rebuilding the corporation. In fact, within 14 months, the company reported its most successful year ever. Foundation Health has since blossomed into one of the most successful publicly traded managed care companies in the United States.

Foundation Health, a California Health Plan, today boasts 572,000 members statewide, making it the fourth-largest HMO in the state. Under Crowley's leadership, operating margins have more than doubled, and net income has more than quintupled. In 1994 Foundation Health's total sales hit a record $1.7 billion. Revenues from the company's specialty divisions reached $378 million in 1994, a fivefold increase over the previous year.

Foundation Health is also rapidly expanding its HMO operations in other states across the country, including Alabama, Texas, Louisiana, Oklahoma, and Florida, and now offers managed health care coverage in the United Kingdom. The company has announced plans to purchase managed care companies with operations in Arizona, Colorado, Florida, Nebraska, Nevada, New Mexico, and Utah.

How has Crowley worked this magic? "We have a bible at Foundation Health, and it's called our business plan," he explains. "You hear people talk about business plans, but you hardly ever run into a company that really has a working plan and sticks to it. We do."

Innovative, Community-based Care

In addition to these bold moves forward, Foundation Health has been among the leaders in development and operation of a large network of community-based

President and Chief Executive Officer Daniel D. Crowley (above) has helped Foundation Health blossom into one of the most successful publicly traded managed care companies in the United States.

health care centers. This "one-stop shopping" approach to medical services offers patients primary care and immediate care, as well as laboratory, X-ray, and pharmacy services—all under one roof.

"People told us that it was difficult to find a personal doctor who takes the time to get to know their families, a doctor who was conveniently located with extended hours," Crowley says. "We knew it was tough to find good primary care doctors who would personally manage the health of their patients. That's why we formed the Foundation Health Medical Group."

Each Foundation Health Medical Group Care Center employs carefully selected primary care physicians including internists, family practitioners, and pediatricians, many of whom have practiced in Sacramento for years. More than 20 Care Center locations in neighborhoods throughout the greater Sacramento area, Ventura, and the San Joaquin Valley are planned for construction by fall of 1995.

As one of the leading health care organizations in the nation to develop the Care Center concept, Foundation Health has made a new level of quality and convenience available. "By providing many services under one roof," says Dr. Jonathan H. Scheff, president of Foundation Health Medical Group, "physicians have immediate access to X-ray and laboratory facilities, and the patient enjoys the convenience of making one visit to have his or her medical needs reviewed, have any prescriptions filled, or have lab work done."

As the Care Center concept takes root in the Sacramento region, Crowley believes Foundation Health is fulfilling a major goal in its business plan. "The strategy here is to serve the employer and the individual," he says. "If we provide care, and they are well served, then we are going to prosper."

FOUNDATION OPERATES A LARGE NETWORK OF COMMUNITY-BASED CARE CENTERS, OFFERING PATIENTS PRIMARY CARE AND IMMEDIATE CARE, AS WELL AS LABORATORY, X-RAY, AND PHARMACY SERVICES—ALL UNDER ONE ROOF (ABOVE).

FOUNDATION'S CARE CENTERS ARE DESIGNED TO MEET THE SPECIAL NEEDS OF EVEN THE YOUNGEST PATIENTS (LEFT AND OPPOSITE).

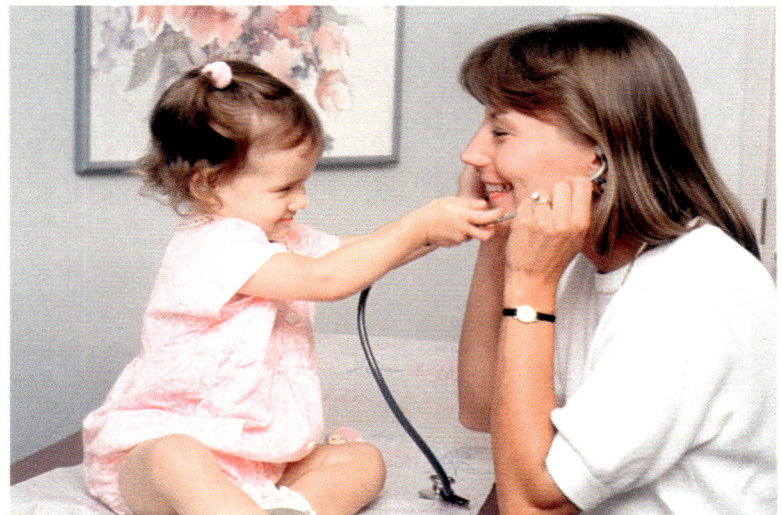

KLEINFELDER, INC.

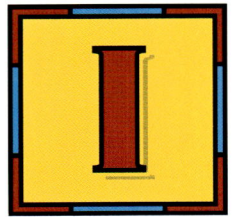

IN 1960 JAMES KLEINFELDER WAS WORKING AS A CIVIL ENGINEER FOR THE CITY OF STOCKTON. WHILE DESIGNING AN UNDERPASS, HE DISCOVERED THAT CONCRETE CYLINDERS WOULD HAVE TO BE SENT TO SACRAMENTO—AN HOUR AWAY—FOR QUALITY TESTING. THE FOLLOWING YEAR, KLEINFELDER INVESTED $8,000 TO FOUND STOCKTON'S OWN SOILS ENGINEERING AND TESTING LABORATORY. SOON

afterwards, the firm expanded and brought its expertise to Sacramento.

From the beginning, Kleinfelder insisted that his firm build on a few basics. "My philosophy has always been simple and direct," says Kleinfelder, who retired as company chairman in 1992. "Always search for what's right, not who's right; be a good listener; be fair in all business dealings; and stay on a learning curve."

That philosophy has allowed Kleinfelder, Inc. to evolve from a local business with $300,000 in revenue in 1969 to today's $55 million company with 26 offices and 650 employees spread throughout the western United States. Recognized as one of the top 100 engineering firms in the country, Kleinfelder is among Northern California's most prominent engineering consulting groups.

Chairman Michael Mahoney, who founded the Sacramento office in 1968, believes a key to the firm's success is attitude. "We are solution-oriented," he says. "We place a high value on teamwork. Whenever a project presents a new challenge, our engineers and scientists meet to combine their knowledge and talent in search of a solution. When you believe the people working with you are the best, as we do, that mutual confidence and respect pay off in tangible results."

A PROVEN COMMITMENT TO QUALITY

During the 1960s, soils testing, laboratory testing of construction materials, and foundation engineering formed the basis of Kleinfelder's services. More than 30 years later—concentrating in the areas of environmental sciences, geotechnical engineering, and construction materials testing—Kleinfelder has become a leader in providing solutions for the industrial, commercial, and residential sectors, as well as for local, state, and federal agencies.

One example of the company's environmental engineering capabilities is the Sacramento Army Depot. Established in 1945, the facility received, stored, issued, and maintained electronics supplies and commodities for the U.S. Army. For some 40 years, wastes created by welding, machining, metal plating, and other industrial practices were disposed of by burning, burying, open-area settling, and evaporation. In 1987 these practices earned the depot a place on the federal Superfund list of environmental hazards.

Retained to assess and oversee the required toxic waste cleanup, Kleinfelder's responsiveness showed why federal and state regulatory agencies continually turn to the firm, and why clients trust Kleinfelder as a reliable, creative adviser. After poring over 50-year-old documents and aerial photographs of the depot, Kleinfelder engineers identified seven environmental hazards. Included on the list were two burn pits, four oxidation lagoons, and a leaky, 1,000-gallon underground tank once used for storing waste solvents.

The firm's innovative solutions to these challenges have received national acclaim. At the underground tank site, for instance, air is circulated through the contaminated soil—collecting, condensing, and treating toxic vapors without costly excavation. Thanks to Kleinfelder's efforts, the Sacramento Army Depot is today well on its way to becoming the first Department of Defense installation to be removed from the Superfund list.

Over the years, Kleinfelder has also gained respect for its work in geotechnical engineering. In the early 1980s, for example, floodplains near downtown Sacramento were routinely forcing millions of gallons of insufficiently treated wastewater into the Sacramento River during floods. A geotechnical study conducted by Kleinfelder indicated that a proposed urban reservoir should be constructed 25 feet below maximum

KLEINFELDER PROVIDED GEOTECHNICAL ENGINEERING AND CONSTRUCTION MATERIALS TESTING FOR THE UC DAVIS ENGINEERING UNIT, A 185,000-SQUARE-FOOT BUILDING THAT FEATURES ONE OF THE LARGEST CLEAN ROOM FACILITIES EVER BUILT IN THE UNITED STATES FOR A MAJOR UNIVERSITY.

river stage, not 40 feet as had previously been suggested. The company's recommendation, one of several made on the project, substantially reduced excavation costs.

Bolstering its expertise in the field of construction materials testing, Kleinfelder maintains laboratories throughout the western United States. Skilled engineers and technicians at these locations provide compliance testing and observation services for wood, concrete, steel, masonry, asphalt, aggregate, soils, and other construction materials on all types of construction projects. Kleinfelder's specialty steel subsidiary, ITI, has complete nondestructive testing capabilities, including a linear accelerator to test aircraft and rocket parts.

IMPROVING ON EXCELLENCE

While the company is an established technical leader, Mahoney believes the firm's true spirit lies elsewhere. "You can look for excellence in many places," he says. "We find it in our people. They take pride in their work and go the extra mile for one another and for our clients." That attitude can be attributed, in part, to the fact that employees own a part of the company through an employee stock ownership program initiated in 1989.

At Kleinfelder, the challenge for the future is formidable: to improve on excellence. "Our greatest challenge in the '90s will be to make the transition from a collection of small offices to a large, national firm," says Senior Vice President Jeremiah Jackson. "We are successfully accomplishing this goal by raising our collective awareness of our capabilities and experience."

And if Kleinfelder's management team knows where they want the firm to go, they also have the vision to identify how to get there.

CLOCKWISE FROM LEFT: RUSS CAREY (LEFT), MANAGER OF KLEINFELDER'S SACRAMENTO OFFICE, AND MICHAEL MAHONEY, CHAIRMAN AND SENIOR PRINCIPAL.

THE FIRM'S INNOVATIVE SOLUTIONS TO THE CHALLENGES OF TOXIC WASTE CLEANUP AT THE SACRAMENTO ARMY DEPOT HAVE RECEIVED NATIONAL ACCLAIM.

THIS KLEINFELDER GROUNDWATER TREATMENT FACILITY AT THE SACRAMENTO ARMY DEPOT PROCESSES APPROXIMATELY 500,000 GALLONS PER DAY.

203

U.S. COMPUTER SERVICES

AS THE HIGHLY TOUTED INFORMATION SUPERHIGHWAY BEGINS TO TAKE SHAPE, U.S. COMPUTER SERVICES WILL BE ROADSIDE, READY TO COLLECT THE TOLLS. THE PARENT COMPANY TO CABLEDATA, CABLEDATA INTERNATIONAL, CABLELEASE, AND INTERNATIONAL BILLING SERVICES, U.S. COMPUTER SERVICES HAS GROWN SINCE 1965 INTO A WORLD LEADER IN TRANSACTION MANAGEMENT AND STATE-ment production. From its headquarters in Rancho Cordova and from International Billing Services operations in El Dorado Hills, the company employs more than 2,000 people worldwide, making it one of Sacramento's largest privately held corporations.

U.S. Computer Services' oldest division, CableData, commands 55 percent of the transaction processing and billing market in the U.S. cable industry. The division provides transaction management systems to 890 cable operators, including Sacramento Cable. For decades, companies around the world have relied on CableData's software and billing services to strategically manage growing subscriber bases, deliver accurate customer statements, and anticipate and respond to change. Today the division serves more than 33 million subscribers worldwide, including 21 of the 25 largest multiple-system operators in the U.S. cable industry. Many of these firms secure financing through CableLease, which provides lease financing for CableData customers.

As the United Kingdom, Australia, the Pacific Rim, and other parts of the world embrace the concept of convergence (a fusion of voice, video, and data services), U.S. Computer Services is strongly positioned to expand its leadership role in the global cable/telephony software and hardware market. In 1993, for example, decades of research and technological progress allowed CableData International to introduce Intelecable,™ the world's first integrated cable and telephony transaction management system.

Another U.S. Computer Services company, International Billing Services, is renowned as one of the premier mailing operations in the country. The largest centralized First Class Mailer in the United States, International Billing Services prints and mails more than 60 million statements each month on behalf of cable television and financial services companies, utilities, and telecommunications entities. In fact, the subsidiary serves approximately 50 percent of the U.S. cellular phone industry and enjoys significant market share in telephone statement production and mailing.

From its 220,000-square-foot facility in El Dorado Hills, International Billing Services generates more than 1 percent of all First Class Mail nationwide. In a competitive, high-speed industry, International Billing Services has achieved an impressive 99.9 percent accuracy rate. On the basis of the subsidiary's technological sophistication and proven expertise in mail handling, the U.S. Postal Service has recognized International Billing Services as the first Systems Certified Mailer in the country.

Focused on future opportunities, U.S. Computer Services remains committed to research and development. At International Billing Services, for instance, the parent company invests more than $8 million annually on automation and software system development. With the vision to anticipate change, the experience to find progressive solutions, and the tenacity to achieve excellence, U.S. Computer Services is well positioned for the fast-paced race along the information superhighway.

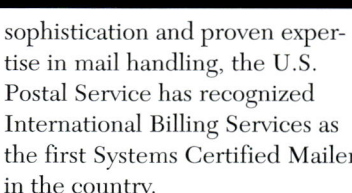

IN ADDITION TO PRINTING AND MAILING MORE THAN 60 MILLION BILLS EVERY MONTH, INTERNATIONAL BILLING SERVICES DESIGNS AND PRODUCES CUSTOM INSERTS, FORMS, AND ENVELOPES (NEAR RIGHT).

SUPERIOR CUSTOMER SERVICE IS THE WATCHWORD OF CABLEDATA. TRAINED SPECIALISTS CAN PINPOINT DIFFICULTIES ANYWHERE ON THE DIGITAL NETWORK AND CAN SOLVE CUSTOMER PROBLEMS ANYWHERE IN THE UNITED STATES—ALL FROM THE TECHNICAL RESPONSE CENTER IN RANCHO CORDOVA (FAR RIGHT).

PHOTOS BY KENT LACIN

Vanguard Security Services

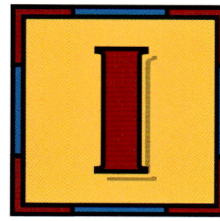

IN THE 1970S AND 1980S, AS SACRAMENTO'S BUSINESS COMMUNITY MATURED AND THE CITY JOINED THE RANKS OF THE FASTEST-GROWING METROPOLITAN AREAS IN THE UNITED STATES, THE NEED FOR PROFESSIONAL PRIVATE SECURITY INCREASED. FOUNDED IN 1970, VANGUARD SECURITY SERVICES HAS EVOLVED INTO SACRAMENTO'S DOMINANT PRIVATE SECURITY SERVICE, AS WELL AS ONE OF THE CAPITAL CITY'S

most explosive business success stories.

In 1980 Vanguard employed 150 people. Today, the company employs more than 2,000. "We've matured with Sacramento," says Matthew Burke, Vanguard's president since 1980, "because we are absolutely committed to delivering on the promises we make when we contract with a client. We conduct ourselves with unfailing commitment to the highest ethical and professional standards. It's something that sets us apart in our business." As the dominant private security company in the Sacramento region, Vanguard today controls approximately 75 percent of the local security service market.

Operated since 1980 under the corporate umbrella of Oakland-based American Protective Services, the fourth-largest security company in the United States, Vanguard provides on-site security to many of Sacramento's industry giants, ranging from hospitals, shopping centers, and manufacturing plants to financial institutions, agricultural operations, and high-rise office buildings. Although the firm also consults on a wide variety of security issues, providing uniformed security officers remains the staple of Vanguard's business. "We are in a service industry and a people business," says Burke. "Our quality officers are our main resource. Our success depends on the well-trained, committed people who work for us on the front line every day making sure that our clients have secure facilities."

Expanding beyond Sacramento

In the late 1980s, as Sacramento's economy leveled off and business growth in the region slowed, Vanguard began to expand beyond its hometown, adding several California branch operations in Silicon Valley, the San Francisco Bay Area, and Los Angeles. The company has also opened offices in Arizona, New Mexico, and Nevada. As the year 2000 approaches, Burke says Vanguard plans to expand its presence in California and the Southwest.

According to Burke, the company is headed for a future filled with tremendous possibilities. "Unfortunately, we live in a society that has problems," he says. "And unfortunately, regular police forces are finding themselves unable to meet the increasing demand for law enforcement services. But luckily, there are companies like Vanguard who can step in and fill the gap. There really is a key role for private security to play in Sacramento and in other communities across the nation. And we are proud to say we give our clients the finest service money can buy."

VANGUARD PROVIDES ON-SITE SECURITY TO MANY OF SACRAMENTO'S INDUSTRY GIANTS, RANGING FROM HOSPITALS, SHOPPING CENTERS, AND MANUFACTURING PLANTS TO FINANCIAL INSTITUTIONS, AGRICULTURAL OPERATIONS, AND HIGH-RISE OFFICE BUILDINGS.

UC Davis Medical Center

The word "special" is often used to describe the care offered at UC Davis Medical Center, the principal referral hospital for 5 million residents in a 38-county region stretching north to the Oregon border and east to Nevada. Opened in 1973 as the main clinical educational site for the UC Davis School of Medicine, the Medical Center blends teaching, research, public service, and patient care for the benefit of the capital region.

Because UC Davis is an academic medical center, patient care is shaped by faculty physicians who are leading teachers and researchers in their fields. The tradition began in 1963. That year, when the University of California, Davis established the first medical school in the Central Valley, Dr. Charles John Tupper was chosen to be its founding dean.

A Pioneer in Modern Medicine

As the medical school steadily grew in the early 1970s, Tupper recognized Sacramento's growing health care needs. Continuing his pioneering spirit, he and other UC representatives led the conversion of an aging community facility into the UC Davis Medical Center. Since then, the Medical Center has developed a national reputation for excellence. In fact, in its 1993 guide to America's best hospitals, *U.S. News & World Report* ranked the UC Davis Medical Center among the nation's best facilities in eight specialties, including cancer.

The UC Davis Cancer Center opened in 1991, offering diagnosis, treatment, and research for virtually every type of cancer. Located in the heart of the Medical Center campus near downtown Sacramento, the facility features full-service clinics for medical and surgical oncology, diagnostic radiology and mammography, a bone marrow and cytogenetics laboratory, and the Resource Center library for patients and their families.

Also recognized nationally is the UC Davis Heart Center—the only university-affiliated hospital setting for cardiac surgery in inland Northern California. Chosen by *U.S. News & World Report* as one of the best in the nation, the center offers the full range of surgeries required for congenital and acquired cardiovascular disease, including heart transplants. Affiliated closely with the UC Davis School of Medicine, surgeons at the Heart Center have access to extensive resources, ensuring that patients benefit from the latest medical technology. A featured component of the Heart Center is the successful Coronary Heart Disease Reversal Program, which offers assistance to patients who are not candidates for bypass surgery or angioplasty.

On the research side, heart specialists at the Medical Center are participating in the 15-year, $625 million Women's Health Initiative, a national project investigating how estrogen replacement therapy, calcium and vitamin D supplements, and a low-fat diet affect cancer, heart disease, and osteoporosis in women aged 50 to 79.

Growing with Sacramento

In a time of rising costs and trends toward managed care, the UC Davis Medical Center remains committed to offering cost-effective health services. To meet future needs in this climate, Medical Center Director Frank J. Loge says the hospital plans to respond with plenty of innovation.

A 300,000-square-foot Shriners Hospital for Crippled Children,

The new UC Davis Imaging Center (below left) houses a high-resolution, high-speed digital MRI unit; two high-speed computed tomography units; and a dedicated breast imaging suite that provides minimally invasive biopsy procedures.

Patient care at UC Davis Medical Center is shaped by faculty physicians who are leading teachers and researchers in their fields (below right).

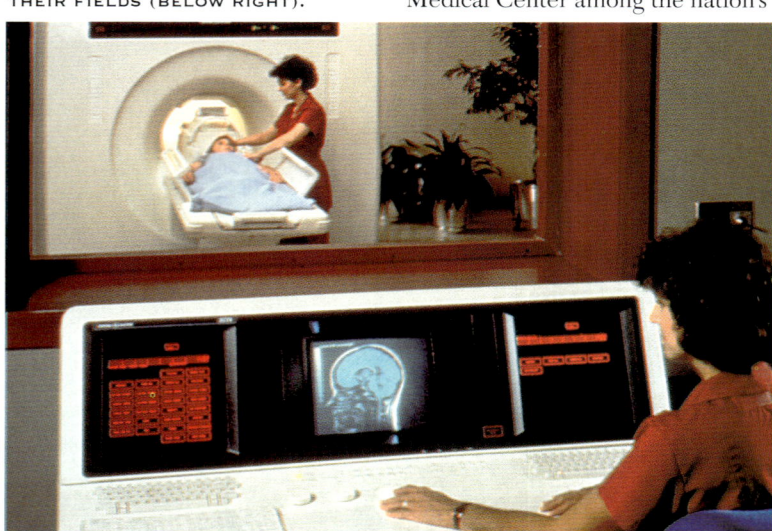
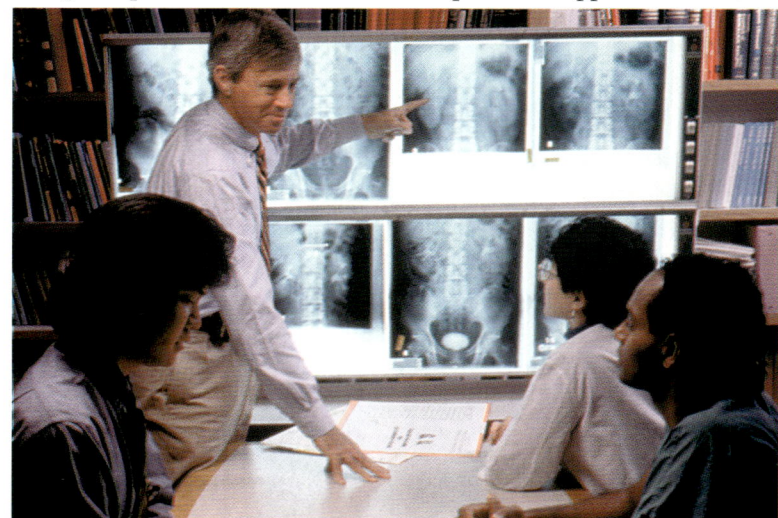

CLOCKWISE FROM LEFT: THE MEDICAL CENTER IS CALIFORNIA'S ONLY LEVEL I TRAUMA CENTER AND ACADEMIC MEDICAL CENTER NORTH OF SAN FRANCISCO.

PATIENTS AND THEIR FAMILIES TAKE COMFORT IN KNOWING THAT DOCTORS, NURSES, THERAPISTS, AND OTHER STAFF MEMBERS RESPECT AND CARE ABOUT THEM AS INDIVIDUALS.

IN 1993 PHYSICIANS AT THE MEDICAL CENTER PERFORMED SACRAMENTO'S FIRST BONE MARROW TRANSPLANT.

THE CANCER CENTER'S MULTIDISCIPLINARY PROGRAM ENCOMPASSES MEDICAL AND SURGICAL ONCOLOGY, RADIATION ONCOLOGY, AND ADVANCED TECHNIQUES SUCH AS PHOTODYNAMIC LASER THERAPY, RADIOIMMUNOTHERAPY, AND LIMB SALVAGE.

for example, will serve as the flagship for all 23 Shriners hospitals, bringing together for the first time an orthopedic service, a burn care unit, and a spinal injury rehabilitation unit under one roof.

The Medical Center also plans to establish satellite health care service centers, some in rural Northern California, to provide better access, continuity of care, and a more efficient approach to meeting regional needs. One of the first of these centers—a medical clinic in Dunsmuir—is a model that will be used to help make the medical expertise in the university available to people who live in more isolated communities. This clinic works in cooperation with and with the support of local physicians and health care providers.

A third key development in the Medical Center's future is construction of a 12-story tower to replace outdated facilities, which will add 416,000 square feet of space to the hospital. With building set to begin in the summer of 1995, the tower will feature three 35-bed nursing units and additional radiology services, plus distribution, receiving, academic, and patient care areas.

Loge says UC Davis Medical Center also will continue its contribution to the fight against AIDS. A national leader in AIDS research, the UC Davis team of physicians, scientists, and veterinarians is collaborating on studies of potential vaccines and therapies. In the past, this team has pioneered much-publicized studies on immunosuppressive retrovirus infections in cats and monkeys, and has developed vaccines for feline and simian AIDS.

With a host of ongoing research efforts and the busiest hospital in California's capital region, Loge foresees a productive future for UC Davis Medical Center. But in the end, he adds, people matter more than new buildings and national headlines. "While patients and their families expect to receive the best in high-tech medical care, they also need to feel that their doctors, nurses, therapists—and even the workers who clean their rooms—respect and care about them as individuals," says Loge. "I'm proud to say that the staff of UC Davis Medical Center has managed to convey this feeling to our patients and visitors."

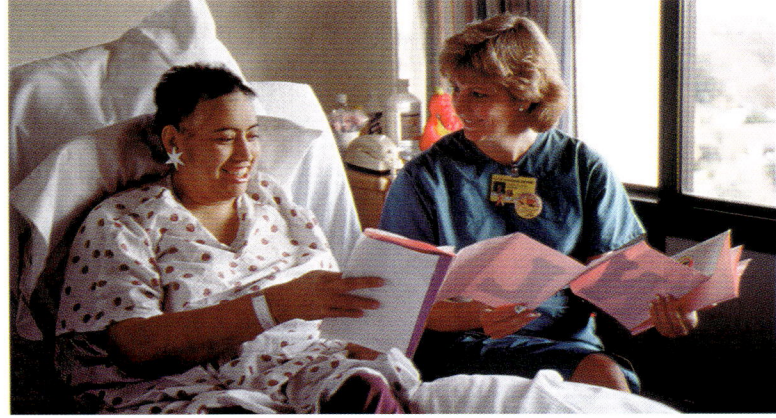

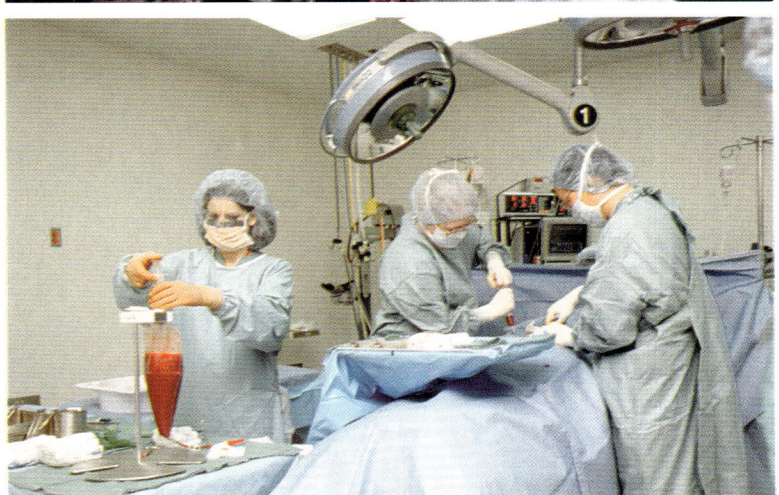

RED LION HOTELS & INNS

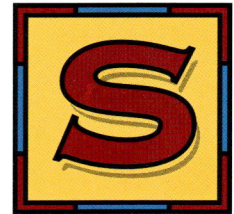

STAFF AND GUESTS OF SACRAMENTO'S RED LION HOTEL ARE NEVER QUITE SURE WHERE THEY'RE GOING TO FIND GENERAL MANAGER JOHN ELSTON. SOMETIMES, FOR EXAMPLE, HE'S POURING COFFEE AT BREAKFAST. OTHER TIMES, HE'S MIXING DRINKS BEHIND THE BAR. ON STILL OTHER OCCASIONS, HE'S FILLING IN ON THE SWITCHBOARD OR INSPECTING A ROOM THAT'S JUST BEEN CLEANED. BUT IT'S NOT because he doesn't trust his staff to get the job done to the level of excellence Sacramento has come to expect at the Red Lion.

For Elston—who began his hospitality career as a bellman at a Red Lion Hotel in 1982 and three years later became the youngest general manager in the $413 million company—the reason is simple. "We are committed to being the best price-value hospitality company in the western United States," he says. "We work toward this goal by making the customer our number one priority at all times."

SUPERIOR SERVICE, PREMIUM VALUE

This focus on superior service has translated into dynamic financial success for the Red Lion chain, which currently boasts 58 hotels in 11 western states. For example, in 1991, Elston's first year as general manager of the Sacramento property, hotel revenues increased 9 percent. Growth in annual revenue continued during the next two years, climbing to $18 million by 1994. In a time when many Sacramento hotels are struggling, both the Red Lion and the Sacramento Inn, a 376-room Red Lion property located across the street, are thriving. Why? "Our customer comes first," maintains Elston. "We'll do whatever it takes to serve the guest."

In recent times, the Red Lion and the Sacramento Inn have put these words into action. In fact, between 1991 and 1994, the hotels invested more than $5.5 million on extensive renovations.

At the Red Lion, new amenities include RJ Grin's, a lively nightclub offering everything from dancing, pool, and shuffleboard to fresh pizza, single-malt whiskeys, and a host of vodkas infused with fresh fruit right on the premises. Big changes have also taken place at

ESTABLISHED IN SACRAMENTO IN 1974, THE RED LION HOTEL HAS DEVELOPED A REPUTATION FOR EXCELLENT SERVICE AND VALUE.

Maxi's, An American Cafe, which now serves superb American cuisine in a light, more intimate setting than in previous years. Nearby, the Coffee Garden provides a casual atmosphere for meals, snacks, and specialty coffees.

Across the street, the Sacramento Inn's new club, Savanna's Lounge, is one of the finest live jazz venues in the city. Intimate and casual, Savanna's hosts local, regional, and national jazz performers Thursday through Saturday nights.

At the Red Lion, superior customer service extends to business and convention gatherings. The hotel features 30,000 square feet of meeting space, ranging from small, flexible, breakout spaces to the spectacular Thunderbird Ballroom, which can accommodate up to 1,500 guests. The Red Lion's comprehensive business services also include computers, facsimile, and audiovisual equipment, as well as full-service catering and management experts who are available to coordinate everything from small group meetings to large conventions and conferences.

Also a favorite for its business services, the Sacramento Inn ranks among the finest meeting venues in the capital city. With 33 percent more meeting space than in 1991, the hotel boasts 17 flexible rooms and a total of 20,000 square feet of business facilities. According to General Manager Lynn Ericksen, the Sacramento Inn is currently adding more meeting space and upgrading existing facilities. But why spend time and money to improve something that's already first-class? "We've set the standard for hospitality in Sacramento for years," Ericksen says. "In the future, our commitment to continue offering the finest full service in the market is strong."

In the Heart of the City

At the Red Lion and the Sacramento Inn, however, superior customer service isn't limited to business customers. In fact, guests find it easy to be pampered without ever leaving the premises. Both hotels feature room, laundry, and valet service, as well as swimming pools, hot tubs, a health club, and a complimentary courtesy car to Sacramento Metropolitan Airport.

But service Red Lion-style also features the unique. Hotel staff members, for example, are experts at locating premium theater tickets in the San Francisco Bay Area, as well as the full lineup of entertainment on the casino stages of Reno and Lake Tahoe.

Back in Sacramento, there's plenty to see and do within minutes of both hotels. The possibilities begin across the street at Arden Fair Mall, where 100 fine shops beckon, including Nordstrom and Weinstocks. Cal Expo—home of the California State Fair, summertime harness racing, and other major events—is just down the street.

A few minutes away, downtown Sacramento features a host of popular attractions, including the state capitol; the old governor's mansion, an 1877 Victorian structure that housed 13 California governors between 1903 and 1967; and the Crocker Art Museum, the oldest art museum west of the Mississippi River. Out in Natomas, the Sacramento Kings, the capital city's NBA franchise, play at ARCO Arena. In addition to professional basketball, ARCO hosts everything from hockey games and tractor pulls to headliner concerts and conventions.

Add to this list convenient access to the American River Bike Trail, Old Sacramento Historic District, golfing, parks, museums, and more, and Elston wonders if he's not understating the case when he calls the Red Lion "the ultimate hotel option in the Sacramento market."

THE SACRAMENTO INN, A 376-ROOM RED LION PROPERTY LOCATED ACROSS THE STREET, RANKS AMONG THE FINEST MEETING VENUES IN THE CAPITAL CITY.

Rio Linda Chemical Co., Inc.

IN 1988, AFTER JUST 12 YEARS OF OPERATION, RIO LINDA CHEMICAL CO. WAS ALREADY AN INDUSTRY LEADER IN THE DEVELOPMENT AND MANUFACTURE OF PATENTED CHLORINE DIOXIDE GENERATING SYSTEMS USED IN VARIOUS INDUSTRIES TO DISINFECT WATER. IN FACT, WITH COMPANY REVENUES AT $3 MILLION ANNUALLY, THE BOTTOM LINE LOOKED QUITE HEALTHY.

"However, Rio Linda was a family-owned business," recalls Glenn W. Holden, president and chief executive officer. "And the company didn't have the funding to capitalize on significant market opportunities."

The solution to Rio Linda's challenge came when Tenneco, Inc. (a $13 billion, Houston-based corporation) and Albright & Wilson Americas (a world leader in large-scale chlorine dioxide generation) purchased the Sacramento company and committed to an aggressive plan of growth. Sales volume climbed to $15 million within five years—a 45 percent per annum increase—while the number of employees quadrupled from 16 to 60. In 1992 Rio Linda commissioned a second manufacturing plant in Monroe, Louisiana, to service the Southeast.

An Industry Leader in Chlorine Dioxide Technology

Today, Rio Linda Chemical Co. is building on its reputation as an industry leader by providing innovative environmental alternatives to traditional disinfection methods. Its patented chlorine dioxide process is extremely fast—1,000 times faster than conventional processes—but is also safe. It is used extensively in the food, dairy, and beverage industries for process water treatment and control of disease-causing microorganisms, such as viruses and bacteria.

In 1991 Rio Linda's commitment to developing safe, innovative disinfection technologies was recognized when two of the company's environmental waste destruction processes were chosen by the Environmental Protection Agency for demonstration under the Superfund Innovative Technology Program. Today, Rio Linda offers more than 75 models of generating systems, ranging from simple manual units to fully automated generators with remote telemetry, flow pacing, multipoint injection, and fail-safe capabilities. With scores of new patents pending, Holden expects the company to broaden the scope of its chlorine dioxide expertise and market penetration.

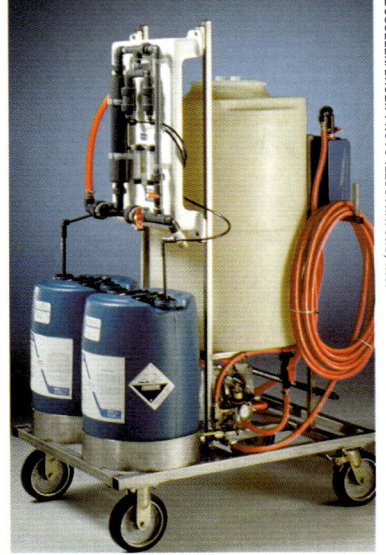

Rio Linda currently provides water treatment systems and service to a large number of cities, including Seattle, St. Paul, and Philadelphia, and Holden sees virtually unlimited potential for increasing the company's share of the market. "There are 300,000 municipalities in the United States," he says. "We currently serve about 300." Rio Linda is also expanding internationally and has already implemented export operations in Japan, Korea, France, Spain, England, and Chile. New relationships are being forged in Mexico and South America.

Fueled by innovation, technology, and the confidence that comes with success, Holden expects Rio Linda Chemical Co.'s future growth to dwarf the already impressive gains made in recent years. "Our goal is to be a $50 million company in five years," Holden says, "and we can do it."

IN THE FOOD PROCESSING INDUSTRY, RIO LINDA'S PATENTED CHLORINE DIOXIDE FOAM SANITIZER SYSTEM IS USED FOR HARD-SURFACE DISINFECTION (TOP).

RIO LINDA'S PATENTED CHLORINE DIOXIDE GENERATOR DISINFECTS MUNICIPAL DRINKING WATER (RIGHT).

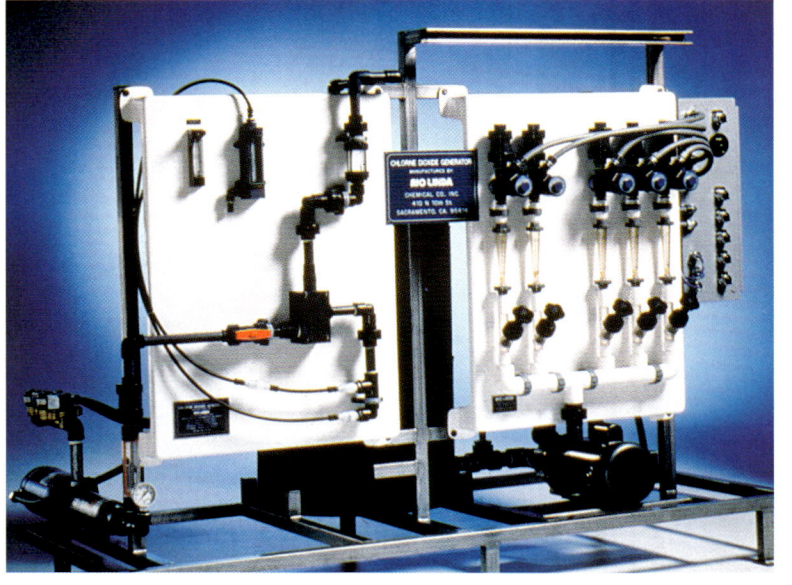

Brown and Caldwell

Until the 1970s, Sacramento residents were served by 21 wastewater treatment plants—located along the Sacramento and American Rivers—that discharged treated effluent upstream of drinking water treatment plant intakes. Something had to be done. Brown and Caldwell, a multidisciplinary environmental engineering and consulting firm, teamed with the County and City of Sacramento and other consulting firms to develop the answer.

As the managing firm in a four-member consulting joint venture, Brown and Caldwell invested more than a decade into the planning, design, and construction of the Sacramento Regional Wastewater Collection and Treatment System. In 1984 the effort paid off, as the American Society of Civil Engineers selected the $460 million treatment plant project as the outstanding civil engineering achievement of the year.

In the early 1980s, Sacramento faced another problem. A burgeoning population was depleting the city's downtown landfill area at the rate of 600 tons per day. Retained to design a 30-acre addition, Brown and Caldwell again found an innovative solution—a 50,000-cubic-yard clay liner that underlies the entire landfill site, protecting the nearby American River from contamination. This design was the first of its kind to comply with new, stringent state regulations.

Innovative Solutions for Government and Industry

The Sacramento office of Brown and Caldwell, established in 1978, has become an important component of the national firm. Headquartered in the San Francisco Bay area, Brown and Caldwell generates more than $100 million in revenue annually. Over the years, the local office has built close relationships with numerous clients in both government and industry. Today, Brown and Caldwell continues to offer its Sacramento clients innovation and superior professional services in the areas of water pollution control and water supply, hazardous waste management, air quality, energy, and solid waste.

Major public-sector clients include the County of Sacramento, the Sacramento Regional County Sanitation District, the City of Sacramento, and Sacramento Municipal Utility District. Brown and Caldwell delivers innovation and quality service to the corporate community as well. The firm has forged ties with industry giants such as ARCO, Aerojet, Southern Pacific, and Pacific Gas and Electric Company.

Currently, Brown and Caldwell is engaged in a host of major projects, including the design of a $20 million cogeneration system at the UC Davis Medical Center. The system will provide power, heating, and cooling for the medical center's 120-acre campus near downtown Sacramento.

According to company Vice President David Jones, the wide range of environmental projects the firm has successfully completed since 1978 is clear testimony to its innovative vision, and the resounding customer satisfaction that Brown and Caldwell has achieved proves its unwavering commitment to quality. "When we've completed a project," Jones says, "we want our clients to know that we have provided them with the best quality service possible."

▲ FRANK PEDRICK

Brown and Caldwell has performed investigations as well as design and operation of remediation systems at numerous ARCO station sites.

▲ SHARON BEALS

The firm invested more than a decade into the planning, design, and construction of the Sacramento Regional Wastewater Collection and Treatment System.

Baxter Diagnostics, Inc., MicroScan

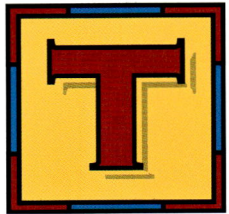

To get fast, accurate results, microbiologists all over the country use the wide range of products offered by Baxter Diagnostics, Inc., MicroScan, a West Sacramento company that manufactures microbiology diagnostic products, including instrumentation and disposable testing panels. These products are used to identify microorganisms and to test their susceptibility to antibiotics. Baxter Diagnostics, Inc., MicroScan is a recognized leader in the microbiology field, and more than half of the nearly 7,000 clinical laboratories in the United States use the company's products.

Today a $125 million, international corporate entity with 600 employees, Baxter Diagnostics, Inc., MicroScan has throughout its history demonstrated leadership and vision, pioneering an unbroken string of successful technologies.

More than a Decade of Innovation

The company got its start in a garage in New Jersey in 1978. Committed to innovation, the fledgling enterprise soon became the first company to manufacture microbiological panels that combined bacterial identification and susceptibility tests. The development was a breakthrough in microbiological testing; prior to the introduction of Baxter Diagnostics, Inc., MicroScan's product, susceptibility and identification tests had to be conducted at different times or by separate technicians with separate equipment. The company's new equipment could conduct both tests simultaneously.

In addition, the exacting dilutions of antibiotics in the MicroScan® panels led to the industrywide use of quantitative, rather than qualitative, susceptibility results. In other words, the tests could now determine not only *which* antibiotics would work on the microbe in question, but also exactly *how much* antibiotic would be necessary to inhibit further growth. The MicroScan® Minimum Inhibitory Concentration (MIC) test for antimicrobic susceptibility enables physicians to accurately and confidently prescribe the most appropriate and effective antibiotic to treat their patients' infections. The ability to provide proper treatment results in faster patient recovery.

In 1980 MicroScan again made history. The company introduced the autoSCAN®-4, the first automated instrument capable of reading microbiological panels.

A year later, the company debuted the MicroScan® Data Management System (DMS), the first computer system dedicated to the needs of clinical microbiology. The connection of the DMS to a semiautomated manual panel reader produced MicroScan's most successful instrument system, touchSCAN®-S/R. The touchSCAN®-S/R instrument features a central view box that illuminates the panel so the technologist can clearly interpret the reactions that have taken place in the wells. The technologist then positions a sonic pen over the area where positive reactions occur and presses the pen button. The results are automatically routed to a computer, which registers and processes the data.

Bringing Industry Leadership to West Sacramento

By 1983, when MicroScan moved its corporate headquarters to West Sacramento, the company had already matured from an unknown start-up business to a leader in the international microbiology industry. In 1985 the company strengthened its reputation for

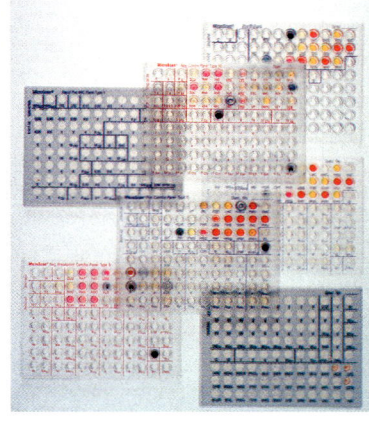

The top-of-the-line WalkAway™-96 (top) and the WalkAway™-40 (not pictured) perform all key functions with MicroScan® panels—incubation, reagent addition, and reading—without the intervention of a technologist.

MicroScan offers a complete line of disposable products contained in 96-well microliter panels (bottom). The Rapids system (white plastic) utilizes fluorescence technology to provide bacterial identification in two hours and susceptibilities in 3.5 to 15 hours—considerably faster than traditional overnight incubation methodologies.

excellence and technological innovation with the development of the autoSCAN®-W/A, a fully automated panel processor that incubates panels, adds reagents, reads the panels, and downloads the information to the DMS. Previously, these steps were performed manually by a technologist.

Today, MicroScan markets more than 75 different panel types to burgeoning domestic and international markets—a far cry from the single panel available in 1978.

What has more than a decade of MicroScan innovation meant to hospital laboratories, clinical reference labs, and the microbiology field in general? Sam Acosta, Baxter Diagnostics, Inc., MicroScan site manager in West Sacramento, explains: "Before automation, some labs would collect all this data and send it to a computer service to compile the information and generate a report. It could take six weeks to get the report, and the hospital would pay handsomely for this service. Now, hospitals collect and process their own data whenever they want it. By incorporating computers and software into our instruments, we're providing physicians with more meaningful information in a more timely fashion. This improves their medical practice and the quality of care they can give to their patients."

In addition to the DMS, MicroScan offers unique and innovative state-of-the-art optional packages, such as the pharmLINK™ software, which allows the microbiology lab to "talk" to the pharmacy. Microbiology results are quickly sent to pharmacists, who can then assess whether the patient is on the most effective antimicrobic therapy, thus leading to patient-focused care.

LOOKING TO THE FUTURE

As the year 2000 approaches, MicroScan continues to exceed customer demands for speed and accuracy in testing for infectious agents and in determining proper treatment for a wide range of infectious diseases. The company remains focused on researching and developing new technologies and on exploring new markets for its expanding array of sophisticated products.

In terms of technological advancements, Baxter Diagnostics, Inc., MicroScan has plans to unveil a host of revolutionary new instruments and products. Coupled with aggressive expansion into international markets such as Japan, Europe, and Latin America, the company is poised to remain a groundbreaker in the Sacramento area's climb to business prominence.

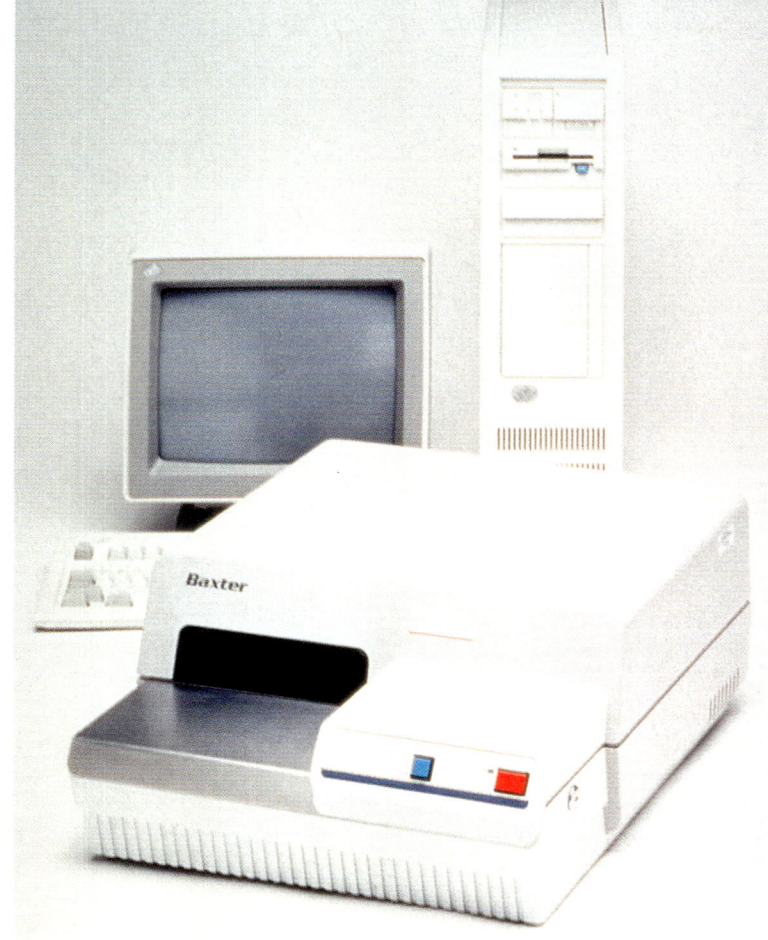

THE MICROSCAN FAMILY OF INSTRUMENTS INCLUDES THE TOUCHSCAN®-S/R, AN ELECTRONIC VIEW BOX; THE AUTOSCAN®-4; AND THE WALKAWAY™ SYSTEMS. EACH IS PROVIDED WITH MICROSCAN® DATA MANAGEMENT SYSTEM SOFTWARE (TOP).

THE AUTOSCAN®-4 SEMIAUTOMATED READER PROCESSES CONVENTIONAL-STYLE MICROSCAN® PANELS IN SIX SECONDS USING A 96-CHANNEL FIBER-OPTIC CABLE AND A SIX-FILTER COLOR-WHEEL SYSTEM (BOTTOM).

Calpo Hom Macaulay & Dong Architects

Calpo Hom Macaulay & Dong Architects begins its second decade with a new name and a continued commitment to excellence. Formerly Niiya Calpo Hom Dong, Inc., the firm was founded in 1984 by Herbert Y. Niiya. Firm principals are Rudy Calpo, Alan C. Hom, Laura Macaulay, and Dennis Dong. Calpo Hom Macaulay & Dong Architects has developed a diverse architectural practice built largely on repeat clients.

In times when discriminating companies desire unique, exciting architectural solutions, how does a smaller firm compete so successfully with Northern California's larger architectural practices? "To us, architecture goes well beyond the concept of shelter," says Dong. "We look at a building as much from the inside as from the outside, and we consider how it enhances the people and the environment it occupies. We do that on every project for every client."

This commitment to excellence includes a strong belief in individual attention for every project. "We believe that design is not based upon a set of rules and formulas," Dong says. "Rather, design is the result of a combination of forces."

From restaurants to fire stations to corporate office complexes, the architects at Calpo Hom Macaulay & Dong deliver quality service and superior results by remaining committed to each project. "This excellence in design, complemented by quality and expeditious professional service, is the cornerstone of the firm's success," notes Hom.

"Architecture is not an eight-hour-a-day, five-day-a-week job," adds Macaulay. "It's a 24-hour-a-day, seven-day-a-week job. Architecture is art, and we believe even the smallest projects are significant additions to Sacramento's architectural canvas."

Pushing the Architectural Envelope

During its first decade, Calpo Hom Macaulay & Dong has consistently contributed to this architectural canvas. The firm has designed $250 million in construction projects, each one unique.

The Hoops Sports Bar and Grille in Sacramento presented a special challenge: to transform a dark interior into a lighter, more playful space to remind patrons of their childhood playgrounds. Calpo Hom Macaulay & Dong fashioned an award-winning architectural solution featuring a bright, open layout and a horseshoe-shaped bar, with corrugated sheet metal, back-lit fiberglass, chain-link fencing, and bright neon. The area even includes a backboard and hoop.

In Roseville, Calpo Hom Macaulay & Dong faced a different design challenge and produced an inspiring result. The City of Roseville needed a new corporation yard that transcended the stereotypical maintenance yard crowded with stark, gray sheds. Calpo Hom Macaulay & Dong met the city's unique demands and designed four major facilities grouped around a landscaped commons area. The design promotes interaction and suggests a small town—complete with a clock tower. The Roseville Corporation Yard, which houses public works facilities, a vehicle maintenance shop, a central warehouse, and administrative facilities, carried a construction cost of $14 million.

For the State of California, Calpo Hom Macaulay & Dong designed an award-winning three-

Strong, clean, playful forms dominate the design of the Roseville Corporation Yard (right). Bold colors, strong forms, and shared views create a healthy working environment with a strong sense of community and pride.

PHOTOS BY STAN KOSLOW

ED ASMUS

Hoops Sports Bar and Grille was designed to re-create the playgrounds of youth, complete with chain-link fencing, industrial lighting, and a playfully "scabbed-together" basketball hoop.

story headquarters building for the Office of Buildings and Grounds. The firm met the challenge of integrating an office and shop complex amid the delicate fabric of residential housing and commercial activity in a central city location, while maintaining efficiency and function. The project involved coordination among state and local agencies and a pension plan asset manager.

These and other projects have earned praise from a variety of clients, including national pension portfolio managers such as Equitable Real Estate Investment Management, Compass Management and Leasing, and Ravel Properties; the State of California; the U.S. Postal Service; UC Davis Medical Center; and the cities of Roseville and Folsom. Calpo Hom Macaulay & Dong has also been recognized with a number of professional awards, including the American Institute of Architects, the American Society of Registered Architects, *Comstock's* magazine's Capital Award for commercial interiors, the Sacramento Old City Association, the Ceramic Tile Institute, and the Illuminating Engineering Society.

Managing Growth for Sacramento's Benefit

Despite its consistent position among Sacramento's prominent architectural firms, Calpo Hom Macaulay & Dong has remained a mid-sized firm. "With a staff of 15 to 20 employees," notes Calpo, "the firm is personal enough to allow the four partners to remain active in a hands-on way. We feel this is important, because it allows the entire firm to stay in an upward creative spiral." In fact, Calpo adds, the four principals do everything from answering telephones to designing multimillion-dollar architectural projects.

By focusing on quality service and the uniqueness of each client, Calpo Hom Macaulay & Dong is able to contribute something special to the Sacramento region. Clients choose the firm, according to Dong, because they sense something special. "There's something," he says, "a feeling perhaps, that they really can't describe in words. I think it comes down to a meeting of the minds. A building can be very uplifting spiritually and enrich the environment of its community. We approach every project with that attitude."

After a decade of fine architectural accomplishments, Calpo Hom Macaulay & Dong plans to continue to push the design envelope. "Sacramento deserves to have excellent architecture," Dong says. "There are qualities about this city that demand nothing but the best."

THE FIRM'S ATTRACTIVE AND FUNCTIONAL DESIGNS INCLUDE (CLOCKWISE FROM TOP LEFT) THE DEPARTMENT OF BUILDINGS AND GROUNDS FACILITY, THE NEW HEADQUARTERS FOR THE CALIFORNIA CORRECTIONAL PEACE OFFICERS ASSOCIATION, AND THE CAPITOL MALL EXECUTIVE CENTER—ALL LOCATED IN THE SACRAMENTO AREA.

HOSE TOWERS AND GABLE ROOFS ADD A SENSE OF PLACE AND FORM TO THE RENOVATED EL DORADO HILLS FIRE STATION NO. 1 (BELOW).

PHOTOS BY STAN KOSLOW

USAA Western Regional Office

USAA (United Services Automobile Association), headquartered in San Antonio, Texas, is one of the nation's leading providers of insurance and financial services. The company serves more than 2.6 million active-duty, former, and retired military officers and their families throughout the world. ■ USAA established its Western Regional Office in Sacramento in 1984. It is now one of the city's 10 largest private-sector employers, with more than 1,000 employees. USAA is responsible for contributing more than $50 million to the local economy through employee payroll, purchases from local vendors, other business-related expenditures, and charitable contributions.

Founded in 1922 by a group of military officers who had difficulty finding reliable and affordable auto insurance, USAA has grown to be the nation's fourth-largest home-owners insurer and the fifth-largest insurer of private passenger automobiles. Although property and casualty insurance is USAA's primary business, the company offers a full array of financial products and services, including life and health insurance, annuities, no-load mutual funds, consumer banking services, real estate investment opportunities, and a discount brokerage.

Good Corporate Citizens

USAA contributes far more to the local community than what it generates as a business. The company's corporate culture encourages community service among employees, who embrace it enthusiastically. "We try to set a good example in the community for corporate citizenship," says Benjamin T. Hacker, USAA's regional vice president. "We feel it's important to make Sacramento a better place to live and work."

USAA devotes an impressive amount of time and resources to local community service. In 1993 the company's employees gave more than 1,500 hours to 130 assorted community service organizations. USAA is also among the

city's largest private-sector contributors to the United Way, helping support some 180 human services organizations. More than 80 percent of USAA's employees give to the United Way. Counting corporate matching funds, contributions amount to more than $300,000 annually.

USAA is especially proud of its mentor program, created to address the challenge of "at-risk" elementary school students. Working with school administrators and teachers, more than 25 USAA employees spend at least one hour a week at one of Sacramento's elementary schools. They serve as tutors, role models, and friends to students in need of academic or attitudinal encouragement. "The willingness of our employees to make a difference in the lives of these young people is something we encourage and applaud," says Hacker. "We have a solid commitment to nurturing the leaders of tomorrow."

USAA has created a strong and beneficial presence in Sacramento. As a company, it has earned a reputation for world-class service. As a corporate citizen, it is known for world-class service to the community. And as an employer, USAA was recently included in *The 100 Best Companies to Work for in America*, with no company rated higher than USAA.

"Our mission as an institution is to serve active-duty, former, and retired military officers and their families," says Hacker. "It is also very important to us that we make a difference in serving the needs of the communities where we are. We are proud to live and serve in a great city like Sacramento."

USAA ESTABLISHED ITS WESTERN REGIONAL OFFICE IN SACRAMENTO IN 1984 (TOP RIGHT). IT IS NOW ONE OF THE CITY'S 10 LARGEST PRIVATE-SECTOR EMPLOYERS, WITH MORE THAN 1,000 EMPLOYEES.

"OUR MISSION AS AN INSTITUTION IS TO SERVE ACTIVE-DUTY, FORMER, AND RETIRED MILITARY OFFICERS AND THEIR FAMILIES," SAYS BENJAMIN T. HACKER, USAA'S REGIONAL VICE PRESIDENT (BOTTOM RIGHT). "WE ARE PROUD TO LIVE AND SERVE IN A GREAT CITY LIKE SACRAMENTO."

Associated Professional Appraisers

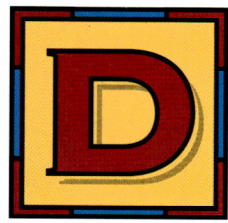

DOLLY DUFF DIDN'T KNOW WHAT THE FUTURE HELD WHEN, ONE DAY IN 1979, SHE ASKED HER EMPLOYER FOR A RAISE OF 50 CENTS AN HOUR. AFTER HER REQUEST WAS DECLINED, DUFF LEFT HER POSITION AS A SECRETARY—EMBARKING ON THE PATH THAT LED, SIX YEARS LATER, TO THE FORMATION OF ASSOCIATED PROFESSIONAL APPRAISERS, A FULL-SERVICE REAL ESTATE APPRAISAL COMPANY.

Associated Professional Appraisers, which opened for business in a tiny, 200-square-foot office in 1985, today shares a 10,000-square-foot building with three sister companies, the Institute for Professional Education, Arbitration & Mediation International, and the American Conflict Resolution Institute. Combined, Duff's four Sacramento-based ventures gross $1 million a year in revenues.

IN 1985 DOLLY DUFF ESTABLISHED ASSOCIATED PROFESSIONAL APPRAISERS, WHICH HAS GROWN INTO FOUR SACRAMENTO-BASED VENTURES GROSSING $1 MILLION A YEAR IN REVENUES.

A Family of Companies

The Institute for Professional Education complements Duff's appraisal business by offering a field-training program in which students learn from licensed appraisers employed by Associated Professional Appraisers. Upon completion of their apprenticeship, students have the ability to become independent contractors. According to Duff, the Institute's mix of classroom education and hands-on experience with trained professionals is the only program of its kind in California.

Another of Duff's ventures, Arbitration & Mediation International, was launched in 1986 as a dispute resolution company and training program for conflict resolution consultants and arbitrators. The company came about, in part, for one very personal reason. Duff says she won't soon forget the time her family was sued over some real estate properties that her husband had purchased with retirement funds. It took eight years for the case to wind its way through the judicial system, and after it was all over, the Duffs had lost $1 million in real estate assets.

The second reason for the new company? The foresight of an entrepreneur who knew her business well. In 1986 settling disputes outside the court system was almost unheard of. Looking to the future, Duff saw a time when court dockets would be so filled with criminal cases that there would be a demand to resolve civil matters before they reached the litigation stage. Later, she established the American Conflict Resolution Institute, a nonprofit corporation dedicated to promoting alternative dispute resolution over litigation.

A Recipe for Success

Having gone from secretary to company owner in less than a decade, Duff is often asked to share her recipe for success. California's first minority female in the appraisal business is more than happy to oblige. "You must be a self-starter," she says. "You must have absolute and complete faith in your own personal abilities. You must be flexible and willing to change your plans without losing sight of your goals."

And Duff always reminds people to continually fuel their inspiration. "You must always nurture your dreams," she asserts, "by taking a few minutes to visualize the potential fruits of your success."

California State Lottery

Created by public vote in 1985 to provide supplemental revenues for schoolchildren, the California State Lottery has contributed more than $6.6 billion to public education. Californians were excited about the new Lottery, and sales during the first week reached $80 million. Since then, Lottery revenues have been distributed to the state's 1,064 public school districts, county offices of education, and governing bodies of public colleges and universities. In the Sacramento metropolitan area alone, from 1985 through 1993, $931 million in product sales has generated more than $270 million in revenues for local public schools.

Helping Schools Help Kids

When state voters approved the Lottery Act in November 1984, California public schools were designated as the sole beneficiary. Intended to provide supplemental funds, the Lottery Act earmarked at least 34 cents of every sales dollar for existing public schools, and the Lottery has exceeded that goal by averaging a 38 percent annual return. Overall, the Lottery's contribution represents approximately 2 percent of the state's total education budget and has averaged $122 per student annually since the Lottery began.

This strong performance has transformed the California Lottery from a fledgling state agency with a single product to a multibillion-dollar player in the state's economic marketplace. From the mom-and-pop market at the end of the street to the large retail outlet in the center of the city, Lottery products are distributed at more than 22,000 locations. Retailers offer as many as 15 different Scratchers® games as well as on-line gaming products such as Keno, Decco, Daily 3, Fantasy 5, and SuperLotto.

In its first nine years, the California Lottery has made a significant economic impact in the state through its $17.5 billion in sales. Fifty cents of every sales dollar is awarded to players as prize money, 34 cents is earmarked for education, 6.5 cents is returned to retailers in the form of sales commissions, 6 cents goes toward Lottery operations, and 3.5 cents supports game costs.

Lottery revenues are evident in classrooms across the Sacramento area. Loomis Union Elementary School in Placer County has used about one-fifth of the $1.5 million it has received to pay instructional aides who help teachers manage growing class sizes. Loomis Union also has used Lottery revenue to purchase photocopy machines, educational film services, health supplies for the school nurse, and hearing and vision testing programs and equipment. At Rio Linda Elementary School in Sacramento County, Lottery funds have supported counselors, psychologists, and music teachers.

And in the foothills above Sac-

Californians were excited about the new Lottery, and sales during the first week reached $80 million. Over 1,000 winners have walked away with prizes of $1 million or more from SuperLotto, the Instant Millionaire Scratchers game, and the weekly "Big Spin" television show.

▼ LOIS GERVAIS

ramento, the Iowa Hills School in the Colfax Elementary School District has been able to create a vibrant learning environment in a rustic mountain setting. In a one-room schoolhouse with only 16 students, the school has been fortunate enough to purchase a computer, a television, a videocassette recorder, overhead projectors, and other audiovisual equipment with Lottery revenues.

The Lottery plays a unique role in the state's education community by providing supplemental funding. In the Sacramento area, the Lottery has created opportunities for students through its model Partners In Education (P.I.E.) program. P.I.E. is a business-education partnership that establishes a direct link between Lottery employees and local schools. It was designed to help students succeed in school by increasing one-on-one attention through tutoring and mentoring programs and by augmenting school needs for equipment and volunteers. The Lottery matches volunteer time hour for hour, up to 40 hours per year.

Looking toward the Future

The Lottery has made an impact outside the classroom as well. Over 1,000 winners have walked away with prizes of $1 million or more from SuperLotto, the Instant Millionaire Scratchers game, and the weekly "Big Spin" television show. Fifty-one of those winners shared the largest single prize in North American lottery history—a jackpot of $118 million in April of 1991. Many of these memorable moments have been captured in award-winning advertising campaigns, including "Dream a Little Dream" and the current "Who's Next?" Billboards across the state add to the excitement by displaying the multimillion-dollar amount of the current SuperLotto jackpot.

Amid the fanfare of actual winners, the Lottery remains focused on maximizing revenues for the benefit of public education. The single Scratchers product of 1985 also launched the popular "Big Spin" television show and today has evolved into a product line of exciting and interesting games with a variety of themes and prize structures. The Lottery has embarked on new research and product design strategies to position its products for wider consumer appeal. Long-range business planning calls for innovative tie-in promotions with corporate partners to produce an interesting mix of cash and merchandise for players.

By maintaining a productive business environment and an ongoing commitment to education, the Lottery is poised to continue its investment in California's greatest asset—its children.

FROM THE MOM-AND-POP MARKET AT THE END OF THE STREET TO THE LARGE RETAIL OUTLET IN THE CENTER OF THE CITY, LOTTERY PRODUCTS ARE DISTRIBUTED AT MORE THAN 22,000 LOCATIONS.
PHOTOS BY SCOTT M. MORGAN

DFI INC.

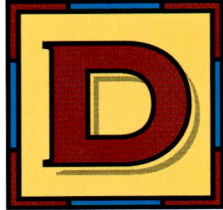

DAVID LU WAS 32 YEARS OLD WHEN HE TOLD HIS FATHER HE WAS LEAVING TAIWAN TO TRY HIS HAND AT BUSINESS IN AMERICA. BACK THEN, IN 1977, THE SENIOR LU WASN'T EXACTLY THRILLED WITH THE NEWS. HE AND HIS SON HAD BECOME QUITE CLOSE, AND BOTH DAVID AND HIS WIFE, GRACE, WOULD HAVE TO GIVE UP GOOD JOBS TO MAKE THE MOVE. IN THE END, DAVID TOLD HIS FATHER HE WOULD TRY

America for a year and return home if things didn't work out.

For David Lu, things definitely worked out.

Today, his Sacramento-based company, DFI Inc. (Diamond Flower), is one of the world's largest manufacturers of IBM-compatible systems, motherboards, interface cards, and peripherals. With seven corporate entities worldwide—in Sacramento, New Jersey, Florida, Arizona, the San Francisco Bay Area, the United Kingdom, and Taiwan—the DFI Group anticipates 1994 revenues of $250 million.

A Big Dream Starts Small

In the mid-1980s, David Lu was working as a comptroller in a Sacramento paper distribution company when his brother, Y.C. Lu, approached him with a business proposition: Y.C. needed a U.S. distributor for his Taiwan-based computer parts company and hoped David would open a distribution center in America.

Because the timing was not quite right for David, he encouraged his wife to try her hand at the venture. In the beginning, Grace started the new computer business out of the couple's garage. Within three months, however, she was so busy that David decided to quit his job and join the effort.

To bankroll DFI, Lu invested $20,000 of his personal savings, and the family back in Taiwan supplied the remainder of the start-up money. While some doubted that DFI Inc. could compete with the big names in the computer industry, Lu's unrelenting commitment to quality and excellence earned the company a reputation as a world leader in the manufacturing and marketing of personal computer enhancement products.

DAVID LU (RIGHT), PRESIDENT AND CEO OF DFI, FOUNDED THE COMPANY IN 1985.

Today the DFI catalog features 60 different products, including notebook computers, desktop computers that feature processor upgradable motherboards, multi-function products, memory upgrade boards, mice, fax boards, network and communications products, and a full lineup of video products and monitors. Each month, more than 100,000 pieces of high-tech equipment move through the DFI Group's warehouses, where the production lines can assemble up to 36,000 computer systems. But establishing and meeting ever-increasing production quotas is only one chapter in the DFI success story.

Success through Innovation

Just how does a business that began in a garage compete with the billion-dollar manufacturers of personal computers? From the outset, David Lu knew the answer. "The personal computer industry is a very high-tech business requiring constant innovation," he says. "New products mature very quickly, and in six months everybody can produce them at a very low cost. At that point, you can only make a small profit. The only way to continue growing the company is through innovation and creation."

Focused on the future, Lu and his talented team have become pioneers in the personal computer industry. In 1987, for instance, DFI introduced the first black-

and-white hand scanner to the U.S. computer market. Two years later, the company unveiled the Color Handy Scanner 4000. Then, in 1991, DFI introduced Model 486-33, a personal business computer featuring a Local Bus Video Graphics Array that sends video signals directly to the central processing unit. Model 486-33, Lu says, delivered a fourfold increase in performance over comparable machines, without the need for an expensive video coprocessor.

Fueled by that spirit of innovation, DFI Inc. (Sacramento) grew its sales of $203,000 in 1986 to $23 million in 1990—an increase of 11,360 percent in a period of five years. That prodigious growth attracted plenty of attention in the business world. In December of 1991, when *Inc.* magazine published its annual list of the 500 fastest-growing privately held companies in America, DFI ranked ninth in the nation and first in California. The following year, Arthur Andersen & Co. named DFI a "Fast Track 25" company. Then, in a *Computer Reseller News* survey of original equipment manufacturers, DFI ranked in the top three in delivery and availability, as well as price and performance.

A Commitment to Sacramento

For David Lu and the entire DFI team, working hard involves more than just making a profit. Lu is proud of the time and money his worldwide staff of 600 contributes to a wide range of community organizations. DFI's 130 employees in the Sacramento metropolitan area support the UC Davis Medical Center, Children's Miracle Network, Easter Seals, Sacramento Urban League, Leukemia Society of America, National Literacy Campaign, churches, and other local associations.

At DFI, the spirit of compassion is deeply rooted within the company. "We have a friendly working atmosphere," Lu says, adding that he strives to establish

and encourage open communication with his staff. Indeed, employees usually find Lu accessible and eager to help solve challenges. In a corporate environment where people are a priority, he believes, profits rise because employees thrive. "We have a very small turnover, less than 5 percent a year," says Lu. "That's one of the reasons DFI continues to grow."

After nearly a decade in business, DFI Inc. shows no signs of slowing down. Even with his company on its way to the Fortune 1000, David Lu has his eye on the future. "I don't feel I'm successful yet," he says. "I just feel I'm a fortunate person. God opened the door for us in this great country, and we worked very hard."

WHAT BEGAN IN DAVID LU'S GARAGE HAS NOW BECOME A MULTIMILLION-DOLLAR BUSINESS THAT CAN ASSEMBLE UP TO 36,000 COMPUTER SYSTEMS PER MONTH.

SILVA STRONG ARCHITECTS

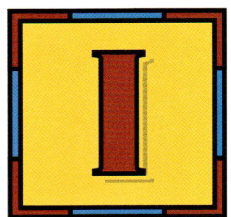

IN A SHORT PERIOD OF TIME, SILVA STRONG ARCHITECTS HAS BECOME ONE OF THE LEADING ARCHITECTURAL FIRMS IN THE REGION. EXPERIENCE, TEAMWORK, AND VISION HAVE POSITIONED THE FIRM FOR CONTINUED SUCCESS. THE YEAR WAS 1987, AND FOR THE PREVIOUS 20 YEARS STANLEY SILVA AND ALLEN STRONG HAD WORKED TOGETHER AT THE SAME SACRAMENTO ARCHITECTURAL FIRM. STRONG

had developed expertise in the area of health care planning, production documents, and construction management, while Silva coordinated and designed a diverse range of educational, commercial, banking, residential, and health care projects, as well as handling public relations and business development.

With their previous firm, Silva and Strong had worked on many of the city's major architectural projects, including Sacramento Metro Airport, Powell-Teichert Office Park, Eskaton American River Hospital, Sutter Memorial Hospital, Sutter General Hospital, the Yolo County Jail, and a host of jobs for the Sacramento Housing and Redevelopment Agency. In addition, the architects had been involved in a number of well-known projects in Sacramento's outlying areas, including the Heavenly Valley Lodge Destination Resort and the Nut Tree Retail Complex and Restaurant. By 1987, Silva says, he and Strong had done about everything there was to do in Sacramento in architecture—except own their own firm.

BUILDING A DREAM

For Silva and Strong, the nation's economic recession made launching their own business risky, and in the beginning, times were tough. But even as their reserves dwindled, Silva and Strong did not question their decision to leave the corporate world to become their own bosses. Soon their persistence was rewarded when a colleague from Carissimi Rohrer Associates Architects & Planners called to request their participation in the $25 million renovation of Sacramento's Radisson Hotel. It was the young firm's first major project.

Following renovation of the hotel, Silva Strong was contacted by a longtime business associate who was developing an office building for Foundation Health, Sacramento's largest publicly held company. Foundation Health needed a new headquarters building to accommodate its rapid growth in the managed health care services field, and in 1988 Silva Strong designed the company's new corporate centerpiece—a striking, three-story structure in Rancho Cordova's Capital Center.

For Silva Strong, the success of the Radisson and Foundation Health ventures led to a string of other major projects, including the $4 million renovation of Sacramento's Cannery Business Park, a mixed-use office complex originally built in 1928 as an aluminum can manufacturing plant. Coupled with design work on Roseville's world-renowned Auto Mall and various efforts for health care giants such as Sutter Health and Kaiser Permanente, it was clear that Silva Strong had become an established firm.

By 1993 Silva Strong Architects had matured into one of Sacramento's 10 largest design groups and one of the city's fastest-growing companies. After only six years of operation, Silva Strong had developed such a solid reputation that leading international architectural firms like Ellerbe Becket and Kaplan/McLaughlin/Diaz began to seek collaboration. "I have known Silva and Strong for 15 years, and

SILVA STRONG DESIGNED THE $4 MILLION RENOVATION OF SACRAMENTO'S CANNERY BUSINESS PARK, A MIXED-USE OFFICE COMPLEX BUILT IN 1928 AS AN ALUMINUM CAN MANUFACTURING PLANT (ABOVE LEFT).

IN 1988 THE FIRM DESIGNED FOUNDATION HEALTH'S NEW CORPORATE CENTERPIECE—A STRIKING, THREE-STORY STRUCTURE IN THE RANCHO CORDOVA CAPITAL CENTER (ABOVE RIGHT).

THE FIRM WAS SUTTER HEALTH'S ARCHITECT OF CHOICE (IN COLLABORATION WITH KAPLAN/MCLAUGHLIN/DIAZ OF SAN FRANCISCO) FOR DESIGN WORK ON THE SANTA CRUZ MATERNITY AND SURGERY CENTER.

they are consummate professionals whose architectural abilities are unsurpassed," says Ken Murai, chief of the Building Design Division, Sacramento County Public Works Department.

SERVING THE MANAGED HEALTH CARE MARKET

As Silva Strong grew, the firm became known for timely production of high-quality architectural projects in a remarkable range of building types—from planning and design to commercial office complexes, detention facilities, and hotels to historical restoration and renovation of hospitals and medical offices. But even with this versatility, it was clear the firm's special talents were in the health care field.

Sutter Health has repeatedly turned to Silva Strong for its expansion design needs. A regional health care system serving more than 50 Northern California communities, Sutter Health has hired Silva Strong for a number of high-priority projects. "Silva Strong's caliber of professional work, level of service, and attention to detail are hard to match," says Dana Ellerbe, assistant administrator of Cancer and Clinical Support Services for Sutter Health. In eastern Sacramento, for example, the firm planned and designed the $11 million Sutter Medical Plaza/Orangevale, an 82,000-square-foot medical facility that will eventually accommodate 24 physicians and a 20-bed recovery unit. In downtown Sacramento, Sutter Health also chose Silva Strong to design its new regional cancer center, a $12 million facility that includes a 45-bed medical/surgical oncology unit and bone marrow transplant unit. Southwest of Sacramento, the firm was Sutter Health's architect of choice (in collaboration with Kaplan/McLaughlin/Diaz of San Francisco) for design work on the Santa Cruz Maternity and Surgery Center. Built for a Sutter Health affiliate, the $10.3 million facility includes an orthopedic medical clinic, four operating room surgery suites, 12 residential-character birthing suites, and 18 recovery beds. "It's always nice to know you will get the two principals' personal attention when you are working with Silva Strong," Ellerbe says.

The Silva Strong team is also associated with Ellerbe Becket Architects in designing a new 40-bed, state-of-the-art facility for Sutter Novato Community Hospital. Programmed around a commitment to "patient-focused care," the physical design will reflect current thinking in the future delivery of health care.

POISED FOR THE FUTURE

Proud of these recent successes, Silva and Strong are looking to the future with great expectations. And why shouldn't they? "We are practicing architects involved in the day-to-day operation of every job this firm does," says Strong. "I don't think you'll find another architectural firm in Sacramento that has two principal partners as active as we are."

IN EASTERN SACRAMENTO, THE FIRM PLANNED AND DESIGNED THE $11 MILLION SUTTER MEDICAL PLAZA/ORANGEVALE, AN 82,000-SQUARE-FOOT MEDICAL FACILITY THAT WILL EVENTUALLY ACCOMMODATE 24 PHYSICIANS AND A 20-BED RECOVERY UNIT (BELOW LEFT).

SILVA STRONG PARTICIPATED IN THE $25 MILLION RENOVATION OF SACRAMENTO'S RADISSON HOTEL, THE FIRM'S FIRST MAJOR PROJECT (BELOW RIGHT).

FOUNTAIN SUITES HOTEL

READING THE NEWSPAPER ONE WINTER DAY, WARREN WILKIE, VICE PRESIDENT AND GENERAL MANAGER OF SACRAMENTO'S FOUNTAIN SUITES HOTEL, CAME ACROSS A STORY ABOUT LITTLE TONY PEREZ. TONY WAS A SIXTH-GRADER WHO LIVED WITH HIS MOTHER IN AUBURN, A GOLD RUSH COMMUNITY NORTHEAST OF SACRAMENTO. TONY WAS TWO YEARS OLD WHEN HIS FATHER DIED IN AN AUTOMOBILE ACCIDENT.

Now 12, Tony was waiting to be matched with a volunteer in the Big Brothers/Big Sisters program. He'd asked for a Big Brother who liked sports, and listed Spud Webb, point guard for the Sacramento Kings, as one of his favorite athletes.

After reading about Tony, Wilkie got an idea. He knew Webb, who was staying at Fountain Suites, a distinctive, 300-room hotel located between downtown Sacramento and ARCO Arena, home of the Kings. Wilkie called Webb and arranged a surprise. One Saturday night soon after, Tony Perez was driven to a Kings game by his new friend Spud Webb. After the game, Tony and his mother enjoyed complimentary accommodations at Fountain Suites.

"I thought we would make a little boy happy," Wilkie says. "Some hotels believe, 'We don't have the money to do this or that.' We believe if you do things right, the money will be there to take care of the bottom line."

Wilkie's "doing things right" approach has paid off handsomely. Since opening in May of 1988, Fountain Suites has forged a solid niche in Sacramento's hotel industry, with occupancy rates averaging 75 percent, well above the industry standard of 62 percent. "We're not a Hyatt," Wilkie says. "We're not a Biltmore or a Hilton. We're Fountain Suites, and we have to be better at the little things that make people want to come back."

GOING THE EXTRA MILE

At Fountain Suites, guests have come to expect service dedicated to meeting their needs. In fact, Wilkie gives his staff the autonomy to serve every guest quickly, completely, and in virtually any situation. For instance, an executive's plane lands late, causing her to miss the complimentary shuttle to the hotel. No problem. The manager drives out in his own car to meet the guest. What if a family is in Sacramento on vacation, and Dad's shaver and Mom's hair spray didn't make it in the suitcase? They make a call to guest services, and within minutes someone from housekeeping is at the door with replacements.

FOUNTAIN SUITES IS A DISTINCTIVE, 300-ROOM HOTEL CONVENIENTLY LOCATED ALONG THE INTERSTATE 5 CORRIDOR JUST FOUR MINUTES FROM DOWNTOWN SACRAMENTO.

ALL GUEST ROOMS ARE LARGER THAN THOSE FOUND AT MANY OTHER HOTELS. THE GOLDEN EYE SUITE OFFERS BOTH COMFORT AND A FEELING OF LUXURY (RIGHT).

A hotel that prides itself on quality, attentive service, Fountain Suites also devotes extraordinary effort to meeting the needs of business travelers and clients. Guest rooms are larger than those found at many other hotels, offering both comfort and a feeling of luxury. Suites are appointed with contemporary furnishings and tasteful color schemes. In addition to complimentary Continental breakfast, blow-dryers, shampoos, and lotions, each guest room includes two telephones, a work area with a desk, and a state-of-the-art voice mail message service, which allows business travelers to remain in convenient, personal contact with their callers.

For business gatherings involving 20 to 200 people, Fountain Suites boasts convenient, first-class meeting space. There are seven meeting rooms, each providing a private, professional setting for business. Business services also feature an experienced staff eager to assist with everything from pads and pencils to security and fax services. Audiovisual equipment is also available.

For the discriminating business traveler, Fountain Suites also offers upgraded guest rooms. Amenities in these Executive Level accommodations include morning newspaper delivery, robes, and coffeemakers. There are even microwaves and refrigerators in Executive Plus rooms.

Fountain Suites' unusual blend of business functionality and comfort is perhaps best illustrated in the hotel's Golden Eye Suite. This spacious guest room features an inviting balcony view, a fireplace, and a separate bedroom with walk-in closet. The Golden Eye Suite also has a large-screen television, VCR, stereo with CD player, wet bar, and spacious Jacuzzi bathtub. With these amenities, it's no surprise that many guests book the Golden Eye Suite as a hospitality room as well.

FOUNTAIN SUITES OFFERS GUESTS NUMEROUS OPPORTUNITIES TO WIND DOWN AFTER A BUSY DAY (ABOVE AND BELOW).

FOR BUSINESS GATHERINGS OF VIRTUALLY ANY SIZE, THE HOTEL BOASTS CONVENIENT, FIRST-CLASS MEETING SPACE (LEFT).

SERVING FROM THE HEART OF SACRAMENTO

In the hotel business, guests often look for accommodations that enable them to get where they want to go quickly. Nestled along the Interstate 5 corridor, Fountain Suites Hotel is positioned to meet the burgeoning service needs of Sacramento's growing travel markets. By complimentary shuttle, the hotel is just 10 minutes from Metro Airport. It's only four minutes from downtown Sacramento, the state capitol, the shopping districts at Downtown Plaza and Old Sacramento, and other entertainment and tourist attractions. Also nearby is a five-mile jogging path, which meanders along the Sacramento River.

While life at some hotels begins to wind down at night, Fountain Suites comes alive. The hotel is within walking distance of a host of fine restaurants, including the renowned Rusty Duck, where fresh fish, top sirloin, and prime rib are the specialties. The Buttercup Pantry, the hotel restaurant, is open 24 hours a day.

With an ideal location and a friendly staff dedicated to service, it's easy to understand why guests enjoy staying at Fountain Suites.

HumanWare, Inc.

In 1988, shortly after HumanWare, Inc. opened for business, founder Jim Halliday called a meeting of his staff. With his young technology company struggling to establish itself in the specialized field of hardware and software for the visually impaired, Halliday told his people that things looked bleak. At the minimum, significant cutbacks would be necessary for HumanWare to stay in business.

The next day, the same employees returned to Halliday's office. One by one, they volunteered to make personal sacrifices—giving up pay, vacations, and bonuses—in a bid to help the fledgling firm succeed. Soon after Halliday accepted their generosities, sales rebounded, and HumanWare was fast on its way to earning $800,000 in first-year revenue.

By May of 1994, such unflagging commitment had created enough momentum that HumanWare generated more revenue in one month than it had during its entire first year. "Our company grew out of the philosophy that a business is only as good as its people," Halliday says. "This philosophy of caring is the driving force behind all of HumanWare's business decisions."

The Link between Technology and People

The idea of "humanware" has always been central to the company's approach to technology. Halliday defines humanware as the point at which technology becomes so sophisticated that it seems simple to the user. "There is a lot of hardware and software on the market, but HumanWare focuses on the link between that technology and the people who use it," he explains. "Our purpose is to build bridges that enable people with disabilities to contribute their unique talents while successfully competing in a world that might otherwise be totally inaccessible."

Halliday believes so deeply in the humanware approach that company business cards feature the team vision: "Our mission and purpose are to help people achieve their highest potential by providing 'HumanWare,' the link between technology and people."

The company's niche centers around identifying and evaluating the needs of individuals who are blind, visually impaired, or learning disabled. Humanized hardware and software compensate for the limitations of a disability and allow the user to perform at a level commensurate with his or her abilities. According to Halliday, the fundamental difference between his company and others in the industry is that HumanWare concentrates on the individual rather than the technology. Ironically, this focus has allowed HumanWare to create more innovations in technology and application than any other company in its field.

In the United States, for example, HumanWare introduced the first eight-dot Braille system and the first 80-cell Braille displays and terminals, proving that users needed and wanted full-line access to their computers. HumanWare also debuted the first high-quality synthetic speech processor, which can be used on a portable basis and built into laptop computers. That same technology

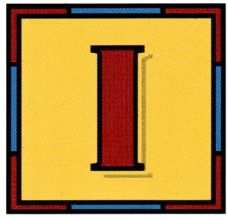

HumanWare's ClearView VGA offers large-print computer access.

THE CLEARVIEW CLOSED-CIRCUIT TELEVISION SYSTEM ALLOWS PEOPLE TO READ AGAIN.

was applied to the credit-card-sized VoiceCard, the first high-quality synthetic speech processor contained on a PCMCIA card for use with notebook and palmtop computers. In addition, HumanWare's Viewpoint and ClearView closed-circuit television systems were the first in the United States to use digital video cameras, which corrected the burn-in and smearing problems that plagued other systems.

Throughout its relatively short history, HumanWare has focused on solutions for people who are blind. Early products included talking laptop computers, Braille terminals, and Braille printers. In order to broaden its reach and stabilize sales cycles, however, HumanWare has entered the low-vision market with print-enlarging devices like video magnifiers and closed-circuit televisions.

"Reading and writing are essential in most job settings," Halliday says, "but they are also important for personal independence and enjoyment. Our closed-circuit televisions make it possible for people with low vision to enlarge the same information that fully sighted people take for granted. This not only includes memos at work or large-print computer output, but 'quality of life' materials like family photographs, personal letters, recipes, and bank statements."

EMPOWERING EMPLOYEES

At HumanWare, responsibility is an essential element of the business philosophy. Every employee, regardless of his or her position, has the blanket approval to respond to a customer's needs. For example, if a customer has a challenge that can be corrected by shipping a replacement unit overnight, no one needs to seek approval from a supervisor. Halliday believes that granting this authority empowers all employees to do and be their best.

"It's almost impossible to make a bad decision," he says, "if it results in a happy customer. This saves time, reduces the need for middle managers, gives employees a sense of responsibility and authority, and enables everyone in the organization to actively exercise the corporate philosophy."

For Halliday, the HumanWare philosophy boils down to the importance of people and the growth gained by working through challenges rather than avoiding or ignoring them. "With growth comes growing pains," he adds. "But who ever heard of an adventure that didn't have a little pain and struggle along the way? Growing pains build character. They ground us. They teach us humility. They give us perspective. They help us to persevere. They teach us to overcome fear. They provide necessary challenges. They define achievement. And they teach us to value people more than things. That is what HumanWare is all about in the first place."

BLIND COMPUTER USERS CAN READ MECHANICAL BRAILLE WITH THE ALVA BRAILLE TERMINAL AND HEAR THE COMPUTER TALK WITH THE KEYNOTE GOLD SPEECH SYNTHESIZER.

Sacramento Cable

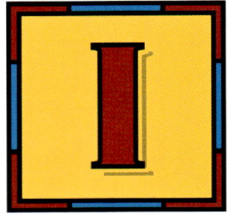

IN A CLIMATE WHERE THE GROWTH OF CABLE SYSTEMS HAS GENERALLY SLOWED, SACRAMENTO CABLE HAS OUTPERFORMED OTHER COMPARABLE COMPANIES AND ENJOYED PHENOMENAL GROWTH. THERE IS A GOOD REASON FOR THIS, ACCORDING TO MARKETING DIRECTOR BRIAN GRUBER. ■ "WE HAVE FOCUSED ON PROVIDING 62 CHANNELS OF QUALITY PROGRAMMING AT A PRICE THAT IS AMONG THE LOWEST in the nation," he says. "And we back it all up with tremendous service." Gruber is in charge of subscriber growth, which totaled 221,000 in summer of 1994.

Sacramento Cable is a relatively new company and was among the last large metropolitan systems to be built in the nation. Now, at less than 10 years old, it is well established and positioning itself for the great information explosion of the late '90s.

Owned by Scripps Howard, a 116-year-old information and entertainment company, the Sacramento system is the largest in the corporation's cable division. The Cincinnati-based firm invested more than $200 million to create a technologically advanced system for the Sacramento area.

"We planned well for the future of cable in Sacramento," says Wayne Vowell, general manager and corporate vice president. "We recently completed 200 miles of fiber-optic cable, which will be the backbone of the great information revolution that is on the horizon."

According to industry statistics, the average cable system in the United States offers about 38 channels. Although Sacramento Cable already carries 62 channels, the addition of about 15 more is expected in the near future. And within a few years? Customers can look forward to hundreds of choices on their cable system—entertainment, information, interactive services, communication technology, and more.

However, Sacramento Cable goes beyond technology and channel choices. The company employs more than 400 people and feels a strong responsibility to them and to the community it serves. There is an active community relations program that supports dozens of charitable organizations, helps local schools, and champions causes important to its customers.

"This intense involvement with the community is an important element in how we do business," says Darby Patterson, who spearheads the company's community relations program. "We contribute to the quality of life in the neighborhoods we serve, and we strive to keep our employees proud members of our team."

According to Patterson, some of Sacramento Cable's financial support is dedicated to low-profile, yet very important causes. "Last year we learned that a three-on-three basketball team had made the national finals but was unable to afford the trip to Colorado to compete," she says. "We picked up the tab for the team and their chaperons (the team was made up of 14-year-olds) and, what do you know, the boys came back with the national championship."

It is this blending of people and technology that distinguishes Sacramento Cable and forms the foundation of its mission.

"We are very excited about the role we play in Sacramento," says Gruber. "It is an opportunity for us to create a premier cable system that delivers excellent service, to run a company that deeply cares for its employees, and to be truly responsible to the community."

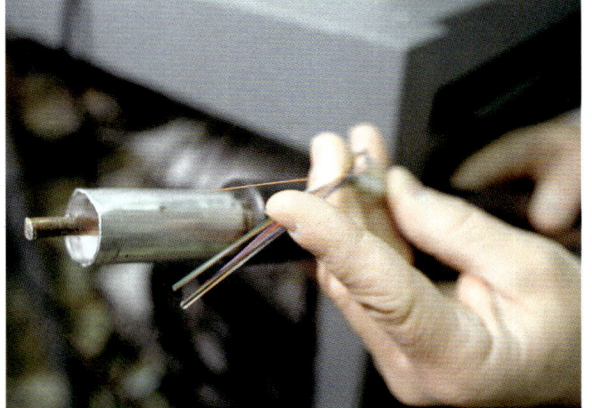

COMBINING CUSTOMER SERVICE AND STATE-OF-THE-ART TECHNOLOGY, SACRAMENTO CABLE HAS ENJOYED PHENOMENAL GROWTH SINCE ITS FOUNDING IN 1985.

Comstock Publishing, Inc.

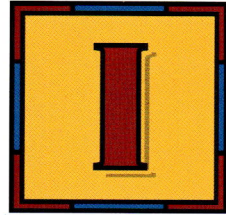

IN THE FALL OF 1988, WINNIE COMSTOCK HAD MANY OF THE THINGS SHE'D ALWAYS WANTED IN LIFE. A NICE HOME. PRIVATE SCHOOL FOR HER DAUGHTER. TWO ARABIAN HORSES. A MERCEDES-BENZ WITH A CELLULAR PHONE. AND A CAREER THAT CHALLENGED AND REWARDED HER. THEN, ONE MORNING, THE MAGAZINE PUBLISHER FOR WHOM SHE SOLD ADVERTISING DECLARED BANKRUPTCY AND CLOSED ITS DOORS.

For Comstock, an enthusiastic dreamer with a tireless work ethic, it was both an end and a beginning.

"At the time," she remembers, "I had about a dollar and a half in my wallet and not much more in my checking account—hardly enough money to start a magazine. But I was furious that something with such potential had died—leaving a gaping hole in the fabric of Sacramento business."

Comstock soon decided to fill the void herself. She mortgaged her home and maxed out her credit cards in order to bankroll her dream, *Comstock's* magazine. Covering the business of the capital region since 1989, *Comstock's* provides a forum for the exchange of ideas on the economic, social, ethical, political, environmental, scientific, and technological issues that impact the practice of business and the prosperity of the Sacramento region.

Growing with Enthusiasm

From the first issue, *Comstock's* has voiced a unique perspective. "Business is seldom reported in a positive fashion," says Janice Fillip, the magazine's editor. "What we do is create an atmosphere for success, a forum where the business leaders of the capital region can get information that helps them to succeed."

Early on, Winnie Comstock couldn't afford to hire a staff, so she contracted with Sacramento's best talent and paid them only for the hours it took them to produce the magazine. Comstock also assembled a distinguished Editorial Advisory Board made up of volunteers culled from all facets of business and industry in the region. The 33-member board helps *Comstock's* keep a finger on the pulse of the Sacramento area's ever-changing business landscape.

As *Comstock's* has matured—the magazine's coverage has expanded from four to nine California counties and nearly 100,000 readers—success has allowed Winnie Comstock to expand her dream. In 1992, for instance, the magazine's in-house advertising department debuted as Design & Litho, the graphic design division of Comstock Publishing. Besides the first-class advertising it produces for *Comstock's* magazine, the award-winning graphic design studio creates corporate identity packages, books, and calendars, as well as posters and publications. As if one magazine were not enough, Comstock launched a new and unique publication in September 1994. Called *Capital Style*, the magazine focuses on leisure and recreational pursuits of the people of California's capital region.

With five years of success already on the shelf, Winnie Comstock is characteristically optimistic about the future of her burgeoning company. "I started the magazine because I wanted to provide something positive and productive for the community," she says. "Because I had faith in my dream and was willing to work to make it come true, we're doing just that."

Comstock's PROVIDES A FORUM FOR THE EXCHANGE OF IDEAS ON THE ECONOMIC, SOCIAL, ETHICAL, POLITICAL, ENVIRONMENTAL, SCIENTIFIC, AND TECHNOLOGICAL ISSUES THAT IMPACT THE PRACTICE OF BUSINESS AND THE PROSPERITY OF THE SACRAMENTO REGION.

IN 1989 WINNIE COMSTOCK ESTABLISHED HER OWN PUBLISHING COMPANY, WHICH HAS GROWN TO INCLUDE TWO MAGAZINES AND AN IN-HOUSE ADVERTISING AND DESIGN DEPARTMENT.

Radisson Hotel Sacramento

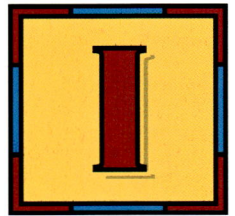

IN 1989, WHEN KINGS COUNTRY OWNERSHIP COMPLETED A RENOVATION OF THE OLD WOODLAKE INN AND REOPENED IT AS THE RADISSON HOTEL SACRAMENTO, THE MINNEAPOLIS-BASED CHAIN DESCRIBED ITS NEWEST HOTEL AS ONE OF ITS "MOST UNIQUE AND PICTURESQUE PROPERTIES." AT FIRST, THAT WAS HARD FOR MANY SACRAMENTANS TO BELIEVE. THEY WONDERED HOW THE OLD WOODLAKE, BUILT IN the 1950s, could compare to other elegant Radisson properties in locales such as New Orleans, Canada, London, Switzerland, Puerto Rico, and Hong Kong. After one look, however, it was easy to see that the new Radisson was indeed a world-class luxury hotel.

Thanks to a $40 million upgrade of the facility, the Radisson Hotel Sacramento is an eclectic retreat for business and leisure travelers to the region. The unique Mediterranean-style exterior, complete with palm trees and Spanish tile, is complemented by a beautiful fountain with a 50-foot spray in the center of the hotel's private, three-acre lake. Inside, all 309 guest rooms and 29 hospitality suites have been upgraded according to the Radisson's matchless standards of distinction. Rooms and suites are beautifully appointed, tastefully combining comfort and luxury. Many of the rooms that overlook the lake feature vaulted ceilings and patios or balconies.

Also featured is the intimate Cabana Room, a richly appointed dining salon offering gourmet cuisine and a sweeping view of the lake. The Palm Court Restaurant dishes up California-fresh selections in a garden setting; the Fanfare Lounge, a stylish lakeside bar, serves cocktails and exotic appetizers on the terrace; and the Grove, a 900-seat outdoor amphitheater, is home to the popular Summer Concert Series running from early June through Labor Day.

All this plus 24-hour room service and complimentary shuttles to both Sacramento Airport and key tourist attractions. The distinction is clear: California's capital now boasts a relaxing, revitalizing resort just five minutes from downtown.

Leading the Way for Business

As home to California's state government, Sacramento has always been a popular convention and resort destination, and the Radisson Hotel Sacramento stays ahead of the competition by offering services tailored to the needs of its guests. From the start, renovation efforts were directed at transforming the hotel into the city's premier business and convention resort facility. Today, it's no accident that the Radisson Hotel Sacramento features more meeting rooms than any other hotel in town, with 50,000 square feet of flexible function space. The hotel is also home to the 2,000-seat Grand Ballroom and Exhibit Area, which is the largest hotel ballroom in the capital city. This versatile, 17,000-square-foot space can be divided into six separate meeting rooms and can accommodate formal dining for as many as 1,500. With a full-production theatrical stage and a loading dock for easy access, the ballroom can host everything from a high-energy social event to a black-tie business dinner.

The Radisson Hotel Sacramento also boasts the city's only hotel conference center. This state-of-the-art facility features 10 meeting

THE RADISSON HOTEL SACRAMENTO IS A RELAXING, REVITALIZING RESORT JUST FIVE MINUTES FROM DOWNTOWN.

THE CABANA ROOM, A RICHLY APPOINTED DINING SALON, OFFERS GOURMET CUISINE AND A SWEEPING VIEW OF THE LAKE (RIGHT).

THE UNIQUE MEDITERRANEAN-STYLE EXTERIOR, COMPLETE WITH PALM TREES AND SPANISH TILE, IS COMPLEMENTED BY A BEAUTIFUL FOUNTAIN WITH A 50-FOOT SPRAY IN THE CENTER OF THE HOTEL'S PRIVATE, THREE-ACRE LAKE.

rooms ranging in size from 700 to 2,068 square feet. Rooms are furnished with data ports, 24-inch video monitors, a dedicated satellite downlink, and comfortable swivel/tilt chairs, all surrounding a spacious outdoor plaza. In addition to meeting the usual needs of business guests, the hotel's comprehensive business center offers teleconferencing, speaker phones, pager rentals, and safety deposit boxes.

For smaller business and social gatherings, the Radisson Hotel Sacramento boasts seven executive board suites. Overlooking the lake and koi pond, the suites include wet bars, refrigerators, living rooms, and conference table seating for as many as 15. In addition, it is possible to adjoin suites with as many as four guest rooms, making the hotel ideal for social or family gatherings.

More Than a Business Destination

The Radisson Hotel Sacramento, of course, isn't just an outstanding environment for business. On the strength of its spectacular Lakeside Terrace, the hotel has become one of Sacramento's favorite wedding locations. In addition to a striking setting, wedding parties can take advantage of comprehensive ceremony or reception packages. Many families choose to have the hotel's wedding specialists coordinate their entire day. Services and amenities include everything from rehearsal on the terrace, a spacious bridal dressing room, and butler service for cake cutting and the marriage toast, to a deluxe lakeside room for the wedding night.

As for leisure activities, the Radisson Hotel Sacramento has something for everyone. Nightly entertainment is available in the Fanfare Lounge. A complete fitness center features a variety of aerobic and weight-training equipment and a 10-station Par Fitness Course. For runners and bicyclists, the American River bike trail beckons nearby with 35 miles of jogging and bicycling trails adjacent to the hotel.

Located less then five minutes away is Northern California's largest shopping center, Arden Fair. Guests can take advantage of the hotel's courtesy shuttle to the mall, where they'll find Nordstrom, Weinstock's, and hundreds of Sacramento's finest specialty shops. The Radisson Hotel Sacramento also claims one of the best hotel locations in town for tourists—only minutes from historic Old Sacramento, the California Exposition Center and State Fair grounds, and Sutter's Fort, which was reconstructed on the original site where John Sutter built his New Helvetia settlement in the late 1830s.

With its assortment of luxurious amenities, the Radisson Hotel Sacramento sets itself apart as not only a "unique and picturesque" jewel in the worldwide Radisson chain, but also as the premier haven for business and leisure travelers to the Sacramento area.

Apple Computer, Inc.

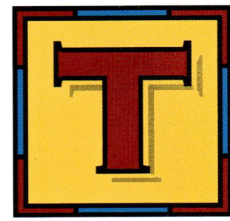

The story of the world's most popular computer began in the spring of 1976, when Steve Wozniak and Steve Jobs finished work on a preassembled computer circuit board they called the Apple I. On April Fool's Day of that year, the two young entrepreneurs—Wozniak was 26 and Jobs was 21—formed the Apple Computer Company in the heart of what would soon become "Silicon Valley."

To finance production of the Apple I boards, Jobs sold his Volkswagen van and Wozniak sold his programmable calculator. That summer, working out of Jobs' garage, the duo built the boards and sold them for $666.66 each. Sales were brisk, and after a few years of strong growth, the fledgling company put together its first formal business plan, projecting sales of $500 million within the decade. Apple, however, hit the $500 million mark in half that time, entering the Fortune 500 within five years.

Today, with annual revenues of nearly $8 billion, Apple Computer, Inc. is one of the most prominent and successful corporations in the world. And the company shows no signs of slowing.

Building on Sacramento's Competitive Edge

Early in the 1990s, in a bid to realign its worldwide manufacturing and distribution activities, Apple went looking for the right site to locate a new logistics center to house distribution activities for the western half of the United States. After an extensive search, the company selected Sacramento. Why? According to Michael Spindler, Apple's president and CEO, the region's exceptional transportation system and excellent quality of life were high on the list of Sacramento's unique and attractive qualities.

But a company that develops, manufactures, licenses, and markets products in 140 countries around the world doesn't decide to build a 500,000-square-foot complex unless it makes sense on the bottom line. Spindler says Apple's Sacramento facility, opened in 1992, has proved to be a critical component in the company's continued growth. "By combining our manufacturing and distribution functions, we're able to respond to customer needs while significantly reducing our manufacturing costs. Apple's new operations model is a key to our aggressive new product plans, and will help us retain our competitive edge throughout the decade."

Located in the master-planned community of Laguna West, the first pedestrian-oriented development in the Sacramento region, Apple's Western Logistics Center is dedicated to distribution functions such as storage, shipping, receiving, quality control, parts supply, testing, and final assembly. According to Spindler, the flexible capabilities of the Sacramento center have allowed Apple to shift from building preconfigured products based on sales forecasts to creating tailored product configurations that meet customer needs quickly and economically.

In Sacramento, 950 employees manage a host of manufacturing and distribution functions for Apple's domestic and international operations, including manufacturing for the U.S., Canadian, Latin American, and Far Eastern markets; finished goods distribution for Texas, Alaska, Hawaii, and the western United States; final assembly for Apple's LC, Quadra, Workgroup Servers, and Power Macintosh product lines; and customized configuration for Apple's Macintosh Performa product line.

Based on the company's performance in recent times, it's clear that the decision to do business in California's capital city has been a shrewd one. In Decem-

Apple Computer was established in 1976 in the heart of what would soon become "Silicon Valley." Today, the company develops, manufactures, licenses, and markets its products in 140 countries around the world.

THE COMPANY HAS COME A LONG WAY SINCE ITS FOUNDERS DEVELOPED THE APPLE I PREASSAMBLED COMPUTER CIRCUIT BOARD (TOP LEFT). APPLE NOW OFFERS A DIVERSE AND GROWING PRODUCT LINE, INCLUDING THE STATE-OF-THE-ART POWER MACINTOSH (BOTTOM LEFT).

ber 1992, for example, just months after Apple announced its intent to set up shop in Sacramento, the company celebrated its first $2 billion revenue quarter. The momentum continued throughout the 1993 fiscal year, with revenues reaching a record $7.98 billion, capped off in the fourth quarter with another sales record of $2.14 billion and a 36 percent increase in unit shipments of Macintosh computers, also an all-time high.

COMMITTED TO ITS HOME COMMUNITIES

At Apple, maintaining the competitive edge also includes high standards of corporate citizenship. In 1992 the company innovated the elimination of chlorofluorocarbons (often used in the industry for cleaning circuit boards) at each of its manufacturing facilities. Responding to environmental considerations, Apple developed a unique manufacturing process that produces high-quality circuit boards without relying on the ozone-depleting propellant. Also in 1992, at the global forum of the United Nations Earth Summit in Rio de Janeiro, Apple shared this process with others, including computer industry suppliers and competitors still using chlorofluorocarbons.

Additionally, the company created a department to manage energy consumption, water conservation, and recycling. Today, Apple employees recycle a wide variety of office and product wastes such as glass, paper, and polystyrene.

In Sacramento, Apple has quickly become a corporate leader in the effort to better the region. The company ranks among the city's most active corporate participants in charitable endeavors ranging from local food and blood drives to Adopt-A-Family programs. Under the leadership of Site Director Clark Winchester, the Sacramento facility is developing a comprehensive community affairs program to further enhance employee volunteerism.

Since 1984 Apple has shipped more than 13 million Macintosh computers. But rather than look back on past successes, the company continues to create winning strategies for the future.

In 1993, following President Bill Clinton's executive order requiring government agencies to purchase only energy-efficient computers, Apple's Macintosh Color Classic became the first personal computer to qualify for the Environmental Protection Agency's new Energy Star rating.

On the strength of these and other innovations, Spindler says the Apple mission—changing the way people use information to work, learn, and play—remains as vibrant today as it was back in 1976, when people first met the computer that smiled back at them.

U.S. BANK OF CALIFORNIA

FREQUENTLY, THE PROFESSIONALS AT U.S. BANK OF CALIFORNIA CHALLENGE THEIR CUSTOMERS WITH SURPRISING QUESTIONS. "DO YOU REALLY NEED A LOAN THAT LARGE?" THEY WILL OFTEN ASK, OR "DO YOU REALLY NEED ANOTHER CREDIT CARD?" U.S. BANK IS TURNING HEADS IN NORTHERN CALIFORNIA BY DOING BUSINESS THE OLD-FASHIONED WAY. "WE TELL IT STRAIGHT," SAYS DANIEL J. DOYLE, U.S. BANK'S president and CEO, "because we aren't here for the short term. We know that if our customers get good advice—even if that advice isn't in the bank's immediate best interest—we're building long-term relationships. That's important because we live here, too, and we want to make Northern California a better place."

U.S. Bank came to Northern California in 1988 and to Sacramento in 1990 after its parent company, Portland-based U.S. Bancorp, purchased an existing banking operation. Backed by this strong parent organization and the deep governing values of integrity, cooperation, caring, leadership, quality, and performance, the bank has grown from 10 branches to 65 in just four years. With more than $2 billion in assets, U.S. Bank offers a wide range of financial services, including commercial loans and lines of credit, services for retail customers and merchants, cash management services, a full range of consumer services, government and international banking, asset management, trust administration, and investment services.

INVESTING IN THE FUTURE

A leader in customer advocacy, U.S. Bank is especially committed to serving the needs of small businesses throughout 30 Northern California counties. As a Certified Small Business Lender, the bank offers the personal services of a hometown bank with the advantages and backing of U.S. Bancorp, the largest financial services institution headquartered in the Northwest and one of the nation's top 35 bank holding companies in terms of size, capital, and profitability.

At U.S. Bank, the commitment to the region goes beyond meeting the customer service and financial needs of its personal and business clientele. Since 1988 the company has invested millions of dollars in affordable housing programs in Northern California. The bank also conducts a variety of educational seminars, covering a wide range of subjects from tips for the first-time home buyer to preparing a loan application for a small business.

According to Doyle, such efforts are paying off—for both the bank and the community. "We are second to none in serving our communities and in sharing the prosperity they have helped us achieve," he says.

Whether it's generous community contributions of time, money, and leadership or innovation in financial services, Doyle believes that the hard work of U.S. Bank's approximately 1,000 employees is a product of their core values of leadership, quality, and performance. "There is a very strong emphasis in this company on being the best at what we do," he says. "We are winners. We believe there is no substitute for outstanding financial performance."

U.S. BANK PLAZA IS LOCATED ON 9TH STREET IN SACRAMENTO (RIGHT).

ARTISTS AND PHOTOGRAPHERS

ED ASMUS is a Sacramento-area architectural photographer. His architectural background and attention to detail have made him popular with a wide range of clients, including Williams and Paddon Architects, Ed Kado and Associates, Nacht & Lewis Architects, Fleming Foods, K.C.S. Development, and Tower Records. In his spare time, "Pepperhead Ed" grows chili peppers, tomatoes, and other produce on his farm in the Delta and markets them to local restaurants.

STAN ATKINSON, the principal news anchor for KOVR Channel 13's 5:00, 6:00, and 11:00 evening news broadcasts, is an experienced writer, producer, and director of documentaries. His work has taken him to some of the most turbulent places in the world: he has been shot at in Cambodia, chased down by a Soviet helicopter gunship in Afghanistan, and held up and robbed by leftist guerrillas in El Salvador. Atkinson was one of 25 reporters selected for the Ford Foundation Journalism Fellowship at Stanford University and has won three Emmy awards. He is the 1989 winner of the George Washington Medal for Individual Achievement from the Freedom Foundation in Valley Forge, Pennsylvania, and is a recipient of the World Affairs Council's Award for International Reporting.

JEFF BURKHOLDER, operator of Life Images in Carmichael, received his photojournalism degree from Sacramento City College. While in school, he worked for the Associated Press and after graduation went on to a number of newspaper jobs, including a stint with the *Sacramento Bee Neighbors*. Since opening Life Images in 1987, Burkholder has focused on providing corporate and advertising clients with images for marketing and in-house communications packages. His work has appeared in many annual reports, brochures, and communications pieces, as well as on posters and billboards. Burkholder's work is also popular with a number of national clients, and his photography has appeared in *Runner's World*, *Triathlon*, *Ultra Sport*, *Sport*, *Fortune*, *Success*, *Comstock's*, *California Business*, *Sacramento Business*, and many others.

ROBERT DI FRANCO, an experienced photographer, gallery manager, and artist, specializes in art and architecture photography. His clients include the Cook Company, the Crocker Art Museum, Los Angeles' Burnett Miller Gallery, the Michael Himovitz Gallery, Brian Gross, Victoria Rivers, *Sacramento* magazine, San Francisco Museum of Modern Art, Yoshio Taylor, and Peter VanderBerge. Di Franco's work has been published in *The Civil War: War on the Frontier* and *The Civil War: Master Index*, both published by Time-Life Books, and in the University of Washington Press' *Norman Lundin: A Decade of Drawing and Painting*.

KURT FISHBACK, a native Sacramentan, is a freelance photographer specializing in general commercial, advertising illustration, executive portrait, and product illustration photography. His clients include Bank of America Foundation, Weinstock's department stores, Girl Scouts of America, *California* magazine, Dearborn Federal Credit Union, and Mercy Healthcare Association. Fishback has had his drawings, paintings, and prints included in a number of exhibitions, and his work can be found in public and private collections all over the country.

DARRELL FORNEY, born in Portland, Oregon, has lived in Sacramento for more than 50 years. A professor of art at Sacramento City College, he is also an active painter, illustrator, and all-around raconteur of the local art scene. His work has been exhibited nationally and internationally in invitational one-man and group shows in Nevada, Utah, Washington, Oregon, Texas, Pennsylvania, Brazil, and Switzerland. In 1978 a retrospective exhibition of Forney's large-letter, postcard-style paintings was held in the Nelson Gallery at the University of California, Davis. Forney is also a published writer on the arts, and his insights have been published in the *Sacramento Bee*, *Sacramento Union*, *WestArt*, *Sacramento* magazine, *American Postcard Journal*, *Canyon Cinemanews*, and art exhibition catalogs.

▲ TOM MYERS

MICHAEL A. JONES has been a photographer for the *Sacramento Bee* since 1989. He has been involved in a number of outside projects, including the *Bee's Book of Dreams* and Viking Studio Books' *The African Americans*. Jones has studied in San Francisco, New York, and Italy. Jones also attended the 43rd Missouri Photographic Workshop in Ste. Genevieve, where he was named Best Photographer at the workshop.

CATHY KELLY, operator of Cathy Kelly Architectural Photography, specializes in all aspects of creative architectural photography, including interiors, exteriors, aerials, and landscapes. Her work has appeared in *AIA Journal*, *Architecture*, *Architectural Record*, *Professional Builder*, and *U.S. News & World Report* and has earned her many awards, including an ASID Design Excellence Award, an AIA National Honors Award, and BIA, BOMA, and Gold Nugget awards.

THE FOOTHILLS EAST OF SACRAMENTO (PAGE 235) ARE A TRANSITION BETWEEN THE VALLEY AND THE SIERRA, AND HAVE THE BEST ASPECTS OF BOTH.
PHOTO BY ED ASMUS

THINK ABOUT THIS: THE STUDENTS AT UC DAVIS WHO BUILT THE "STEALTH STURGEON" (RIGHT) MAY SOMEDAY BE FLYING THE STEALTH BOMBER AT NEARBY MCCLELLAN AIR FORCE BASE (OPPOSITE).

GREG KONDOS has been painting and drawing for over 50 years. He has had numerous solo exhibitions at galleries all over the country—including many at Sacramento's Crocker Art Museum—and his paintings were featured in a solo exhibition at San Francisco's California Palace of the Legion of Honor, where he had won Winter Invitational awards in 1962 and 1963. Kondos' work was included in *The West—80 Contemporaries*, organized by the University of Arizona at Tucson; *A Sense of Place: The Artist and the American Landscape*, organized by Alan Gussow for the University of Nebraska's Gallery and the Joslyn Art Museum in Omaha; and the American Academy of Arts and Letters' Invitational Exhibition of Painting and Sculpture in 1993, where he won an award. Kondos also won the Dillard Collection prize in the exhibition *Art on Paper*. When he retired from teaching at Sacramento City College in 1982, the college's Little Gallery was renamed the Gregory Kondos Gallery. Kondos is a close friend and neighbor of Wayne Thiebaud, and the two are the central figures in what has come to be called the Sacramento River School of painting.

KENT LACIN is the operator of Kent Lacin Media Services and specializes in food, people, medical, and conceptual photography. His clients include Access Health Marketing, CableData, Sutter Health, and Hughes Aircraft, and he has won a number of awards for his work, including *Studio* magazine awards, Sacramento Advertising Club Gold awards, IABC Crystal awards, and the American Society for Health Care Marketing & Public Relations' Touchstone Award.

PAT LIVINGSTON opened the Graphic Impressions Gallery on Balboa Island shortly after graduating from the University of California in 1971. Livingston soon outgrew the space and moved the gallery to Belmont Shore in Long Beach, where he currently works with interior designers and art consultants to provide photographic art for commercial and health care facilities. He was commissioned by Langdon & Wilson Architects to produce Cibachrome murals for State Mutual Savings and by Lonny Gans to produce computer airbrush murals for Fluor Corporation.

JEFF MYERS has grown up working in the photography business but has also pursued an interest in art. He is one of the rising stars in the Sacramento art scene and his paintings are exhibited in galleries throughout the United States.

TOM AND SALLY MYERS have been full-time freelance photographers for 30 years and have been published in many national magazines, including *National Geographic*, *National Wildlife*, *Newsweek*, *Animals* (London), and numerous travel publications. Their photos appear in books and educational CD-ROM materials throughout the world, advertisements, album covers, and Hallmark cards and calendars. With their son, Jeff Myers, the family has over 400,000 color images in their files covering a variety of geographic areas, including Europe and the Pacific coast from Mexico to Alaska and inland to Colorado.

▲ TOM MYERS

BRYAN PATRICK, a native Sacramentan, is a photographer for the *Sacramento Bee*. Prior to joining the *Bee*, he worked for 14 years at the now-defunct *Sacramento Union*. Patrick is a six-time runner-up for Photographer of the Year awards given by the California Press Photographers' Association and the National Press Photographers' Association.

MICHAEL POWERS, a Sacramento resident since 1988, specializes in advertising, product, and food photography. His clients include Dole, the Rice Growers Association, Starwest, Ford, Pacific Bell, *Comstock's*, *Sacramento* magazine, ADVO, and Backscratchers Nails. Powers operates his own studio, Michael Powers Photography, and enjoys windsurfing, snow skiing, and golfing in his spare time.

ALLEN QUINN, originally from Corpus Christi, Texas, has lived in the Sacramento area since 1979. From his studio, Allen Quinn Photography, he specializes in photojournalism and corporate and travel photography, and his clients include the *Los Angeles Times*, Agence France-Presse, United Press International, Pacific Bell, University of the Pacific, AT&T, Fairchild Communications, Wells Fargo, *Il Massagero*, and others. Quinn recently completed an 800-kilometer motorcycle trip through the Zagros Mountains in western Iran, which "seemed like a great idea," he says, "until we became hopelessly lost."

WAYNE THIEBAUD has received numerous honors for his prints, drawings, and paintings. Since his first one-person exhibition at Sacramento's Crocker Art Museum in 1957, Thiebaud has garnered national attention for his work. Embraced early on by the American pop art movement, his work has come to transcend the bounds of any specific genre and he has become a major figure in the pantheon of American art. In 1985 he was elected to the American Academy and Institute of Arts and Letters, and in 1986 was named an Associate of the National Academy of Design, where he was named an Academician in 1987. Thiebaud was chosen as a Fellow in the American Academy of Arts and Science in 1988, won California's Governor's Award for Lifetime Achievement in 1991, and received the Grumbacher Gold Medallion Award for Painting from the American Academy of Design in 1993.

GEORGE TURNER grew up in the Sacramento area. An education in commercial art preceded a brief stint as an illustrator and a 17-year career as an aviator and part-time photographer. In 1980 he left aviation to pursue a career in photography. For the past 10 years Turner has worked as a corporate photographer in Sacramento. He continues to build his stock files, concentrating on wildlife and natural history subjects.

ROCKY WIDNER, a resident of Sacramento for 10 years, is the official team photographer for the Sacramento Kings.

JAMES WOODSON, a graduate of the Brooks School of Photography, is originally from Stockton. He specializes in people and still-life photography, and his work has been acquired by San Francisco's Museum of Modern Art, the National Gallery of Canada, the University of New Mexico Art Museum, the Stills Division of the National Film Board of Canada, and others. Woodson lives in Valley Springs.

Index to Patrons

Adams Group	164
Aerojet	182
Apple Computer, Inc.	232
Associated Professional Appraisers	217
Baxter Diagnostics, Inc., MicroScan	212
Brown and Caldwell	211
California State Lottery	218
Calpo Hom Macaulay & Dong Architects	214
Comstock Publishing, Inc.	229
CSUS School of Business Administration	190
DFI Inc.	220
Foundation Health Corporation	200
Fountain Suites Hotel	224
Giselle's Travel Bureau	194
Graphic Center	192
HumanWare, Inc.	226
Kleinfelder, Inc.	202
KOVR Channel 13	188
KVIE Channel 6	195
Lionakis-Beaumont Design Group	166
Mather Federal Credit Union	186
McDonald's Corporation	191
Mercy Healthcare Sacramento	160
Pacific Gas and Electric Company	172
Physicians Clinical Laboratory, Inc.	198
Port of Sacramento	196
Radisson Hotel Sacramento	230
Raley's	176
Red Lion Hotels & Inns	208
Rice Growers Association of California	168
Rio Linda Chemical Co., Inc.	210
Sacramento Cable	228
Sacramento Credit Union	178
Sacramento Light Opera Association	184
Sacramento Metropolitan Chamber of Commerce	162
Sacramento Municipal Utility District	180
Silva Strong Architects	222
The Spink Corporation	173
Sutter Health	170
Tenco Tractor, Inc.	174
UC Davis Medical Center	206
U.S. Bank of California	234
U.S. Computer Services	204
USAA Western Regional Office	216
Vanguard Security Services	205